WOMEN
IN INDIA'S
FREEDOM STRUGGLE

When the history of India's fight for independence would be written, the sacrifices made by the women of India will occupy the foremost place.

—Mahatma Gandhi

WOMEN IN INDIA'S FREEDOM STRUGGLE

MANMOHAN KAUR

STERLING PUBLISHERS PRIVATE LIMITED

STERLING PUBLISHERS PRIVATE LIMITED
L-10, Green Park Extension, New Delhi-110016

Women in India's Freedom Struggle
©1992, Manmohan Kaur
First Edition: 1968
Second Edition: 1985
Third Edition: 1992
ISBN 81 207 1399 0

PRINTED IN INDIA

Published by S.K. Ghai, Managing Director, Sterling Publishers Pvt. Ltd., L-10, Green Park Extension, New Delhi-110016. Laserset at Vikas Compographics, A-1/256 Safdarjung Enclave, New Delhi-110029. Printed at Elegant Printers, New Delhi.

PREFACE

This subject was chosen with a view to recording the work done by women in various phases of the freedom struggle from 1857 to 1947. In the course of my study I found that women of India, when given an opportunity, did not lag behind in any field, whether political, administrative or educational.

The book covers a period of ninety years. It begins with 1857 when the first attempt for freedom was made, and ends with 1947 when India attained independence. While selecting this topic I could not foresee the difficulties which subsequently had to be encountered in the way of collecting material. The subject relates to the recent past and hence not much has been written even about the freedom movement as a whole, not to speak of the work done by women in this field.

At the very commencement of my work I was able to get permission from the Government of India to consult its records up to 1946. But later the permission was withdrawn in pursuance of a Government policy and scholars were forbidden to use the records pertaining to the period beyond 1917. This embargo on the official records also deprived me of the official interpretation of various events relating to the freedom movement. As a result, for the period 1917-47, I had to depend mostly on contemporary newspapers, journals, correspondence, personal interviews and records maintained in the offices of the political parties.

The National Library, Calcutta, where I spent over three months, has a good collection of newspapers and journals, etc. Information available from these sources was, however, very limited due to the fact that whenever any major political agitation took place in the country, rigorous censorship was clamped down on the newspapers.

The next source could be the pioneer women themselves who had played a prominent part in the freedom struggle. These ladies are no more. Probably if women like Sarla Devi, Madam Bhikaji Rustum K.R. Cama, Annie Besant, Sarojini Naidu, Satyawati and many others could be contacted they would have been able to give a good deal of information.

The women in politics today and who participated in the struggle for freedom were contacted through correspondence and personal interviews. But the information collected from them is not very comprehensive.

In certain cases men who had been in the political field for a long time were approached but they perhaps were not aware that they would be called upon to give information on their counterparts, the women, and as such the information from this source was also scanty.

The women of India, it is evident from quite a few sources, had started taking part in the political agitation of the country, but because the police was hesitant to arrest them in the early stages of the struggle, even the police reports are far from complete in this respect.

This, however, should not lead the reader to think that women's part in the freedom movement was negligible. In fact, the role played by them was quite significant. I spent about three years in the National Archives of India, New Delhi, and collected some valuable information pertaining to the period 1857-1917 from the records of the Foreign Political and Home Political Departments. The census reports, native paper reports, Imperial Gazetteers and a number of official reports give an insight into the social conditions of the country.

The offices of the different political parties had been victims of many a police raid and the records were either burnt or kept so indifferently that to go through them entailed a lot of work. However, the files and reports available in the All India Congress Committee office, New Delhi, are of interest for the years 1930 to 1947. Some material was also collected from the Central Secretariat Library, New Delhi, and Panjab University Library, Chandigarh.

Small bits of information gathered from different sources when put together do reveal the fact that women in India exhibited courage and patriotism and that the part played by them in the struggle for political freedom was important in nature and vital in its consequences.

I express my grateful thanks to Dr. Hari Ram Gupta, former Head of History Department, Panjab University, without whose liberal help and able guidance this work could not have been completed.

In 1968 and 1985 two earlier editions of this book were published under the title *Role of Women in the Freedom Movement (1857-1947)*. and *Women in India's Freedom Struggle.*

Manmohan Kaur

ABBREVIATIONS

A.I.C.C.	—	All India Congress Committee is the deliberative standing committee of the Congress elected annually
Congress	—	Indian National Congress
Ed.	—	Edited
Govt.	—	Government
N.A.I.	—	National Archives of India, New Delhi
N.L.C.	—	National Library, Calcutta
N.W.P.	—	North Western Province
U.P.	—	Uttar Pradesh

CONTENTS

INTRODUCTION

Women in ancient India occupied a dignified place. They participated in the outdoor life as circumstances and situations demanded and there were hardly any prescribed positions exclusively earmarked for men.[1] All the high avenues of learning were open to women. During this period we come across a reference to some women who excelled in learning and their hymns were included in the Vedas. There were women known as Brahmavadinis who could continue their studies throughout their life. Some of the outstanding women of that age were Lopamudra, Apala, Kadru, Ghosha, Paulomi and others. The notable philosopher of the time was Gargi.[2] However, absence of legal rights, keeping female slaves[3] in an aristocratic Aryan family and polygamy tended to lower the status of women.

The Buddhists maintained the traditions of Brahmanical religion and gave an honoured place to women in the social life of the country. Women were admitted in the order of nuns by virtue of which they gained opportunities to learn and to serve. They participated in the public life and won distinctions. Some of them were amongst Buddha's chief disciples. Many a women gave up wealth and ease and took up missionary work. Prominent among them were Dharmapala, Anupama, Queen Kshema, Chapa and others.[4]

Women continued enjoying the same position more or less until the Muslim invasions from the north-west. A slow and steady but imperceptible decline in the position of women had begun with the advent of Huns. With the coming of the invaders this process accelerated, and the decline was marked and discernible. Continuous invasions made the conditions in the Indo-Gangetic plain unsettled. The political instability, consequent migration of population and economic depression extending over a period of about three centuries affected the women adversely.

Infanticide, child marriage, sati, purdah system and prejudices against women's education were some of the measures adopted by the Hindu society to save the honour of their women, against invaders and foreign conquerors. All these customs hampered the progress of women, yet there appeared throughout the ages some women who excelled as administrators, warriors, reformers and as religious teachers. The names of Padmini, Razia Begum, Durgawati, who fought against Akbar, and Chand Bibi who defended the Ahmednagar Fort, represent the warriors and administrators amongst the women. Mughal princesses like Nur Jahan, Jahan Ara and Zebunnissa are prominent women of the medieval India. South India was not much affected by the intruders, as a result education was fairly spread in the region. One hears of poetesses like Ganga Devi, the author of *Varandanbika Parnaya*. Amongst the Maratha rulers Tara Bai, who was instrumental in putting up a powerful resistance against the onslaughts of Aurangzeb, and Ahalya Bai Holkar, whose administration won admiration of English-men, were famous women of this time. Punjab had a courageous and good stateswoman in Sada Kaur who helped Ranjit Singh in conquering Lahore and consolidating the Sikh empire.

The old order slowly changed with the coming of the British. The economic structure built by them to exploit the Indian resources for their benefit proved ruinous to the economic and cultural set-up of the land. Western education and contacts with the West opened new opportunities for the people of India. The Western form of education, however, did not appeal to men and especially to women in the beginning, but before long they began to adjust themselves to this change.

Even before the provisions made in the Wood's despatch[5] on education could be implemented, the British felt the first tremors against their regime. The part played by women in the great outbreak of 1857-58 invited admiration even from the English. It was the Rani of Jhansi about whom Sir Hugh Rose observed, "She was the bravest and best military leader of the rebels."[6] The Rani of Ramgarh met her death in the battlefield while Begum Hazrat Mahal had to escape to Nepal and died there as an exile.

The period followed by this outbreak was one of social reforms and social reconstruction. Social reformers, both men and women, appeared on the stage of India to uplift the womanhood of the land. The need of educating women in India had by now started receiving some attention.

Girls began to join schools and colleges. In 1888, Anandibai Joshi went abroad to study medicine. There were still several impediments in the way of women's freedom on par with men, as conservative minds had continued to disapprove of the imparting of higher education to women. But by now social reformers like Pandita Rama Bai, Rama Bai Ranade and others had come out openly to advocate women's cause.

The birth of the Indian National Congress in 1885 furnished a political platform to women. It was in the year 1900 that Swarnkumari and J. Gangoli attended the Congress session held in Calcutta as delegates from Bengal. Smt. Gangoli was the first woman to speak from the Congress platform. This was perhaps a beginning of the new era and then onwards the women took an increasingly active part in the political activities of the country.

The first decade of the twentieth century witnessed the revolutionary activities in the political field. Sarla Devi and Bhikaji Rustom K.R. Cama openly supported the cause of the revolutionaries and rank amongst the outstanding leaders of this period.

Then came the Home Rule Movement of Annie Besant between the years 1916 and 1918. She had adopted India as her home and it was her work that threatened the roots of the British Rule in India. As a result Annie Besant was imprisoned. Later, on release, she enjoyed the highest honour by being elected President of the Indian National Congress.

In the following years women of India got a new tool, in the form of passive resistance, introduced by Gandhiji. O'Malley observed that "at the very moment when the Congress and Mahatma Gandhi were calling on them for a national effort, they recognised that the prophet and the paramount had each placed a valuable weapon within their reach. With one hand they grasped passive resistance and with the other the vote."[7]

Thousands of women joined the Satyagraha army of Gandhiji. They raised their voices against the Rowlatt Bill, Salt Laws, Forest Laws and went to jail as a consequence of their defiance.

During the Civil Disobedience movement women like Sarojini Naidu, Kamala Devi Chattopadhyaya, Lado Rani Zutshi, Durga Bai and many others became War Dictators. Sarojini Naidu was not only the first Indian woman to become the President of the Indian National Congress in 1925 but was also the first woman to lead the biggest salt raid in Bombay.

While the men were in prison it was left to the women of India to guide and lead the people during the critical periods. In a bid to achieve their aim they had to face lathi blows and bullets, but once they had decided to come out and work for freedom, there was no going back from it. Swaroop Rani Nehru, wife of Motilal Nehru, was one of the many who received lathi blows.

The demand for independence brought in other concessions for Indians in the form of Government of India Act, 1935. By virtue of this Act, ministries were formed in the provinces after the general elections. Women contested the seats and were elected. Vijayalakshmi Pandit became the first woman minister while Ansuyabai Kale and Sipi Milani became the duputy speakers of Central Provinces and Sindh Assemblies respectively.

The ministries did not last long. They hardly functioned for two years when the Second World War broke out and the Governor-General thrust India into the whirlpool of war on the British side. Thereupon the Congress ministries resigned. This crisis was followed first by the individual Satyagrahas and later by the Quit India Movement in 1942.

The leaders who initiated the movement were arrested in the first round-up. So the women of India stepped forward to carry on the movement for independence. In places like Assam, Bombay, it was the women and students who were responsible for the fight for freedom. They took out processions, held demonstrations and organised camps for women to give them the required training. Women like Aruna Asaf Ali, Sucheta Kriplani and Usha Mehta worked underground during this period.

Indian women outside India also took up the cause of their motherland and joined the ranks of the Indian National Army. Lakshmi, Colonel of the Rani Jhansi Regiment, was another personage who was also a member of the Azad Hind Government.

The war ended in 1945 and in the same year elections were held in England. The Labour Party came into power with Attlee as the Prime Minister. He made an announcement that his government desired to transfer power to the Indians. For this purpose negotiations between the British authorities and Indian leaders were set in motion as a consequence of which Indian Independence Act of 1947 was passed. This marked the ending of the British rule in India.

The post-independence period, particularly in case of women, has been a continuation of an era of social reforms, economic upliftment and political recognition. Struggle for equity, justice and parity between two human beings continue. It may be mentioned that there have been women during this period who have played significant role in the development of the country. There has been a woman Prime Minister, Mrs. Indira Gandhi. She led the country for many years as its Prime Minister. There have been other women who have honoured the chair of Chief Ministers, Governors, educationists and legal experts etc. But to say that they have been freed from the social bondage and that their status is on par with men would be far from truth. Efforts are however on to right the wrong through social legislation education, and increase economic and political opportunities. The last chapter now being added gives an overview of these problems.

Notes and References

1. Kane, P.V., *History of Dharamashastras, Ancient and Medieval Religions and Civil Law*, Poona, Vol. II, Part I, p. 556; Mukerjee, Radha Kumud, *Hindu Civilisation*, 1936, p. 73.
2. Altekar, A.S., *The Position of Women in Hindu Civilisation from Prehistoric Time to the Present Day*, Banares, p. 13.
3. Bahadur Mal writes: "We find a lamentable feature in the last phase of the Vedic period in the form of a custom of slave girls being given away to the husbands along with the brides. The slave girls could be treated as Vadhus or wives, whenever the husband wanted to give them that status. It is also a fact that the kings used to present to the priests slave girls along with cows, horses and gold." Bahadur Mal, *A Story of Indian Culture*, p. 60.
4. Horner, I.B., *Women Under Primitive Buddhism*, London, p. 104.
5. Wood's despatch of 1854 on education made provision for women's education. Details are given in Chapter I.
6. Forrest, G.W., *Selections from the Letters, Despatches and other State Papers*, Vol. IV, p. 139.
7. O'Malley (Ed.), *Modern India and the West*, 1941, p. 475.

1

POSITION OF WOMEN: 1857-1900

> The impact of West on Indian civilisation has brought about changes
> that are more fundamental in the case of women than men. To men it
> brought a new conception of the world, of its material resources,
> ethical standards, and political possibilities, but to the women it
> brought slowly but potentially a new conception of themselves. If
> men reassessed themselves as citizens in a new India, women
> revalued themselves as human beings in a new social order.
>
> —*O'Malley*[1]

Men and women are two inseparable parts of human society and they
have always shared sorrows and joys together. If men have endeavoured
to free themselves from slavery, women have not lagged behind.
History is full of heroic deeds of both men and women who have fought
for independence of their motherland. The history of the struggle for
India's freedom is like many others a story of joint endeavour of both
men and women. The contribution made by women cannot be studied
independently of the study of social and economic position of women in
the society about the opening period of this thesis.

As late as the middle of the nineteenth century it was a common
belief that women were fit only for household work, that their place was
in the kitchen and at best they might come in the drawing room.
Margaret Cousins,[2] one of the founders of Women's India Association
and the one who worked for almost two decades for the betterment of
women's conditions and status, held the opinion that the condition of
women in general all over the country was at its lowest ebb from the
point of view of literacy, health, social status, and economic
independence.[3]

The Friend of India in its issue of August 31, 1866 supported the view expressed above: "Born and bred up to strictest seclusion, and married whilst yet a child, she is devóted to a life of domestic quietude, varied only by the rites of religion and the ordinary events of the family. Of the world around her, she can know little or nothing and the world knows little or nothing of her. Her mental faculties are either under-developed altogether or wasted upon frivolities, whilst her notions of right and wrong overlaid by a superstition and credulity, until they have become almost as devoid of moral meaning as the instincts of an animal."[4]

Some of the customs which affected their contribution to Indian nationalism were: infanticide, child marriage, conditions of widows, polygamy, offering girls to the deity and prejudice against women's education.

Infanticide

Infanticide was a custom of killing girls at birth. It was practised in most parts of Northern India. A son carried on the family name. So the birth of a son was celebrated with a lot of pomp and show. *Putra* (son) was needed to perform certain religious ceremonies to enable the parents to go to heaven after death. If there was no son in the family one had to adopt one. So the son was a "spiritual and a religious necessity" in the Hindu family. Thus man came to possess all the importance. On the other hand, the birth of a girl was looked down upon. Tod writes that Rajputs were often heard to exclaim: "Accursed the day when a woman child was born to me."[5] The girl was considered to be an economic burden as a lot of money had to be spent at the time of her marriage.

Secondly, the custom of hypergamy was strictly in force amongst certain classes of people. This restriction presented many difficulties.[6] Hypergamy was not the only law in operation. There was another important law whereby marrying a girl from one sacred group or from one sacred village to another was forbidden. A Sayid (high caste Muslim) could not give his daughter in marriage to an ordinary person. At the same time a person of a lower caste would deem it a sacrilege to have such an alliance even if the Sayid was willing to marry his daughter to him.

The high caste Hindus looked upon the birth of a daughter as a great humiliation for them as they had to bow their heads to the persons, to whom they were to marry their daughters, at the time of marriage.

Amongst the Rajputs and other high caste people their pride was injured if the bridegroom was from the lower caste.

As a result of all these customs and prejudices, the practice of putting girls to death immediately after birth got a kind of sanction. This crime was common in Uttar Pradesh, Punjab, Rajasthan and Gujarat. Infanticide was a speciality of the Rajputs but it was practised by some Kshatris, Bedis and Sodhis (Sikhs), Jats and Muslim Sayids also. Though the system had firm roots in the above enumerated sections of the people, it was reported in 1853 that the crime prevailed among all classes to a greater or lesser degree.[7] This hideous custom had neither the sanction of religion nor was it recognized by society, all the same it was tolerated by both guardians of religion and society.

The innocent creature was put to death in a variety of ways:

(i)   As soon as the child was born opium was administered. Sometimes a pill made out of "bhang" and tobacco was placed on the palate of the infant where it softened with the saliva and went into the system of the child causing her death.[8]

(ii) In some cases the placenta of the new-born girl was placed on its mouth which caused suffocation and death.[9]

(iii) Amongst Rajputs it was a common practice that a mother's breast was smeared with a preparation from *dhatura* or Mudar plant or the poppy. The infant drank the milk along with the poison, while in Punjab juice of *aak* plant (*calatropis gigantea*) was given to the child with her first feed.

(iv) Another method of killing the child was that a big hole was dug in the ground which was filled with milk, the child was placed in it thus causing death by drowning.[10]

(v)   In Punjab the infant was put into a *Ghara* or earthen water-pot, and buried in the ground.[11] Sometimes the mother starved the child to put an end to the innocent life. Punjab had still another way of infanticide. The baby was buried with a little *gur* (a variety of brown sugar) in her mouth and twisted cotton placed in her hand. The following couplet was recited as she was laid down:

> *Gur Khaen, Puni Kahthon*
> *Ap na aion, bhyaiyan ghallen.*
> (Eat gur, spin your cotton,
> Don't come, send brother instead).[12]

Infanticide was first detected by Emperor Jahangir in the early part of the seventeenth century and he disapproved of this custom.[13]

The second person to raise his voice against this crime was Raja Jai Singh of Jaipur State of Rajasthan who acceded to the throne in 1755. He "submitted to the prince of every Rajput State a decree, which was laid before a convocation of their respective vassals, in which he regulated the 'deeja' or dower and other marriage expenditure with reference to the property of the vassal, limiting it to one year's income of the estate."[14] This plan of the Raja did not meet the required success.

In the more recent period female infanticide was brought to light by Jonathan Duncan,[15] in 1780, then Resident at Banares. He was later appointed Governor of Bombay and he was largely responsible for putting an end to this crime.[16]

It was reported that in Surat, Kutch, Gujarat, Jodhpur and several other states of Rajasthan, it existed as a regular system. In the neighbourhood of Baroda there was a powerful clan of Rajputs known as Jarejahs, among whom the crime was universally practised.[17]

The English tried to dissuade the people and undertakings were obtained from some of the Rajas and chiefs with a view to putting an end to this crime. Infanticide fund was also introduced and the poor people were helped financially at the time of marriage. Rewards were instituted for the informer of an infanticide. The Rajas and chiefs who tried to discourage the custom were given honours. In the beginning, however, the chiefs were reluctant to make promises[19] for the preservation of their daughters.

Two regulations were also passed by the Government, to suppress infanticide, i.e., Regulation XXI of 1795 and Regulation III of 1804. Even though it was reported in 1821 that the crime was on the decline yet after 15 years it came to light that "not less than twenty thousand infants were annually destroyed in Malwa and Rajputana."[20]

The Government persuaded the Rajputs to enter into an agreement among themselves to reduce the expenditure on the marriage of a daughter so that it did not exceed one-tenth of the annual income of the bride's father. This plan was first put into practice in Jaipur and later was followed by some other States.

These regulations and agreements were only half way measures and had little effect. Nothing substantial was done till 1836 when

Thomson, Magistrate and Collector of Azamgarh, while making settlement of the district (a district of Uttar Pradesh), discovered the prevalence of this crime. He reported that the custom was common amongst the Rajputs on the border of Oudh territories. "Among a body of Rajputs numbering some 10,000 not a single daughter was forthcoming."[21]

Enquiries were again made at this time at Banares. Moore made detailed investigations in three hundred villages. In 62 villages he found that there was no female child under the age of 6 years.[22]

In one such sub-division he visited 38 villages and found no girl at all. The marriage of a girl was a rare occurrence. In some villages there had not been any marriage within the recollection of the living people.[23]

Moore found another territory of Hara Rajputs inhabiting villages on the border of Oudh regarding whom he says: "Not only are there no girls to be found in their houses now but there never have been any nor has such an event as the marriage of a daughter taken place for more than two hundred years."[24]

In 1839 Montgomery in the Magistracy of Allahabad discovered that the practice of killing female babies was prevalent in Barra, a place on the border of Rewa, amongst the Rajput tribes. He (Montgomery) appointed a peon in each village to report the birth of a female child. The watchman and the midwife (local *dai*) were instructed to report each birth in the Police Station. In the event of death of a female child, the Sub-Inspector of Police was instructed to hold enquiries and to send the body to the Civil Surgeon for examination. The people of this area migrated to Rewa to avoid these restrictions. The Raja of this principality was addressed on the subject with a view to putting an end to this crime.[25]

In Punjab the practice was prevalent almost all over the State. It is reported the Bedis were generally known by the title of *Kurimar* or "daughter slayer". Sodhi residents of Ambala, Patiala and Nabha, Jat residents of Multan, Gujranwala and Jhelum and Muslim residents of Jhelum and Ferozepore also killed their girls.[26]

Repeated proclamations were made during the period 1832 to 1846 condemning this crime in the Cis Sutlej States.

In 1846 when Jalandhar Doab was annexed to the British territories, it was reported by Lawrence that the crime was prevalent in that place and was mostly practised amongst the Bedis. Lawrence made an announcement thus: "*Bewa mat Jalao; beti mat maro*; *korhi mat dabbo.*" (Thou shall not burn thy widows; thou shall not kill thy daughters; thou shall not bury thy lepers.)[27]

Customs die hard with people. A deputation of Bedis waited on Lawrence to demonstrate with him against the prohibition of their time-honoured practice of destroying female children.[28]

The practice had taken roots in the district of Hoshiarpur. It was reported in 1867 that in the Police division of Hajipur[29] in 36 villages consisting of 1,013 houses of Rajputs, ten per cent of the female children, had died within a year.[30]

Enquiries made in Uttar Pradesh in 1869 by Hobart revealed an appalling situation. He examined a group of ten villages and found 104 boys and one girl. The people admitted that in the previous 10 years only one girl was married.[31]

In another 27 villages he found 284 boys but 23 girls only and in another ten villages he discovered the marriage of a girl was an unknown happening.[32]

These circumstances impressed upon the Government the necessity of having a legislation on the subject. The Act VIII of 1870 was enacted whereby a watch was to be kept over the people and the registration of births and deaths was strictly enforced.

However, after more than three decades of the enactment of this special legislation it was reported by the Superintendent Incharge Census for Punjab for 1901 that "infanticide had not quite disappeared."[33]

Farquahar wrote as late as 1913: "So ingrained was the habit in many Indian castes and tribes that the determination of the British government to put it down was in many places baffled for years; and the best authorities are doubtful whether it does not persist in certain quarters to some extent even today."[34]

The practice of killing the female child has by now slowly died. O'Malley said (1941): "Its abandonment is due to a combination of causes including the operation of the Act, the pressure of public opinion, the influence of more enlightened ideas, and even more perhaps the relaxation of rules of hypergamy by the castes concerned owing to the action of law of supply and demand which has taken a direction opposite to that already noticed, the paucity of women having given them a market value and enabled parents to demand bride prices."[35]

Child Marriage

The girls who escaped the cruel custom of infanticide were married very young, i.e., between the ages of five and ten years, having no opportunity for the improvement of their mental or physical self. It might be argued that since girls did not go to school and had no social life, they were married young. It also secured their purity. Marriages were arranged by parents. Early marriage was convenient because the younger a girl the easier her adjustment to the new environment.

The custom involved a number of abuses. The awareness of the importance of marriage and its responsibilities were absent in such marriages. For the child-wife, marriage was associated with sweets, beautiful dresses, fireworks and for a few days to be the centre of attraction with perhaps a ride on the horse or in a palanquin in the gay evening procession. After the marriage her companions, most often, were a husband much older in age or a few elderly women in the house.[36]

The life in the new home was not always happy. Thus "the girl child from the moment of her birth to her death undergoes one continuous lifelong suffering as a child-wife, as a child-mother and very often as a child-widow."[37] The system marred all developments—physical, intellectual and even spiritual. It resulted in crushing the individuality of the child-wife. Early marriage and early consummation curtailed freedom and joy of girlhood. Before even she could taste the carefree years of girlhood, she was compelled to be a mother. The practice of child marriage was responsible for the high rate of infant mortality. Fuller observes: "Of the children born every year, only about half the number reach the age of 30 years."[38] The custom was answerable for millions of widows in the country, abnormal deliveries, prolonged illness of mother after confinement, sterility in some cases and prolonged debility of chronic diseases in others.

Better social status for women was a prerequisite for India's progress. Foreign missionaries started taking interest in the social conditions of the country, but people were doubtful of their motives. As a reaction to their method of work, western contacts and western education, the men of India rose to the need of the hour. In the beginning it was men who laboured hard to improve the conditions of women but slowly the women of India also came forward to take their place in the society outside their home.

The social reform movement for the emancipation of women was set in motion by Raja Rammohun Roy who stood on the threshold of the old and the new. He interpreted the East in the light of the West. He was a socio-religious reformer, a politician and an educationist. Rammohun Roy was the first man who espoused the cause of women. From then onwards, women, who were not only the slaves of the ruling nation but also of the customs and usages of the society, started receiving attention which with the advent of Mahatma Gandhi, became a national issue.

Associations like the Brahmo Samaj and the Arya Samaj took up the cause of child marriage. There was the need of a special law to save the child-wife from physical suffering and harassment at the hands of the husband. It was at the instance of Ishwar Chandra Vidyasagar that the first step was taken in this direction in 1860. The Indian Penal Code prohibited the consummation of marriage if the girl was less than ten years old. This age was considered low by later reformers like Keshab Chandra Sen and Behramji Malabari.

Keshab Chandra Sen of the Brahmo Samaj introduced a novel marriage ceremony whereby the consent of the bridegroom and bride had to be secured. It was a step toward the recognition of women's individuality, and marriage ceased to be a contract between the parents. Moreover, a marriage ceremony could now be performed without any restrictions of caste, creed or religion.[39] Sen also issued circulars to the medical authorities with a view to ascertaining the marriageable age. Thus he initiated a propaganda against child marriage. The marriageable age fixed under the Brahmo Act 1872, (it later came to be known as the Native Marriage Act), for girls was 14 years and for boys 18 years. Under this Act, bigamy, polygamy and infant marriages were made impossible.[40]

Sen sought to promote social reforms through schools and organisations which would educate people against social evils. The British-India Society (1854), the Calcutta Evening School (1855) and the Goodwill Fraternity (1857) were some of the institutions which owe their origin to him.

In his campaign for the liberation of women, Keshab Chandra Sen adopted new methods. In those days women were not supposed to come out even to perform divine service. Sen took his wife from Calcutta to Jorasanko, the centre of Brahmo Samaj activities, to participate in divine services. For this act he was forbidden to enter his ancestral home, but the punishment did not worry him in the least and he continued his efforts with the result that the Brahmo Samaj was thrown open to women.

After his return from England in 1870, Sen started an "Indian Improvement Society"[41] with the objective of promoting physical and mental improvement of women.

Malabari was another social reformer of this time. He took up the cause of enforced widowhood and child marriage in the nineties of the last century. Malabari wanted to have legislation on the subject. Although he was well aware of the weakness of the Government interference, yet he argued that State support was needed. He submitted his proposal to Lord Ripon who in turn circulated it to the local governments. The request for reforms did not receive the required attention. Lord Ripon's answer to the reformers was: "Although there is much to be said in favour of each of these suggestions, the Governor-General in Council as at present advised, would prefer not to interfere even to the limited extent proposed, by legislation until sufficient proof is forthcoming that legislation has been asked for by a section important in influence or number of the Hindu Community itself."[42]

Malabari had given enough publicity to this case before he approached the Government. He started the crusade against this evil all over again. He published a pamphlet entitled 'Infant Marriage and Enforced Widowhood'. This pamphlet with its unsparing criticism roused a great deal of interest and did much to mould the public opinion. He toured the country, arousing and enlightening people on the harmful consequences of this system. After six years of hard work in India he went to England to enlist the help of the people there, especially of women.

By this time another social reformer, Daya Ram Gidmul, joined hands with Malabari to put an end to this custom. In January 1885, the Surat widows addressed an appeal to the 'Gaikwad', supporting Malabari's point of view. In March 1886, a memorandum was addressed by Sir T. Madhavrao and other leading citizens to the Viceroy requesting for the fixation of marriageable age for girls at ten. Another petition from Meerut praying that marriageable age be fixed at 12 for girls and at 16 for boys,[43] was submitted to the Government of India.

These reforms were accentuated by the famous case of Rukmabai that occurred in 1885. Rukmabai was married to Dadaji, a Maharashtrian gentleman, at a very young age. When she attained the age of maturity she refused to go to her husband's house on the plea that her husband was uncultured and illiterate. The case was taken to the court. A defence committee was organised to fight this case for Rukmabai in which Govind Ranade took a prominent part. The court gave its verdict in favour of Dadaji.[44] It stirred many hearts and the question of child marriage gained prominence. The Indian National Social Conference, which was founded by Mahadeo Govind Ranade in Bombay in 1887, further supported the case for reforms.

Another event which accelerated legislations on the subject was the lawful case of Phulmani Dasi, a child aged 11 years who was married to an adult husband. He raped her, as a result of which she died.[45] The death of Phulmani Dasi was an important factor in forcing the lady doctors to send a memorandum to the Government requesting suitable legislation to prevent child marriages. This request was supported by 1,500 Indian women who sent a representation to Queen Victoria beseeching similar reforms.[46]

A committee of influential persons was formed to go into this question. On the recommendations of this committee in 1891 the Age of Consent Bill was passed by the Government whereby cohabitation with a wife under the age of 12 years was prohibited.

This question was examined by the Joshi Committee (1925) and on its recommendations the Child Marriage Restraint Act commonly known as Sarada Act was passed in 1929 which raised the marriageable age for girls to 14 and for boys to 18 years. The Act, however, remained a dead letter. It was obeyed in its breach more than in its observance. Moreover, the Act did not reach the population in the villages for lack of publicity. Another cause of its failure was that there was no adequate machinery to enforce it. The Act was complicated by the fact that a complaint against the offending parties had to be lodged before they could be punished. The only way of punishing the party was by imposing fine. The contracting party considered it as an extra expenditure on marriage and thus the fine was paid.

Two years after the enactment of Child Restraint Marriage Act, 1939, the census of 1941 revealed the high rate of child marriages being performed.

Age Group	Percentage Married
0 to 1	0.3
1 to 2	1.2
2 to 3	2.0
3 to 4	4.2
4 to 5	6.6
5 to 10	19.3
10 to 15	38.1

However all these secular causes which encouraged child marriage are disappearing. The joint family system is disintegrating, the economic struggle is harder and the theory that girls need not be educated like boys does not appeal to society.[47]

Conditions of Widows

Child marriage had its repercussions and many girls became widows even before they had attained maturity. In some cases they had to burn themselves on the funeral pyre of their husbands. This rite was popularly known as 'Sati'. It was an old custom. In the fourth century B.C., Alexandar's soldiers discovered 'Sati' in Punjab. "It was practised," writes Smith, "by the half foreign city of Taxila along with other startling customs and that it also prevailed amongst the Kathavi who dwelt on the banks of the Ravi."[48]

Sati was not a universal practice. This rite was performed to glorify the warrior caste and was compulsory for princesses. Many women were burnt on the funeral pyre of a single Raja. It had slowly become a social convention with the result that unwilling widows were also forced to abide by this custom.[49] The widow was given a drink of 'bhang' (a kind of intoxicant) to remove the fear of death. In Telugu country including Vijayanagar, widows were buried alive. Those women who managed to escape from the funeral pyre were dragged into it again. Such a case took place in 1863 at Monghyr in Bihar. Makesh Lal, resident of Sarnamya, Pargana Balliah, died on August 9, 1863. His widow expressed her desire to become a Sati. Her faith and determination was put to test by applying 'ghee' to her little finger and setting afire. She passed through this ordeal successfully and was allowed to share the funeral pyre of her husband. Later her courage failed and she tried to escape but this was intolerable to friends and relatives who forced her back. The agony was unbearable and she again rolled off the burning pyre and falling on the ground tore the burnt flesh of her body in excruciating pain. The major portion of her body had already burnt. When people saw her in this miserable state, they left her to her fate with a chowkidar to guard her. She died the next morning.[50]

Some of the widows who showed reluctance to become Satis were either drowned or they had to spend their days in utter misery. They were regarded as untouchables and were not retained in their caste and families. Naturally these widows had to throw themselves at the mercy of low people.[51]

The widow was compelled to lead a forlorn life and was deprived of the minimum comforts of life. She had to live on one meal a day, sleep on the floor and could not wear nice clothes. If she happened to be under 20 years of age, she was allowed to wear a white sari with a small border. But if a widow was older, she was supposed to wear an all white sari. She was burdened with work. In a family of ordinary means she had to be a kitchen maid, menial servant, a nurse and a housekeeper, all in one.[52] The sight of a widow was considered inauspicious. So she was kept out of all festivities.

Behramji Malabari, a staunch advocate of widow re-marriage said, "Suttee was one single act of martyrdom or heroism as the victim conceived it, and an act of religious merits as popularly believed, while the life which caste imposed on an unwilling widow was a perpetual agony, a burning to death by slow fire without any chastening or elevating effect on the sufferer or any moral advantage to the community at large by way of compensation."[53]

Ishwar Chandra Vidyasagar was able to get an Act passed in 1856 which legalised widow re-marriage. The first widow re-marriage was performed in Calcutta in December 1856. Ishwar Chandra set an example by marrying his first son to a widow. He also bore the expenses of such marriages and in a number of cases provided for the maintenance of married couples and their families.

However, the Act did not receive the required publicity and as such remained on the statute book. The outbreak of 1857 hindered the progress of reforms.

In May 1870, a young widow sought protection from a district official. She complained that her father, Sita Ram, an agent of Shankaracharya, a Hindu high priest, wanted to shave her head forcibly. The Magistrate showed his inability to interfere in a religious matter.[54]

Another case where force was used against a widow was reported on August 5, 1872. A widow teacher in a girls school at Kerwada, Bharoch District (Bombay), wanted to marry a school-master of Katpor, a place near Kerwada. She invited friends for the marriage and made necessary preparations. Her relatives, who were opposed to the marriage, assaulted the girl, her intended husband and their friends. They forcibly shaved off the head of the widow and confined her to the house.[55]

South India was equally backward in this respect. Viresalungam Pantulu,[56] who initiated this reform, faced much opposition. He celebrated the marriage of a Brahmin widower and a young widow on December 13, 1881, in Rajamundry. This caused a lot of excitement. "The engines of social oppression were brought into play and were most vigorously worked against the little bond."[57]

However, reformers had taken up the cause of widows. Widow re-marriage associations were started and widow homes were opened to train them for an independent career and thereby save them from dependence on their relatives. The first such home was started by Saispada Banerjee in 1877 at Calcutta. Slowly more such homes came up in Bombay and other places. The problem of widows became less acute with the raising of marriageable age and the spread of education.

Polygamy

Polygamy was another custom which tended to lower the status of women. It was not universally practised. Bengal, Uttar Pradesh and Punjab were the worst affected areas. This system reduced women to a state of perpetual subjection among those classes which practised this custom. The girls were married at a very early age and naturally the child-wife was under the domination of the husband and mother-in-law. But in case the wife showed independence of spirit, the threat of second marriage was used to cow her down.[58]

Polygamy was permissible among the Hindus and there was no limit to the number of wives one could have. But due to economic reasons the system was confined to upper strata of society. Among the ruling chiefs it was a common feature. The usual practice with the common man was that if the wife failed to bear him a son, or suffered infirmity or disease or was infidel or on account of some differences in the two families, the husband took recourse to second marriage.

Among the classes which allowed widow re-marriage polygamy was permitted in certain cases. The deceased brother's wife was married to the surviving brother in order to keep the family property. This ceremony was known in Punjab as 'karewa' or 'chadar andasi'.[59]

In Bengal, the custom of polygamy was prevalent amongst the Coolin Brahmins. A Coolin who had married "a hundred wives was considered a model of respectability."[60] Plural marriages were common amongst this caste and it led to many deplorable abuses, Even in the middle classes, instances were not infrequent of multiplying the number of wives without any resonable cause and even in cases where they were unable to afford suitable maintenance to their living consorts. Ishwar Chandra Vidyasagar writes that "with the Coolin Brahmin the sacred rite of matrimony had been notoriously degraded to a system of shameful traffic. These men, for some sordid gain of some paltry sum visited village after village accepting the hands of scores of maidens, the great majority of whom were destined never to enjoy the blessings of a wedded life."[61] There was another class of Coolin Brahmins, inhabiting the various parts of Uttar Pradesh called Konojeas, practising polygamy but on a limited scale.

A Muslim can have four wives at the same time with religious sanction. However, monogamy seems to have been the general practice. There is a custom whereby a Muslim can marry four wives by 'Nikah'[62] and he can marry a number of wives by 'Motah.'[63] A Well-known Persian proverb bears witness to this custom. "A man should marry four wives, a Persian to have somebody to talk to, a Khurasani for his housework, a Hindu woman for nursing her children, and a woman of Mavarunnahr to have some one to whip as a warning for the other three."[64]

The census report of Punjab 1911 reveals thus: "the first thing a Mohammedan will do, when he can afford a luxury is to marry a second wife and if means permit, he will very soon go to the full limit of four."[65]

In West Punjab polygamy was the rule rather than an exception amongst the rich Muslims. The second marriage was the outcome of a love affair, as soon as the man was able to gain independence. Then came the third marriage of his own choice in mature years and the fourth wife, in most cases, was taken when the first and second grew old.[66] Even where this custom was prevalent it did not gain approval of the society as is apparent from the following couplet:

Dun zalin da vanera, jun dun kuttian vich sur.[67]

(A husband of two women is like a pig between two dogs.)

It is really unfortunate that no law has been passed by the Government of India to ban this evil and degrading custom amongst the Muslims. In the Hindu community, however, this custom was viewed with disfavour and was condemned by the social reformers of this period vehemently.

The Maharaja of Burdwan and Rani Shurnomoyee of Cassim Bazar presented petitions in 1856 to the Bengal Government to pass a legislation banning polygamy. In the petitions they narrated the pitiable plight of women who were victims of this system.[68]

Ishwar Chandra Vidyasagar also raised his voice against this custom and drafted a Bill. However, nothing substantial was done to curb this evil. In 1938 three Private Bills on the subject came before the Central Legislature. One of the bills allowed the taking of a second wife with the permission of the District Judge under exceptional circumstances. The other two bills were for the total prohibition of a second marriage unless the first marriage was dissolved. None of these bills were passed.

The Baroda State Government was the first to pass an Act in 1942, declaring the second marriage illegal if the first spouse was alive or if the first marriage had not been dissolved. Bombay followed Baroda and in 1946 passed the Prevention of Hindu Bigamous Marriage Act, but this could not be effective as the intending parties could go to the neighbouring areas and contract second marriages.[69] The Hindu Marriage Act, 1955, passed after independence, has declared bigamy an offence.

Purdah System

"The last downward step," writes Farquahar, "faithfully possible because of all that had gone before it, was the acceptance of the custom of secluding the women of the upper castes in the women's apartment and cutting them off from all participation in public life."[70]

There was no purdah amongst the women in ancient India, but it slowly crept into the Hindu society. The purdah was introduced partly to shield them from the insults and cruelties of the invaders and partly in imitation of the custom of alien conquerors. Child marriage was also responsible for this custom. The girls were married so very young that a jealous husband had to guard them from outside influence. The child-wife had also to be protected from her husband who was an adult.

Purdah was more strictly observed in North India than in the South. In fact, wherever the influence of Muslims was strong, the women were kept in seclusion.

Purdah did not become popular with the Marathas, but it had become a common custom with the ruling chiefs of Rajasthan.

In the lower strata of society, for instance, the peasants and working classes, this custom could not be observed as the woman had to help the man in his economic pursuits. But even amongst these classes an unmarried girl was not allowed to go unescorted. The married woman would hide or cover her face in the presence of elders and also from the husband when he met her in the company of others.[71]

Amongst the Muslims, a woman was not supposed to appear before a man to whom it was possible to be married. The women who observed purdah went out in covered palanquins. Those who could not afford this luxury had to go in *burqa* or with a sheet covering them from top to bottom.

The Zenana[72] system was in vogue. Among the rich the Zenana was spacious and luxurious while among the poor the 'purdah' was less common, where it was observed it was so rigid that a woman was confined in a small house with practically no windows or with openings high up in the walls. She could do no work except cooking which was done inside the house. It had been said that a Rajput woman could not leave her house to fetch water though the house might be in a jungle and the well in front of it.[73]

While writing about the Zenana, Roy observes: "There the women lay condemned to lifelong prison, a helpless, prostrate and pathetic figure with feebled health, her naturally keen senses dulled through inaction, without the light of knowledge illuminating her vision, steeped in ignorance and prejudice, groping in the dark, a martyr in the conventions of the society in which she had been born."[74]

Purdah had become a hallmark of respectability and importance. In Punjab it was said:

> *Andar bhaithi, lakh di—*
> *Bahar gayi kakh di!*[75]

(The one who stays indoor is worth lakhs; who wanders about

is worth a straw.)

Tre kam kharab—
Mard nun chakki
Sandhe nun garb
Ran nun rah.[76]

(Three things are bad: grinding for a man, pregnancy for a bull and wandering for a woman.)

This custom was so ingrained in women that they did not feel the restriction much. As late as 1922, H.H. Nawab Sultan Jehan Begum, ruler of Bhopal, wrote a book in defence of Purdah—*Al-Hijab* or "Why Purdah is Necessary". She writes, "To expect Muslim girls to go to schools and colleges with open faces or with veils on, and sit with boys and obtain instructions in different branches of knowledge is tantamount to the death of their finer sentiments, morality and religion."[77]

Its bad effects were specially apparent in the middle class families which observed purdah strictly, but could not afford to provide spacious apartments. No consideration to light and fresh air was given. What mattered was how best the privacy could be secured, with the result these Zenanas were the places where tuberculosis thrived.[78]

Dr. Vaughan who made special studies of this custom in *The Purdah System and Its Effects on Motherhood,* observed that osteomalacia was the direct result of purdah. Her studies revealed that this disease was prevalent among women in the child-bearing age. It often started before marriage when the girl went into seclusion and away from sunlight. Purdah deprived the women of any significance in the life outside home. Even in the house, women's economic dependence on man and the belief that man was superior to woman left them with no individuality of their own.[79] The reformers like Raja Rammohun Roy, Keshab Chandra Sen, and leaders of the socio-religious reform movements were well aware of this evil custom and worked for the removal of purdah.

Mahatma Gandhi criticised the institution of purdah. He said, "Chastity is not a hothouse growth. It cannot be superimposed. It cannot be protected by the surrounding walls of the purdah."[80]

Offering Girls to the Deity

Another custom which lowered the importance of the girls in society was offering them to the deities in the temples. In Maharashtra there is a deity known as Khandaba—the incarnation of Shiva. Girls were offered to him by the parents in infancy or early childhood and these girls were known as Muralis. This custom was prevalent in Poona and Satara districts.[81] A woman in a bid to be the mother of many children promised to sacrifice her first-born daughter to Khandaba. The first born was set apart for him. When the girl reached the marriageable age she was married to the 'khanda' or dagger of Khandaba and became his wife. Her fate was sealed as she could not become the wedded wife of a man and in consequence usually led an infamous life. Some of these girls became Muralis while others became ordinary public women.

The parents of such girls were not ashamed to take their earnings because they belonged to Khandaba. Kunbis, Mahars, Mangs and other low caste people gladly converted their daughters into Muralis. The higher caste people also bought the girls from low class poor people and offered them to Khandaba.[82]

The Muralis performed night workship and sang in the service of their gods at different places and earned their living. They were invited by people who held the night service. So long as they were young they were called, but once old they were left as destitutes.

The Muralis found their counterparts in Devdasis in the South. Their duty was also to sing and dance before the temple gods and in the processions. There were 11,573 women dancers in the Madras Presidency in 1900. These girls were the common property of the priests.[83]

Some of the widows who visited Brindaban for pilgrimage fell victims to the lust of the priests. Once a girl stayed in the temple, she came to be known as 'Vaishnavis'. In that capacity she was either used as a mistress or hired out to other people. When they were old they lived a life of misery. Vaishnavis were found in Bengal as well. Their number in this province in 1925 was 2,03,610.[84]

In Western India there were the 'Bhavins'. The term was applied to women in the service of gods. These girls were presented to gods in infancy. Their business was to light the temple lamps and keep them trimmed, to sweep and mop the floor, to turn the 'chauri' over the idol, serve the 'hooka' to the congregation and attend to the visitors in the temple.[85]

In South India Devdasis and dancing girls were identical but not so in Western and Central India. In the latter two provinces they formed a separate class or caste called Kalanwantin. They visited the temple at the invitation of the temple authorities. They were professional singers and dancers and differed from common public women, and even from the Muralis and Bhavins.[86]

In 1900 Fuller wrote: "In the Punjab, dancing girls enjoy public favour, they move more freely in native society than public women in civilised society. With these women around, many a family's happiness has been ruined and estrangement made complete between husband and wife by the husband coming under the influence of the *nautch* girls."[87]

A movement against dancing girls was organised in 1892. Slowly it spread to other parts of the country. Appeals were also made to the Government on this account. The question of Devdasis was taken up by Smt. Muthulakshmi Reddi when she became a member of the Legislative Council in 1926. With her efforts, Prevention of Dedication Act, 1929, was passed.

The Bombay Government followed the example set by the Madras Government and passed in 1934 the Devdasis Act.[88]

The practice of selling girls also needed condemnation. The father of the girls received a certain sum of money in exchange for his daughter from the party to whom she was to be given in marriage. The girls sold and purchased could not be treated better than slaves.[89]

Education of Women

The absence of education amongst women was largely responsible for their low status in society. William Adam, who made enquiries in Bengal on the problem of education in his second report (1835), observed that it was a common superstition that women taught to read and write became widows soon after their marriage; secondly, people believed that intrigues were facilitated by imparting knowledge of letters to women.[90] As a result of these superstitions and beliefs the education of women did not receive encouragement either from the government or the people. Some elementary education was imparted to girls in a few rich families but there were no public schools. The author of the *Census of 1881* admitted that the exact number of women who could read or write was not available as the ability of women to write was not considered a sign of respectability.

Long before the government took up the cause of women's education, missionaries were already at work. The progress in the work was rather slow, because female teachers from suitable social position were not available. The shortage of teachers could be judged from the fact that as late as 1881-82, the total number of girls in normal schools throughout India was 515.[91]

The inspection of girls schools was also in the hands of male inspectors. The custom of child marriage and Purdah system curtailed the school life of the girls. They were not expected to earn their livelihood after being educated and so their education was considered useless. Lastly, the textbooks were prepared to meet the needs of boys and those books were often not suitable for girls.[92]

Adam observed that the first organised effort to teach the girls was made in 1818 at Chinsura but this attempt met with failure.[93] However, the missionaries were out to meet these failures and their constant efforts brought about the establishment of girls' schools both in Bombay and Bengal in 1823. In fact, the education of women between the years 1823 and 1854 mainly remained in the hands of missionaries. By this time people also started taking interest in female education. A praiseworthy development in the history of education was the organisation of the Elphinstone College Students' Literacy Scientific Society founded by Prof. Patton of the college. As a result of discussions of this society and mainly under the inspiration and guidance of Dadabhai Naoroji, four new girls' schools were established in 1849, in Bombay. In these schools teaching was done by college students.[94] In 1851, an endowment fund of Rs. 20,000 was created by Maginbhai Karam Chand for the establishment of girls' schools in the same city.[95]

In Madras the education of women was first taken up by the missionaries. It was for the first time in 1881 that the missionaries of the Scottish Church started working for the education of Hindu women. Schools for Christian converts were in vogue long before this. In 1845, the first girls' school was opened under the joint management of Indians and Europeans.

However, the Government of India recognised the importance of women's education when it made provision in the despatch on education in 1854.[96] At this time (1854), the position of female education in the various provinces was insignificant.

In Uttar Pradesh, Gopal Singh, Deputy Inspector of Schools, working single handed, founded a large number of schools for girls. He also succeeded in getting the government to extend its patronage to these ventures. The schools were attended by girls of all classes. The masters were selected by the parents of the pupils. A committee of respectable gentlemen was constituted for general supervision. There were 288 schools in Agra in January 1857.[97]

Female education on the Western model could hardly be said to have begun at this time in Punjab. In fact, this province needed a revival and not a new start. Before annexation there were several indigenous schools in the Punjab. The foreign missionaries had a weak hold in this area and these indigenous schools were run by the Indian ladies themselves. Nawankot and Moranwali in Lahore, Vairowal in Amritsar district and Asand in Karnal district had schools run by the Punjabi ladies. They also ran 6 girls schools in Delhi. There were 108 schools opened by Bedi Khem Singh[98] and these schools were not open to inspection. Later they were closed. A textbook was also written by him for the use of girls.

G.W. Leitner, who made enquiries into the indigenous education in Punjab in 1882, observed that there had been a gradual decline in the female education after the annexation of the State. With the introduction of the new regime and new language the teaching capacity of the mother who could teach Punjabi to her children was lost. The English rule was also responsible for weakening the religious feelings which caused the decline of all indigenous schools including those conducted by women. The method of education adopted by the English, i.e., the inspection of the schools by male inspectors and keeping of schools in public places was not appreciated by the people at large.[99]

Lastly, during the Sikh rule, a woman guilty of misconduct was severely punished by the local Panchayats, but with the coming into force of the English Law, adultery, for instance, could be committed with immunity. As a consequence the male population watched with great jealousy and contempt the emancipation of women. The education of women in Punjab remained restricted. There were only 17 schools with 806 students in 1854.

Lord Dalhousie was the first to give grants of public money for girl schools and to honour the gentlemen who founded them. He also sustained the Benthune School at Calcutta after the death of its founder.

Zenana Missions helped in spreading the education among women. These were started in 1855 in Calcutta. The classes were conducted in the homes of the individuals and certificates were issued to the students. Fortnightly meetings were also held. These meetings were arranged with a view to bringing the ladies together in a common place and it gave opportunity to those who could not join the class to show their skill in needlework.[100] The Zenana Mission schools taught Christianity besides other subjects. Trained staff of Indian Christians or Anglo-Indians along with one or two Europeans was appointed and this staff taught in the house allotted to them. Later came the Secular Zenana Agencies which had both Indian and European members which imparted education without religious bias.[101]

In spite of the sentiments borne out in the education despatch of 1854, the Government was still hesitant to take bold steps to promote the education of women. As late as 1865, Government issued instructions that girls' schools should be opened only if they had the material support of the people.[102]

Miss Mary Carpenter who visited India twice between 1866 and 1869 was able to secure a grant of £ 12,000 per annum, for five years on matching basis, for the establishment of normal schools. But the support of the Government was not wholehearted and was not readily available. It was in 1868 that the Madras, Bombay and Uttar Pradesh Governments recommended to the Government of India, to open Normal Schools, a step necessary for the promotion of female education. But the latter did not favour this move.[103]

In the year 1866-67 the position of education of women in various provinces is given below:[104]

The people had begun realising the importance of women's education and a number of schools sprang up in the country. But the girls were not permitted to take any university examination till the early eighties of the last century. This period also witnessed many a social reform movement like the Brahmo Samaj, Arya Samaj, which helped in the promotion of women's education. The Education Commission of 1882 further recommended the expansion of girls' education with the result that posts of Inspectoress of Girls Schools were created and a few training schools for women teachers were also established. By the end of the nineteenth century there were 12 colleges, 467 secondary schools and 5,628 primary schools for girls with a total enrolment of 4,44,470 students.

Name of Province	Schools	Number of schools	Number of pupils
Bengal	Government	1	97
	schools under grant-in-aid	183	} 4767
	Schools receiving allowance under other rules	60	
Madras	Government	Nil	...
	aided schools	75	3109
Bombay	Government	61	1935
	Aided schools	12	1193
	Schools not aided by Govt.	17	902
Uttar Pradesh	Govt., lower classes	479	8981
	Aided & unaided middle classes	9	934
	Aided & unaided lower classes	105	2056
Punjab	Government	296	6198
	aided female schools	651	14243

The percentage of educated women slowly increased. The following figures taken from the Census Report give an insight into this development of women's education:

Year	Percentage of literate women
1891	0.5
1901	0.7
1911	1.1
1921	1.9
1931	2.4
1941	6.9

Women's education was given a fresh impetus with independence and as a result their literacy rate is 18.70 per cent.

Notes and References

1. O'Malley, L.S.S. (Edited), *Modern India and the West*, Oxford, 1941, p. 445.
2. For details regarding Margaret Cousins see Chapter 8.
3. Cousins, M.B., *Indian Womanhood Today*, Allahabad, 1941, p. 15.
4. *Friend of India*, August 31, 1866, Vol. XXXII, p. 1018.
5. Tod, J., *Annals and Antiquities of Rajasthan*, Vol. I, p. 505.
6. Browne observes thus "Every step we ascend up this ladder of caste we find females become fewer and fewer, till on reaching the top, they altogether disappear." The Brahmins, one of the high caste Hindus, appear to be innocent to this crime.
   Browne, John Cave, *Indian Infanticide, Its Origin, Progress and Suppression*, London, 1857, p. 11.
7. Browne, Jone Cave, op. cit., pp. 108-129.
8. ibid., p. 8
9. Walker, Alexander Col., *A Report on Infanticide*, 1808, p. 66, (Printed, N.A.I. Library).
10. In the year A.D. 802 Smt. Gujra Bai, a descendant of one of the Gaikwad Rajas of Gujarat who was in Bombay for political reasons complained about this crime being prevalent in Kutch. This information was later confirmed by Captain Slaton who was on a political mission to that State. He writes: "The custom mentioned in Gujra Bai's relations is in force to this day; every infant born in Raja's family of Rani or lawful wife is immediately dropped into a hole dug in the earth and filled with milk where it is drowned."
    Wilson J., *History of the Suppression of Infanticide in Western India*, Bombay, p. 46.
11. *Hoshiarpur District Gazetteer*, 1883-84, Lahore, p 40.
12. ibid.
13. Tod, J., op. cit., p. 506.
14. Tod, J., op cit., p. 506.
15. He was born on May 15, 1756, came to India in 1772, and was Governor of Bombay for 16 years.
16. Cormackam, Rev. J., *Accounts of Abolition of Female Infanticide in Gujarat*, London, 1815, p. 14.
17. Browne, J.C., op. cit., p. 31.
18. ibid., pp. 52-53.
19. The Jehrajahas Jahajee, a chief of Gujarat informed Walker, the British Political Agent, that out of regard for friendship he was prepared to preserve his daughters, provided the chief of Nawanagur and Gonal Wallas also agree. If they did not preserve them he declined to do so.
    Walker, Alexender, *A Report on Infanticide, Appendix* 17.
20. Browne, J.C., op. cit., London, 1857, p. 58.

21. *Abstracts of the Proceedings of the Council of the Governor-General of India*, 1870, Vol. IX, p. 5
22. ibid., p. 6.
23. *Abstract of the Proceedings*, 1870, op. cit., p.6.
24. ibid., p. 7.
25. Browne, J.C., op. cit., p. 71.
26. ibid., p. 143
27. *Census Report*, Punjab, 1911, part 1, p. 243.
28. *Hoshiarpur District Gazetteer*, Vol. XIII A, Lahore, 1904, p. 30.
29. It is a place about 18 miles from Dasuya in Hoshiarpur district.
30. *Hoshiarpur District Gazetteer*, Vol. XIII A, Lahore, 1904, p. 30.
31. *Abstract of the Proceedings*, 1870, op. cit., p. 8.
32. ibid.
33. *Hoshiarpur District Gazetteer*, Vol. XIII A, Lahore, 1904, p. 31
34. Farquahar, J.N., *The Crown of Hinduism*, 2nd Edition, (Oxford), 1915, p. 91.
35. O'Malley, L.S.S., op. cit., p. 357.
36. Fuller M., *The Wrongs of Indian Womanhood*, New York, 1900, p. 33.
37. ibid., p. 36.
38. ibid.
39. Buch, M.L., *Rise and Growth of Indian Liberalism*, Baroda, 1938, p. 77.
40. *Report on Native Papers*, Bengal (Confidential), for the week ending 3 December 1870.
41. ibid.
42. *Indian Social Reformer*, 1899, Vol. 9, p. 250.
43. ibid.
44. Rukmabai did not abide by the verdict of the court. She was sentenced upto rising of the court. Later she took up her studies in medicine and became one of the prominent doctors.
45. Fuller, M., op. cit., p. 18.
46. *Indian Social Reformer*, 1889, Vol. 9, p. 250.
47. *Hindu Marriage Act*, 1955, has raised the marriageable age of girls to 15 years and that of boys to 18 years.
48. Smith, A. Vincent, *Oxford History of India*, p. 665.
49. Pegg writes in his *India's Cries to British Humanity* that "a widow who would turn with natural instinctive horror from the hint of sharing her husband's pyre will be at length gradually brought to pronounce a reluctant consent, because distracted with grief at the event without one friend to advise or protect her, she is little prepared to oppose the surrounding crowd of hungry Brahmins and interested relations, either by argument or force."
    A magistrate at Bhuj reported in 1819 that since 1816 there was only one case where a woman wanted to burn herself and she appeared firm

in her resolution. The ceremony was delayed for 24 hours and this made her change the decision. 2nd Edition, 1913, pp. 16-65.

50. This account is taken from an article entitled "Story of a century old Sati case in Bihar" contributed by Dr. K.K. Basu of Bhagalpur to the History Department, Panjab University, Chandigarh. For further details, see Appendix A.

51. Tavernier, Jean Baptiste, *Travels in India*, New York, 1889, Vol. II, p. 160.

52. Mullik, B., *The Hindu Family in Bengal*, Calcutta, 1882, p. 117.

53. Nehru, Shyama Kumari, *Our Cause*, Allahabad, pp. 270-271.

54. *Report on Native Papers*, Bombay (Confidential), for the week ending May 28, 1870, p.5.

55. *Report on Native Papers*, Bombay (Confidential), for the week ending August 10, 1872, p. 4.

56. Viresalungam was born at Rajamundry in Andhra State on April 16, 1848. He was a bitter critic of child marriage. He also raised his voice against dancing of girls. His mission was to support the widows by opening schools and widow homes.

57. *Indian Social Reformer*, Madras, 1900, Vol. 10, p. 279.

58. Farquahar, J.N., op. cit., p. 108.

59. *Census of Punjab*, 1911, Part I, p. 289.

60. Buch, M.A., op. cit., p. 53.

61. *Friend of India*, March 30, 1865, p. 362.

62. Lawful marriage.

63. It is a kind of ceremony and is binding like the lawful marriage for a stipulated period.

64. Abul Fazal, *Aine-e-Akbari*, Vol. I, English Translation by Blochmann, 1873, p. 327.

65. *Punjab Census Report*, 1911. Part I, p. 290.

66. ibid.

67. ibid.

68. *Proceedings of the Legislative Council of India from January to December*, Vol. II, Calcutta, 1857, p. 417.

69. By the *Hindu Marriage Act*, 1955, bigamy became an offence throughout the country.

70. Farquahar, J.N., op. cit., p. 101.

71. *Census Report Punjab*, 1911, Part 19, p. 295.

72. Women's apartment.

73. This custom is still prevalent even though not with the same rigidity in the districts of Rohtak and Hissar, especially in the villages which are mostly inhabited by Rajputs.

74. Roy, P.C., *Life and Times of C.R. Dass*, 1927, p.4.

75. *District Gazetteer, Multan, 1901-02*, p. 98.

76. ibid.

77. H.H. Nawab Sultan Jahan Begum, *Al-Hijab or Why Purdah is Necessary,* (Calcutta), 1922, p. 194.
78. Health Officer of Calcutta, *Report for 1913,* p. 126
79. Nehru, Shyama Kumari, op. cit., p. 208.
80. Gandhi, M.K., *Women and Social Injustice,* Ahmedabad, 1945, p. 101.
81. Fuller, M., op. cit., p. 101.
82. *Report on Native Papers,* Bengal (Confidential), for the week ending April 30, 1876, p. 1.
83. Fuller, M., op. cit., p. 101.
84. Gandhi, M.K., op. cit., p. 144
85. Fuller M., op. cit., p. 120.
86. ibid., p. 131.
87. ibid.
88. Government of India passed an Act in 1956 whereby traffic in women and children was prohibited. This law came into force in 1958.
89. *Report on Native Papers,* Bombay, for the week ending November 6, 1869, p. 4.
   Report on Native Papers, Bengal, for the week ending June 5, 1869, p. 1.
90. Long, J., *Adam's Report* on Vernacular Education in Bengal and Bihar, submitted in 1835, 1836, 1839, with a brief review of present conditions, Calcutta, 1868, p. 132.
91. *Census for India,* 1881, Vol. I, p. 254.
92. *Report of Indian Education Commission,* 1882 p. 521
93. Long J., op. cit., p. 44.
94. *Report of Indian Education Commission,* 1882, p. 524.
95. British Parliamentary Papers—*Education in India,* Vol. 47, 1854, p. 16.
96. The despatch on education of 1854 partly reads: "The importance of female education in India, cannot be overrated, and we have observed with pleasure the evidence which is now afforded of an increased desire on the part of many of the natives of India to give good education to their daughters. By this means a far greater proportional impulse is imparted to the educational and moral tone of the people than by the education of men. We have already observed that schools for females are included among those to which grants-in-aid may be given; and we cannot refrain from expressing our sympathy with efforts which are being made in this direction.

   Our Governor-General in Council has declared in a communication to the Government of Bengal, that the Government ought to give native female education in India its frank and cordial support...."
   British Parliamentary Papers—*Education in India,* Vol. 47, 1854, p. 16, Paragraph 8B.

97. Selections from the Records of the Government of India, Home Department, No. LXVII, p. 52.

98. Bedi Khem Singh was born in 1830. He was a great reformer and was also a member of the Legislative Council, Punjab.

99. Leitner, G.W., *History of Indigenous Education in the Punjab*, Calcutta, 1882, p. 107.

100. *Indian Social Reformer*, Vol. 10, 1900, p. 59.

101. *Report of Indian Education Commission*, p. 535.

102. *Calcutta Review*, Vol. 60, 1936, p. 74.

103. The Government of India wrote: "The supreme Government in dealing with this question requires not only Native co-operation, but Native initiation. They are prepared to grant a generous measure of assistance but the intervention of the State must according to their resolution be preceded by an earnest and genuine effort on the part of the local community.

   "The Governor-General in Council is far from satisfied that (except in the immediate neighbourhood of the Presidency towns) the Native community has not yet really shown any spontaneous desire for extension of female education. Indeed, there is ground to fear that the action already taken in that direction on the part of Government has in some places, being regarded with mistrust, nor is it surprising that this should be the case. The true value of education even for males is hardly as yet fully appreciated by the Native community at large, while on the other hand it must be obvious even to the most ignorant among them, that the natural result of the general extension of female education would be to place the domestic relations of every family on a new footing and to break up existing social habits and traditions. Even when these results are themselves beneficial, the interference of foreign rulers to effect them will probably be distasteful. Far more must this be the case when such changes are opposed to widely prevailing customs deeply rooted and long established.

   "The Governor-General in Council, therefore, considers it a grave political necessity to maintain the principles of the rules which have been already prescribed, that is to say, that as a condition of pecuniary aid from Government, it should be always required that Native in every case be taken bonafide by the Native local community itself and that they should contribute a reasonable share of the requisite outlay as a pledge of their earnestness and sincerity."
   Selection from Records, Home Department, Papers connected with *Education in India*, Calcutta, 1868, pp. 1701-71.

104. Selection from the Records of the Government of India, Home Department, No. LXVIII, p. 56.

2

WOMEN FIGHTERS' ROLE IN 1857-1858 WAR

The upheaval of 1857-58 was the first organised armed attempt by the Indians to free themselves from the political grip of the English. The period was one of great tribulation for the Indians and the English alike, because the fate of both experienced such convulsions which were unmatched in the history of the country. The British emerged victorious, but the Indians gained too because the movement became a symbol of strength and sacrifice for the subsequent generations.

In the decade preceding the outbreak the political map of India was radically changed. Lord Dalhousie had intensified the process of annexation through a vigorous application of the policy of 'lapse'. The years of his regime (1848-56) saw the absorption of nothing less than eight States which meant that a quarter million square miles of territory was added to the East India Company's territorial limits.

The period also witnessed the missionary activities against early marriage, purdah system, the passing of the Widow Re-marriage Bill in 1856, activities of some English officers engaged in proselytising, the introduction of railways, telegraph and the greased cartridges.

The atmosphere of the country, and especially of northern India, was clouded with vague suspicions. The people felt confirmed in their faith that the British authorities were not satisfied with mere annexation of the States but wanted to interfere in their religious affairs and end the caste system.

The first signs of unrest were felt in the first quarter of the year 1857 when the sepoys at Berhampore (five miles east of Nowgong), Barrackpore and Ambala resorted to incendiarism. The Indian Regiments were disbanded and the culprits punished. This, however, did not quieten the situation and proved only a prelude to the open rebellion which followed in May.

The leaders of the outbreak were both men and women, most important amongst the latter being Begum Hazrat Mahal, Rani Lakshmi Bai, Rani of Ramgarh and Rani Tace Bai. Some of them led troops to the battlefield and fought, while others accepted the sufferings and privation, imprisonment and death.

It was on April 24, 1857, that C. Smyth, Commandant, 3rd-Light Cavalry, ordered a parade to test the loyalty of the soldiers, at Meerut. Out of ninety sepoys present, 85 refused to accept new cartridges. As a result they were court-martialled and were sentenced to varying terms of imprisonment extending up to 10 years.

The sentence thus passed was announced on May 9, 1857, in the presence of a gathering with an aim to create a consternation and fear. The sepoys were stripped of their uniforms and then were handed over to the smiths for fastening shakles round their arms and legs.[1] The sight might have been picturesque for the English Commander but the whole affair was distasteful to the Indians assembled. "There was a good deal of murmuring in our ranks," says Gough, "and had it not been for the presence of the British troops it is impossible to say what might not have taken place."[2]

Later in the evening the 'women of bazar' jeered at the sepoys. "Your brethren have been ornamented with these anklets and incarcerated and for what? Because they would not swerve from their creed and you cowards as you are, sit still indifferent to your fate. If you have an atom of manhood in you, go and release them."[3]

The taunts inflamed their hearts. "The spark which fell from female lips ignited it at once and the night of the May 10, 1857, saw the commencement of a tragedy never before witnessed since India passed under British sway."[4]

The flames of fire which broke out at Meerut, on May 10, spread rapidly over a large part of northern India.

Begum Hazrat Mahal

While the women of Meerut were partly instrumental, in accelerating action on the part of sepoys, conditions in Lucknow, a place not very far away from Meerut, were inspiring Begum Hazrat Mahal to take up the leadership.

Hazrat Mahal was a dancing girl and later became an acknowledgd wife of King Wajid Ali Shah of Oudh by 'Motah'. The annexation of Oudh which was completed in 1856 came as a heavy blow to the royal family, chiefs and the people. Hazrat Mahal discontented as she was, decided to stay back in Lucknow, while the deposed king went to Calcutta and made his abode there.

The queen mother, however, could not bear this injustice and left for England. "An aged queen brought up in all the pomp and luxury of the East, the soles of whose feet were scarcely allowed to tread the ground, laying aside the prejudices of travel, and undertaking a journey of some ten thousand miles, appealed to the people of England for justice." Her efforts bore no fruit.[5]

As a consequence of the absorption of Oudh into British territory, as many as 60,000 people were thrown out of employment. Artisans and craftsmen lost their only means of livelihood. Another factor which caused annoyance was that Jackson, the Resident at Lucknow, had converted Chatar Manzil, a palace for the royal family, into his residence. Qadim Rasul, a building of sanctity, was converted into a storehouse. Added to these causes were: (a) new revenue settlements did not provide any relief which, therefore, caused frustration; (b) judicial system remained cumbersome, expensive and lengthy; (c) some of the old taxes though abolished were replaced by the new; (d) the payment of pensions, according to the pension list, prepared at the time of annexation, was unduly delayed.

In the early part of April, Dr. Wells, a British medical officer in Lucknow, tested the quality of medicine by applying the bottle to his mouth before administering to patients. This was disliked by the soldiers and they refused to take it lest the taint of a Christian should degrade their caste. The complaint went up to the Commandant of 48 Native Infantry who reconciled the excited soldiers. That night the doctor's bungalow was destroyed by fire. The culprit was untraced. After a couple of days a number of huts of the 13th Regiment were burnt under mysterious circumstances.[6]

The wounds received as a result of absorption of Oudh were still fresh when rebellion broke out at Meerut on May 10, 1857. The injury caused by annexation was combined with the opportunity afforded by the outbreak at Meerut and people with a hope to establish their own rule lent their support to the rebel cause, and the banner of revolt was raised in Lucknow on May 30, 1857.

The revolution spread rapidly to other towns of Oudh and the rebels were successful in establishing their authority in many places one after another. Consequently by the middle of June, the British regime in this province lay prostrate. Lucknow was the only place where the English did not leave the Residency building and faced the rebels till they were able to regain their lost power.

Hazrat Mahal was an influential lady and was the primary figure in bringing about this insurrection. "She has excited all Oudh," said Russell, "to take up the interests of her son, and the chiefs have sworn to be faithful to him."[7] The boy's name was Birjis Qadir who was then eleven years old.

Hazrat Mahal who became the regent queen exercised all authority. She ruled the State diplomatically and exhibited qualities of a good leadership and statesmanship. The high offices in the State were distributed between the Hindus and Muslims. She also honoured brave soldiers.[8]

Hazrat Mahal Begum was perhaps not fated to rule the State for a long time. In September 1857 came the news of the defeat of the rebels in Delhi which was not only discouraging but was also ruinous for her designs. Added to this was the arrival of Outram[9] and Havelock[10] from Kanpur to relieve the British garrison in the Residency of Lucknow. After a few encounters with the rebels Outram was able to occupy Alam Bagh[11] on September 23, 1857, and finally reached the besieged Garrison on September 25.

The victory of the English in Kanpur was another setback to her plans. But nothing deterred her from the path she had chosen. The Begum kept up the spirit and held Durbars. One of her ideas was to cause her own death by taking poison instead of becoming a prisoner of the English.[12]

In the month of November Sir Colin Campbell, Commander-in-Chief of the British Forces, along with a small reinforcement arrived at Lucknow. The Begum gave a tough fight. Her soldiers became panicky and began to run away. The rebels also became disrespectful to her. The difficult situation made her doubtful of the outcome of the struggle. The English Commander was able to escort the besieged garrison out of the Residency to Alam Bagh.

The rebels again became active in Kanpur and their activities compelled Campbell to retrace his steps. This move of the English helped the Indian troops to pick up courage again. The Begum took this opportunity and ordered for the occupation of Banaras and Allahabad. She also sent instructions to Nazims and Talukadars to march on Azamgarh and Jaunpur (Dist. of Uttar Pradesh). She called a meeting of the chiefs on December 22, 1857, and criticised the leaders for not exhibiting courage. She denounced them for their indifference and callousness. The Begum is reported to have complained, "Great things were promised from all powerful Delhi and my heart used to be gladdened by the communications I used to receive from that city but soon the king had been dispossessed and his army scattered. The English have brought over the Sikhs and Rajahs, and communications are cut off. The Nana has been vanquished, Lucknow is endangered— what is to be done? The whole army is in Lucknow, but it is without courage. Why does it not attack Alam Bagh? Is it waiting for the English to be reinforced and Lucknow to be surrounded? How much longer am I to pay the sepoys for doing nothing? Answer me now, and if you won't fight, I shall negotiate with the English to spare my life."[13]

She tried to encourage the soldiers and is reported to have appeared on the battlefield on February 25, 1858, mounted on an elephant.[14] Alam Bagh was vigorously attacked by a force sometimes led by Maulvi Ahmedula Shah[15] and at other times by the Begum in person.[16]

Russell observes thus: "Begum declares undying war against us; and in the circumstances of the annexation of the kingdom the concealment of the suppression of the treaty, the apparent ingratitude to the family for money lent and aid given at most critical times has many grounds for her indignant rhetoric."[17]

It was on March 2, 1858, that the British started operations against Lucknow with a strong force of thirty thousand under the command of Sir Colin Campbell and Jung Bahadur (Nepal). The British forces occupied one place after another till the rebels found their positions precarious and decided to evacuate. In the Central Court, Lucknow alone, 860 defenders became the victims of this battle.

Hazrat Mahal "never lost heart and moved among her men with spirit that deserved better success."[18] She went about in the battlefield inspiring her troops. By March 18, 1858, all the strong points in Lucknow were in the hands of the English. But "a powerful force probably inspired by the Begum held Musabagh, a palace in Lucknow, till the 19th March 1858."[19]

Later the Begum reinforced Maulvi Ahmedula Shah in his attack on Shahjahanpur. On October 1, 1858, she issued instructions to the troops in a long letter, directing them the line of attack. "This document," wrote the Chief Commissioner, "appears to be genuine and many of the movements ordered have been made and failed." She wrote: "Imtizamood Dowlah is requested to concentrate a sufficient force including artillery for the defence of Pilibheet on the Bheera and Jugadpur roads, the leaders to be Enayat Ali Khan...."[20] She not only issued instructions but also led the troops to the battlefield. Sarfras Begum writing to Akhtar Mahal, wife of Wajid Ali who was at Calcutta, made mention of Hazrat Mahal thus: "I did not know Hazrat Mahal was such a brave lady. Seated on an elephant she led her troops against the English without any fear. Alam Bagh was the scene of a pitched battle. Ahmedula Shah joined Hazrat Mahal and they fought with valour and courage but luck did not favour them."[21]

Another Begum, Sayda, wrote to Wajid Ali thus: "Hazrat Mahal showed such courage that the enemy was terrified. She turned out to be very daring. She has brought name to the Sultan Alam."[22]

Under adverse circumstances the Begum had to escape to Nepal[23] with her followers and her son Birjis Qadir. The Nepalese authorities were hesitant to give asylum to the rebels. The Nepal Government in a strongly worded letter on January 15, 1859, wrote that if she was to honour the treaty with the British Government the rebels must be surrendered to that government. And therefore, "If you should remain or seek an asylum within my territory and frontier, the Gorkha troops will most certainly, in pursuance of the treaty agreed upon by both the high States, attack and make war on you.... And be it known that the Nepal State will neither assist nor show mercy to, nor permit to remain in its territories or within its frontiers to those who have been so faithless and ungrateful as to do mischief and raise animosity and insurrection against their master...."[24]

These threats, however, were all in vain as the Begum refused to surrender to the foreign Government. The Nepalese authorities had to change the decision and asylum was given to her on the condition that she will not communicate with the rebel leaders or with their troops or with the people of India.[25]

She faced many difficulties in Nepal. Only women and boys under 12 were allowed to stay in her camp. The lieutenant incharge of her at Noakote (Nepal) observed the Begum complaining thus: "The Gorkhas have reduced me to dust, they have joined the British, they have neither assisted my troops nor allowed them to remain in the country, neither have they allowed me to join them."[26] When the Prime Minister of Nepal proclaimed in the rebels' camps the Governor-General's terms and invited them to surrender, the Begum said, "They would sooner die than surrender."[27]

The British authorities offered her the terms that "The Begum Hazrat Mahal will receive all the consideration which is due to her as a woman and member of a royal house. But political powers she shall never have, and she will do wisely to secure by prompt submission a generous treatment and an honourable position for the rest of her life."[28] It was further added that "The rebel leaders must submit themselves to the mercy and generosity of the Government unconditionally, their lives and honour being safe, if they have not taken part in the murder of the British subjects. This applies to all from Begum down to those of the lowest rank amongst them."[29]

The Begum did not agree to these terms as she was not prepared to see herself deprived of all political powers, though it may be said that there might have been a remote fear in her mind about revengeful treatment from the British as it was alleged in some quarters that she was a party to the murder of Europeans.[30] Instead of surrendering she asked for armed assistance from the Nepalese authorities for the purpose of making conquest of the British Province.[31]

After the mutiny was quelled, the Queen of England issued a proclamation to appease the people. She promised to respect the agreements entered into by the Company and also to respect the religious rites, etc. But it did not receive an unqualified success. Begum Hazrat Mahal issued a counter proclamation challenging the truth and sincerity of the promises made by the British Queen in the proclamation. She warned the people not to have faith in these promises "for it is the unvarying custom of the English never to forgive a fault, be it great or small."[32]

She condemned the article relating to agreement and contracts and asserted that there was nothing new in them. "The Company professed to treat the chief of Bharatpur as a son, and then took his territory; the chief of Lahore[33] was carried off to London and it has not fallen to his lot to return..."[34]

The Begum dealt with each article in detail and uncovered the lies in it.

She did not surrender to the British authorities, so she was refused a pension. Nepal Government, however, allowed her a *pension of Mohri* Rs 400 a month. The Begum tried to come back to India in 1877 but orders were issued, whereby any request made by either Birjis Qadir and his mother who, or was, a very clever and designing woman, should not be allowed to visit British India."[35] The Government of India clearly explained that "If they did enter the territories of the British Government they would on no consideration receive any assistance or allowance from Government and would be required to be under the surveillance of the magistrate of the district in which they might take up residence."[36]

As a result of the attitude of the British government she could not come to India and hence had to reside in Nepal permanently. Thus, the Begum died for the great cause in exile, in 1879, in a land foreign to her.[37]

There were other women who laid their lives in the battlefield but whose names still remain unknown. Gordon Alexandra observes: "Among the slain at Sikendra Bagh there were a few negresses. They fought like wild cats and it was not till after they were killed that their sex was even suspected."[38]

Forbes Mitchell makes mention of a woman who was shot at Sikendra Bagh. She was armed with a heavy old pattern piston. Seated on the pipal tree she killed half a dozen people. [39]

Russell also discovered a woman a few days after the battle. She was dead but near her body was an enormous mine.[40]

In Delhi there was another woman who became famous under the name, Maid of Delhi. She would go to the battlefield in a Sawar's uniform and was reported to have been worse than five sepoys in the battlefield. *Saddiq-Uli Akhbar* (newspaper) reported that she had been given a horse by the King.[41]

Rani Lakshmi Bai of Jhansi

While Hazrat Mahal was busy in exterminating the British from Oudh, Jhansi gave a quick response to the rebel's cause. On June 5, 1857, there was an open rebellion at Jhansi.

Jhansi was a small Maratha State but its geographical location was strategically important. It could serve as a nerve centre for the Central Indian States and this consideration prompted Dalhousie to hasten its annexation in 1854.

The management of the state, till it became British territory, was with Gangadhar Rao.[42] He had an able wife in Rani Lakshmi Bai. She was the daughter of Moropant Tambe who was in the service of Peshwa Chimmaji Appa on a monthly salary of rupees fifty. The Rani was born on November 19, 1835, at Banares. She was named Manikarnika but she became known by the name she was given after her marriage, Lakshmi Bai. She lost her mother Bhagirathi Bai, when she was a child. The burden of bringing her up rested on her father. She was married at the age of 14 years to Gangadhar Rao then 40 years of age.[43] An interesting account of her has been written by John Lang who became her chief consultant after the annexation of Jhansi.[44]

A son was born to Gangadhar Rao and Rani Lakshmi Bai in 1851, but he died after three months. The ruler of Jhansi fell ill in 1853 and an adoption became necessary. He adopted Anand Rao,[45] a five-year-old boy, who received his new name, Damodar Gangadhar Rao, after adoption on December 19, 1853, in the presence of Major Ellis, the Assistant Political Agent and Major Martin, Commanding the Jhansi Contingent. Gangadhar Rao handed over a letter to Ellis with the request to get the necessary sanction of the Government of India for this adoption.[46]

Instead of giving approval to the action taken by the Raja the doctrine of 'lapse' was put into force by Dalhousie in the case of Jhansi and the decision was conveyed in an official letter to Major Ellis, the Superintendent of Jhansi, dated March 7, 1854. The letter in part reads: "The State which was a tributory and dependent principality held by grant from the British Government has reverted to that government."[47] When Ellis informed Lakshmi Bai, widow of the late Raja, whom Major D.A. Malcolm, the political Agent described as a lady "who bears a very high character and is much respected by every one at Jhansi,"[48] about the decision of the government she is reported to have said, *"Meri Jhansi, Nehi Dungi"* (I shall not surrender my Jhansi).[49]

By the new terms provided to her, a pension of rupees five thousand per month was fixed for her and she was given a palace at Jhansi for her residence. The Rani and her personal female attendants were not amenable to the British Court during their life time. Personal ornaments of the late Maharaja and the balance remaining in the public treasury after closing accounts of the State were considered her private property.[50] She repudiated these terms and expressed dissatisfaction to Ellis and also requested the Governor-General to allow her a period of 31 days to enable her to represent her case,[51] but the representation was of no avail since the government was averse to revert the decision. The Rani was no ordinary person and as such the irrevocable decision of the government did not help her to lead a life of acceptance and quietude. Instead it aspired her to fight for her rights to represent her case further.[52]

She addressed a 'Khureetta' on December 21, 1854,[53] to the Court of Directors reminding them that the right of adoption was by Hindu Law absolute, fixed and indefeasible and this indefeasible right was not transferred to the East India Company nor was it lost or forfeited by the ruler of Jhansi by any breach of treaty or by conquest and it was not acquired by the East India Company.[54] The Rani felt that the adoption was not disputed as Damodar Rao was permitted to succeed to his father's property—it was the effect of that adoption which she presumed that the government disowned. Lakshmi Bai, therefore, questioned the justification and legality of the annexation of Jhansi. She, however, held that if it became necessary on grounds of expediency the course followed should have been that of negotiations and agreement and not that of "exercise of the powers without right of the great and strong against the weak and small."[55] In the same petition she informed the authorities that the merger of Jhansi was a gross violation and negation of treaties of the Government of India and that the case of Jhansi had created a disquietude among the princes and chiefs of Upper India and they awaited the result of an application submitted by her with great interest because the decision given in case of Jhansi would help them to decide whether they were to have faith or distrust in the British rule.[56]

Over and above, she asserted that "The people of Jhansi did not desire to be made the subject of the East India Company. On the contrary, without a single exception they testified their willingness and desire to remain the subject of your memorialist and her ward."[57]

It is evident from this petition that the Rani not only demanded justice for her cause but she also gave an expression to the sentiments of the people in general and to the wavering faith of the chiefs in the English regime in particular, and, hence, made it clear that the treatment meted out to her was being viewed with concern.

Since the petition did not bring any tangible results, she sent a mission to England to represent her case which cost her rupees sixty thousand. The Rani did all that was in her power to regain her lost position, but these protests were of no avail. It was like a cry in the wilderness which went unheard and uncared for. Its effect on the mind of the young Rani is described by Forest in these words: "Thus the Maratha Queen tall in stature, handsome in person, young, energetic, proud and unyielding from that moment indulged the stern passion of anger and revenge."[58]

As a mark of her displeasure she had declined the offer of a pension, but after some time she revised her judgement and accepted it. Her rage was further aroused when she was asked to pay the unliquidated debt of her ancestors amounting to 'Nanashahi', i.e., thirty-six thousand rupees. Lakshmi Bai protested that these debts were not her debts and were not contracted by her late husband and hence she was not responsible for them. The Deputy Superintendent supported her in his recommendation[59] to the Lt. Governor, but the government did not yield. She was asked to pay them from the private funds of the Raja made over to her, otherwise she was threatened with a deduction from her monthly pension. Another act of the British authorities which earned the Rani's displeasure was the refusal to advance money to celebrate the sacred thread ceremony of Damodar Rao, unless four sureties for the repayment of the sum were furnished. Such negative attitude of the government towards each of her requests helped her to keep alive the issue of annexation and to look forward for a chance of redressal. The Rani was "ready to take any opportunity of gratifying her revenge and being like many other Maratha women of rank, possessed of masculine spirit[60] she was well fitted to carry out her designs, and was ripe when the outbreak occurred in 1857."[61]

So far the Rani had personal grievances to nurse; but before long an opportunity was provided by the rulers which enabled her to make a common cause with the people of Jhansi who had continued to brood over the injury and the disgrace of annexation. Kaye writes that "She hated the English with the deadliest hatred. And soon she began to cherish new-born grievances. Foremost among these were the killing of cattle by the English."[62]

Slaughter of cows was an unknown thing in the Brahmin State, but the *British government was unmindful* of the religious sentiments of the people. They not only authorised slaughter of the cows but also established slaughter houses. The Rani and the people petitioned against this wrong but it was of no avail. Hence an excuse was given to "increase the fear and religious passions which had been aroused among the sepoys by the question of greased cartridges and to scatter among them the seeds of disloyalty and contention."[63]

Still another cause which created dissatisfaction was the government's verdict in favour of the two mistresses of the late Gangadhar Rao, allowing them to have the rent of village Sumberadah.[64]

In May, there was a widespread rumour in Jhansi as in other places that ground bones were mixed in the flour and that cow's and pig's fat had been used for making cartridges for the use of the army.

In the beginning of June 1857, a letter is reported to have been received from the mutineers at Delhi to say that "the whole army of the Bengal Presidency had mutinied and as the Regiment at Jhansi had not done so men composing it were outcaste and had lost their faith."[65]

This quickened the passage of revolt and Jhansi witnessed an open rebellion on June 5, 1857. The English had to take shelter in the city fort on June 6. The next day the Rani's adherents also joined the rebels. They released the prisoners, set fire to the "kutchery" and murdered all those officers on whomsoever they were able to lay their hands. The rebels also attacked the fort occupied by the English. Fire was exchanged between the besiegers and the besieged till the night of June 6, when the troops retired and the Rani's men kept guard on the fort.[66]

The following morning three persons, Messrs Scot, Purcells and Andrews, were sent from the English Camp disguised as Indians with a view to obtaining help from the Rani. All the three of them were murdered. Andrews is reported to have been killed by a servant of the Rani at the palace door. The same night rebels were successful in getting some guns and men[67] and the fort was again attacked on the morning of June 8, with added strength and renewed energy. The English could not hold on any longer and thus surrendered on a promise that they would be allowed to leave Jhansi unmolested. But as soon as they came out they were seized and taken to Jokham Bagh where all of them,[68] except Mrs. Multov, her two children and Mr. Crawford, who managed to escape, including women and children were murdered.

In the evening a proclamation was made by the rebels: "The people are God's, the country is the King's (Padshah) and the two religions govern."[69]

The victory of the rebels was followed by a dispute over the possession of Jhansi territory between the Rani and Sadashiv Rao Narain Parowala, a relation of the late Raja. However, Lakshmi Bai was able to get the territory after paying a large sum to the rebels and a proclamation was made: "The people are God's, the country is Padshah's and the Raj is Rani Lakshmi Bai's."[70] She, however, was to govern on behalf of her adopted son.

There are different versions regarding the actual complicity of the Rani in the rebellion. In the official *Narrative of the Events,* the facts are recorded in the following manner: "Mr. Scott, Head Writer in the Deputy Commissioner's office, who lived near the lines and mixed much with natives and had much better information of what was going on, and placed his property in the keeping of a loyal native in the town of Jhansi. He persisted in avowing that he had good reasons to know that a mutiny was intended and that the Rani and the troops were one."[71]

The above statement is partly corroborated from the papers relating to the mutiny of 1857 compiled in the Intelligence Department of the Government of India. It is stated that about this time one Chatajee, an agent of an Indian Chief, informed Captain Gordon, Deputy Superintendent of Jhansi, that Bhole Nath, adherent of the Rani, convened meetings with the Indian officers who frequently visited the Rani's palace and that treachery was intended.[72] However, it is not clear whether these proceedings had the sanction of Lakshmi Bai. It appears that the Rani apprehended danger and so sought permission to keep an armed guard for her protection.

Kaye, while referring to her share in the rebellion, writes that "with the Maratha instinct she was in danger from the enemies of the English and thus intimated that her interests were identical with our own while she was plotting our overthrow."[73]

It has been mentioned above that the Rani asked permission to keep an armed guard for her protection as she said she was afraid of the enemy of the English. It is interesting to refer here to Skene's letter who was in charge of Jhansi district at that time. He wrote on May 8, 1857: "I do not think that there is any cause of alarm about this neighbour-hood."[74] This is curious enough to find that, while the English were not aware of their enemies, she should have apprehended danger from them. It is clear, therefore, that she was familiar with the designs of the rebels and tried to please both the parties. By asking for an armed assistance she showed the rebels on one hand that her interests were identical with them and that she had already started the recruitment of armed men while on the other hand she could tell the British authorities that she had warned them of the danger if the rebels' plot was ever discovered.

It is an established fact that the Rani was popular and influential. She mentioned in the petition made by her against the annexation that the people of Jhansi wanted her to be the ruler.[75] Sir Hugh Rose, who fought against her, while referring to the resistance put up by her soldiers writes: "The reason was sufficiently clear, the people of Jhansi fought for the Queen and the independence of their country. Even after the city had fallen her bounty and liberality rendered her an influential and dangerous adversary."[76] It is unbelievable that a person of her standing and influence should not have been taken into confidence by the rebels while designing the overthrow of the British Government.

Rani's father, Moropant, was one of the chief instigators of the rebellion in that part of the country. He could not have possibly kept her in the dark about the intending revolt. Her advice and assistance must have been sought by him.[77] The preceding account, therefore, nullifies Majumdar's statement that "Rani Lakshmi Bai of Jhansi not only did not instigate the sepoy mutiny but had nothing to do with their plan or programme."[78] As far as the Rani's role in the events that led to the massacre of Europeans is concerned, Major Ellis, writing to the Secretary to the Government of India on June 26, 1857, i.e., about 18 days after the massacre, reported thus: "Sjt Kirchaff in the Canal Department who arrived here yesterday evening from Mohaba gives an account of the conspiracy of Jhansi and Nowgong mutineers. Sadashiv Narain Rao Parolwala has been declared a rebel at Jhansi by order of the Agent of the Governor-General, Central India, but he has little or no influence there, and it cannot be doubted that the cold-blooded atrocities committed by our troops on the Europeans would not have been perpetrated had the Rani not encouraged them."[79]

Thornton, Joint Magistrate and Deputy Collector, in an official letter, informed Captain Bruce, Superintendent of Police at Kanpur on August 18, 1857,[80] that the mutineer sepoys intended to leave Jhansi after they had seized the treasure. It was at the instance of "a Bundelkhand chieftainess, the Rani of Jhansi, wishing to regain power in the district, bribed them with large presents to take the fort and put all the Europeans to death before they finally departed for Delhi."[81]

The official report, recorded eight months after the actual occurrence, held the Rani responsible for the murder of English people in Jhansi. It (report) says: "Through the treachery of the Rani the fortress of Jhansi whither the European residents had fled, on the native troops mutinying, fell into the possession of mutineers and a general massacre of all Europeans of every age and sex took place."[82]

Thomas Lowe, a medical officer with Sir Hugh Rose's forces, while referring to his entry in the palace at Jhansi writes: "In most of the rooms we found some relics or other of the unfortunate officers who perished here in the mutiny. These things showed that the Rani had not only participated in their murder but had positively shared in the plunder of their property."[83]

The worst charge was brought against the Rani by Shahab-ud-Din, Khansama of Major Skein, who was at Jhansi and moved about the town carrying messages for and from his master. He was hauled up by the rebels on a couple of occasions but somehow or the other fortune favoured him and he was let free. Shahab-ud-Din states: "He saw Karuk Bijlee (Gun) was put in order by Rani's order to be used against the officers and that the town people, mutineer sepoys and Rani's servants were firing.... One day before the murder of the officers it was proclaimed in the town by the beat of the drum that the country belonged to the King, the Rani had the rule and that the officers will be killed tomorrow." It was further stated by him that after the massacre of the Europeans "the Rani, jail daroga and sawars went to the *pultan* and orders to free the prisoners were given."[84]

Shahab-ud-Din's statement is not corroborated wholly and seems to have a tinge of fiction at places and as such cannot be taken as the whole truth.

Madar Bakhsh, another person attached to Gordon, was engaged in helping the Europeans. He recorded in his statement that he took a letter from his master to the Rani. In this letter Gordon had requested the Rani to get them down from the fort and to send them to Duttia or Orchha. The letter under reference was handed over to the Rani's father who in turn took it to her. She forwarded the same letter to the Risaldar through her lawyer Ajudhia Prashad. Madar Bakhsh later heard from "one of the Rani's chobdars who had been dismissed" that the Rani sent another messenger named Zabita Khan to the Risaldar apparently with another message. After the return of Ajudhia Prashad she sent a letter to the besieged Europeans, but the contents of this letter were not known to him. Madar Bakhsh further stated that he heard that the Rani's sepoys took Europeans to the parade and killed them.[85]

As against these statements Bhagwan Brahmin who was at that time at Jhansi says that Lal Bahadur subedar and Bakshish Ali, the jail daroga, brought the Europeans out of the fort after pledging safety to them. It is recorded in his statement, "I did not hear that the Europeans were killed by the order of the Rani."[86]

Sheikh Hingan, hookambardar of Captain Gordon, appears to have carried some messages to the Rani from his master. He stated that when Gordon heard that the Rani had supplied guns and sepoys to the mutineers, he wrote a letter to the Rani "to say it was her Raj and he and other gentlemen would go where she liked." He further stated that Rani sent a message through her servant to the besieged and the contents were to this effect: "What can I do? Sepoys have surrounded me, and say I have concealed the gentlemen and that I must get the fort evacuated, and assist them to save myself. I have sent guns and my followers; if you wish to save yourself, abandon the fort, no one will injure you." According to Sheikh Hingan the mutineers promised that the Europeans would be able to leave Jhansi safely.[87]

There is still more evidence which throws further light on the occurrences. A Bengali[88] attached to the Writer's Establishment of Jhansi Custom Collector's Office who was in Jhansi during these troubled days and also was ill-treated for having sympathy with the Europeans states: "The Rani placed guards at her gate and shut herself up in her palace. Captain Gordon sent a message to the Rani soliciting her assistance at this crisis, but this was refused as the mutineers threatened to put her to death and to set fire to her palace in case of her compliance with Captain Gordon's request. The Rani's guards then joined the mutineers." He further held that three persons, Messrs Andrews, Purcell and Scott, disguised as Indians went to the Rani for help; but the feint being discovered, they were taken to the palace of the

Rani and she did not even agree to honour them with an interview. She sent them to the mutineers. Her words were to the effect: "She had no concern with the English swine." While referring to the attack on the fort he says that the Rani was threatened with instant assassination provided she refused to side with the rebels. She accordingly consented and supplied them with a reinforcement of 1,000 and two heavy guns which she had ordered to be dug out of the earth.

As regards the murder of the Europeans, he observed that as soon as the Europeans came out of the fort, they were seized by the rebels and taken to Jokham Bagh and "then commenced the horrid massacre, the daroga of the jail first raising his sword and killing Captain Skein."[89]

Kaye, a celebrated historian writes: "I have been informed that none of the Rani's servants were present at the occasion of the massacre. It seems to have been mainly the work of our old followers. The irregular cavalry issued the bloody mandate and our jail daroga was foremost in the butchery."[90]

Mrs. Multov who was in the fort with the garrison and was able to escape with the help of an 'ayah' recorded her impression thus: "Mr. Skein and Mr. Gordon went to the Rani and got about 50 or 60 guns and some powder and shots and balls and she sent about 50 of her own sepoys to the fort to assist us and about 2 o'clock during the day they killed the gentleman who was with them and commenced burning the bungalow and speared Mr. Taylor who belonged to the cavalry, so he galloped his horse and came to the fort. As soon as the Rani heard of it she got all her sepoys down from the fort. The Rani and her sepoys joined with the Regiment." In her evidence she also mentioned that the Europeans agreed to come out of the fort on a solemn promise from the rebels that their lives would be spared. This promise is reported to have been countersigned by the Rani. But as soon as they came out of the fort sepoys put their guard around them.

Mrs Multov further stated: "I went out with 'Ayah', they did not take notice of me. She brought and left me in the Jokham Bagh in those Hindoo graves made like a house. I remained there about a month. Dowlut Ram came from Saugor, and heard of me, he came to me that very evening. I sent Dowlut Ram twice to Saugor, he was caught twice on the road. Those letters came to Jhansi to the Rani and she was looking out for me and Dowlut Ram. So Dowlut hid himself and hid me and two children. It was the Rani's order, if any one catches us going out of town that she will give one hundred rupees as a present, in those days."[91]

Mrs. Multov's statement is not corroborated fully by any other person. Secondly, she took her abode in Jokham Bagh, a Hindu cemetery. This place was also the scene of massacre of the English. It is unbelievable that she stayed, in those troubled days, in a graveyard, a place not very secure, for a month and could not be discovered by the rebels in spite of the announcement of the reward. So much reliance cannot be put on her evidence.

Majumdar and Sen seek to support the Rani's innocence by referring to a letter written[92] by Martin, on August 20, 1889,[93] to Damodar Rao, the Rani's adopted son. Martin, while referring to the occurrence at Jhansi, writes: "The poor thing took no part whatever in the massacre of the European residents of Jhansi in June 1857. On the contrary she supplied them with food for two days after they had gone into the fort—got 100 matchlock men from Kurrua and sent them to assist us."[94]

The Rani's letter written to the British authorities does not make any reference to the help rendered by her to the Englishmen stationed at Jhansi. In fact she writes "that she could render no aid for want of guns and soldiers as she had only 100 or 50 people engaged in guarding her house."[95] If the Rani had helped the British in their difficult hour, she would have never forgotten to mention it.

Secondly, Martin's name does not appear anywhere in the official reports or enquiries nor does it occur in the statements made by various servants in the service of the British officials at Jhansi. The official reports indicate that there were only two persons, i.e., Mr. Crawford and Mrs. Multov who were fortunate to escape from Jhansi.

It is curious that Martin was not even with his compatriots in the fort as is apparent from his letter.

In view of the aforesaid facts much weight cannot be given to Martin's letter.

Sir Robert Hamilton who made enquiries into these events referred to the dispositions of Sepoy Aman Khan of 12 Native Infantry. He says that "his assertions are corroborated by and corroborate those made by others and as far as they go should say entitle up credit." Aman Khan took service with the Rani after the rebels left for Delhi. He was under death sentence when he made this statement. Aman Khan reported that "the insurgents, previous to the mutiny, did not consult the Rani. He also stated that the mutineer sepoys placing their guns in position threatened all the rest with immediate death if they refused to join them. Then all went to the palace of the Rani with loaded guns and demanded assistance and supplies. She was obliged to yield and to furnish guns, ammunition and supplies."[96]

Hamilton did not expressly accuse the Rani of complicity with the rebels. He, however, observed that Aman Khan was very reserved in any matter relating to his own regiment and averse to give more than the bare answer. This assertion of Hamilton shows that Aman Khan might have kept back certain information and even this statement may not be the whole truth.

It might appear from the later statements that the Rani was obliged to lend assistance to the rebels. There seems to have been no question of obligation. If she was really faithful to the English she should have left the State and taken refuge with them as was done by the Maharaja of Gwalior whose army had joined the rebels.

Secondly, she could have given proof of her loyalty by helping some of the English people to escape. Two persons, i.e., Mrs. Multov and Mr. Crawfort were able to get out of the grips of the rebels. In neither case she rendered any help. It is interesting to note in this connection that the Rani of Chattapur gave asylum and helped some of the Englishmen to escape.

Thirdly, if the Rani was interested in retaining the goodwill of the British Government, there was no need for her to offer to pay a larger sum of money to the rebels than Narain Rao Parlowala in exchange for Jhansi, her lost kingdom.

Fourthly, there is an authentic account available of the first day's event, i.e., June 5, 1857, relating to the revolt at Jhansi. Captain Gordon, Deputy Superintendent of Jhansi at that time, informed the higher authorities in a letter dated June 6, 1857, that trouble had started at Jhansi and that the magazine and all the treasure amounting to four and a half lakhs of rupees was seized by the rebels. In this letter Gordon did not make any reference to the help given by the Rani of Jhansi or of the help expected from her. He writes: "I have applied to Sumthur and Orchha for assistance. None can be expected from Duttia where the Raja has just died and a state of anarchy prevails."[97] Thus from the very beginning, her conduct as far as her loyalty to the British Government was concerned was doubted.

In fact, it would not be wrong to say that Lakshmi Bai moved in that period in a diplomatic way. For her, the main problem was regaining her lost power and status. She, like a shrewd person, watched which way things would take a turn for the better. When she saw the British power dwindling and the sun rising on the rebels, she did not hesitate to join the insurgents openly.

Moreover, the evidence elaborated in the aforesaid pages is based on hearsay. None of these people were in a position to be associated with the Rani's plans and for that matter with the high officials who were responsible for bringing about this insurrection. In the light of this conflicting evidence it is not possible to arrive at a definite conclusion. However, it is not ruled out that the Rani might not have ordered the murder but she accepted the massacre of Europeans as an outcome of the revolt on the part of the sepoys.

Immediately after taking over the reign of Jhansi on June 9, 1857, the Rani issued orders to the chiefs and officials of the State that she was seated on the 'gaddi' and that they were to carry on business. Receipt of such a 'perwanah' was reported by an Indian Magistrate of Mauranipur on June 10, 1857.[98] She also started recruiting men from Jhansi. Sepoy Aman Khan says that "after the mutineers left the station I entered the service of the Ranee on four rupees a month. None of the mutineers remained here—all the muskets left by the mutineers and their uniforms that had been given to the poor people of the station were collected and given by the Ranee to those who entered her service. In this manner 100 men, all from the people of the town, were raised by the Ranee. Besides these about 80 men from the Scindias' Contingent that were disarmed and disbanded at Asseer came in here and were employed by the Rani."[99]

This statement is further corroborated by Hingan, hookambardar of Captain Gordon thus: "The mutineers went away after three days and the Rani then raised two Companies of Sepoys and gave the command to three mutineers who had remained behind."[100]

June 12, 1857,[101] is presumed to be the date on which the Rani wrote her first letter to the Commissioner informing him about the happenings in Jhansi and requesting for help. A second letter was written on June 14, 1857.[102] Some other letters followed later.[103]

It is apparent from the 'parwanah' issued by the Rani on June 10, that she had chosen the line of action and that her letters to the government were an eyewash. This correspondence was a clever piece of diplomacy as the Rani needed time to build up her forces if ever she had to face the formidable foe and that she could safely do by identifying her interests with the British.

However, the Rani was able to impress upon the Commissioner, Saugar Division, with these letters the sincerity of her action and as such was authorised[104] by him to collect the revenue, to raise police and to do everything in her power to restore order.[105]

The Governor-General doubted the sincerity of the Rani and accorded a conditional approval on the basis of the account supplied by Major Ellis: "Rani did lend assistance to the mutineers and rebels and she gave guns and men."[106]

Later the Rani raised a body of fourteen thousand men and unearthed the guns which had been concealed by the former Raja and of which British authorities knew nothing. She began to cast cannons, and make ammunitions. The Rani negotiated with the rebel Rajas of Banpur and Shahgarh. She also established a mint of her own. From the evidence of Deokeemunder Sahar, former orderly of the late Lt. Gordon of Jhansi, it appears that the Rani proclaimed in the town that her reign had commenced and that the English Raj was over.[107] She raised her own flag on the fort and assembled the 'mahajans' to present her their 'nazranas'.[108]

The period, however, was fraught with danger for the Rani, Sadashiv Rao, who failed to get the territory of Jhansi, posed himself to be a ruler at Kurrua (a town 30 miles West of Jhansi) on June 13, 1857. He issued a proclamation to the fact: "Maharaja Sadashiv Rao Narain has seated himself on the throne of Jhansi at Kurrua." [109] This came as a challenge to the Rani and she sent her forces against him. Sadashiv Rao was defeated and was taken prisoner.

The second enemy she had to face was the Rani of Tehree. The latter's forces took over Mauranipur on August 10, 1857. The Rani of Jhansi suffered reverses in the beginning but in the battle which ensued on October 23, with the Tehree's forces, she came out victorious. The Rani of Jhansi then sent a word demanding from the Rani of Tehree either the immediate surrender of Tehree and Orchha or retribution for the loss she had sustained.

Rani Lakshmi Bai wrote to Hamilton again on January 1, 1858,[110] informing him about the battle with Rani Tehree's troops thereby professing to be loyal to the British government. But it was reported on January 5, 1858, that the "Rani of Jhansi continued to rule over Jhansi, all disaffected and mutineers men that go to Jhansi are kept by the Rani. At this time she had 400 mutineers with her and the rest of the force was composed of the relatives of the surrounding Thakoors. Although the news of the total defeat of the rebels at Kanpur and that of the advancing of the British Forces has been received by the Rani she seems to entertain no fears."[111] This statement showed the hollowness of her sincerity to the British government.

The letter of the Rani was not acknowledged by Hamilton. This added to her determination to fight. Secondly, it served as a warning to the Rani to be on guard. Combining in herself the qualities of a warrior and a stateswoman she set about performing her duties with speed.

Lakshmi Bai wrote letters to other Rajas and Chiefs "exerting them to save their faith and sacrifice everything for its sake."[112] She also wrote to the Nana Sahib that "something must be done to cherish the State and afford it protection."[113] This letter makes it clear that she was in touch with Nana Sahib.[114] Within a short time "she gained a great influence over the heart of her people. It was this influence, this force of character added to a splendid and inspiring courage that enabled her some months later to offer to the English troops under Sir Hugh Rose a resistance which made to a less able commander might even have been successful."[115]

There were several discouraging factors. After the defeat of the Kanpur rebels, came the news of the defeat of the Raja of Banpur. In a letter dated March 13, 1858, the Raja of Banpur wrote, "I, who appeased the English, inevitably fall and your force cannot face the English. I advice you to save your life as you can."[116] Later, on March 16, the Raja of Banpur with 2,500 horses and two guns took refuge in Jhansi. The Rani sent him supplies. Her officers told the military officers that if there should be a fight with the English they must strike, and whosoever had no mind to do this, let him at once resign his appointment.[117] By March 1853 she had 15,000 men in her service. The Rani got all the large and small guns which escaped destruction at the time of the annexation, repaired them and had eight new guns manufactured, thus making a total of twenty.[118]

The newswriter writing on March 17 stated: "that Rani's officers sent 'khureeta' to the officers commanding at Tel Bhat. The officers in rebellion against the English said to the Rani's officers that "we believing the Rani to be the enemy of the English, took service with her. We will not fight inside the city walls. Give us guns and we will fight outside the walls. And if it be your object by the 'khureeta' which you have sent to the English to make peace with them, pay up our arrears and dismiss us." The Rani's officers replied, "Rest assure you will be satisfied."[119]

Later she ordered Rana Bouru Singh of Nirwar who had taken refuge in Jhansi to leave the town as she did not intend to fight the English. The report further adds: "It is believed that although the Rani publicly directed him to go... she in her heart wishes him to remain."[120]

It was reported on March 18 that the messenger who took the letter to the Agent to the Governor-General returned with a message from him, "Let the Rani come hither."[121] She then sent another letter. The Rani's mind inclined both ways. To peace and to war. To war from fear of her rebel servants, to peace from the advice of her other servants."[122] In fact the Rani was in a dilemma at this critical period. However, she decided to face the enemy.

On March 20, the Rani sent out all her men in the district to repair to the town. The houses near the city wall were vacated. The same day two small guns were placed on the city walls and ammunition was distributed. The next day, the city being besieged, the Rani and her advisors wrote a 'khureeta' to the Agent stating that they were ready to pay obedience to the British Government. Before the 'khureeta' was finished the Rani and Gangadhar Bhaee Singh, one of the prominent rebel leaders in Jhansi, saw some sowars surrounding the town. Firing was ordered.[123] Thus began the historic fight. "The Rani had", writes Ball Charles, "bravely determined to defend herself to the last, nor was there at any time during the continuance of the siege any symptom weakness or vacillation on her part or that of her personal adherents."

Sir Hugh Rose,[125] a seasoned soldier, held the command of the British forces. The siege began on March 22, the Rani's troops showed undaunted courage and returned shot for shot. Women were noticed working in the batteries and carrying ammunitions.[126]

"It was sure," writes Malleson, "that the Rani had infused some her lofty spirit into her compatriots. Women and children were se assisting in repair of the havoc made in the defence by the fire of besiegers and in carrying food and water to the soldiers on duty. It seemed a contest between the two races under the conditions unusually favourable to the besieged."[127]

The Rani of Jhansi would go to the batteries to rouse the zeal of her soldiers by her presence and her fiery words.[128]

On March 28, 1858, shells falling into the fort blew up five maunds of gunpowder and the building in which it was stored. Forty men were killed. The Rani was much distressed and distracted by this havoc caused by the enemy and did not take meals till the evening. She took up her quarters in an underground house in the fort. On 29th, 30th and 31st March, much damage was done to the building and a hundred men were killed.

On 31st March, twenty-two thousand men under Tantia Tope,[129] at the request of the Rani, marched against the British camp before Jhansi. Sir Hugh Rose defeated him (Tantia Tope). Tantia Tope's defeat on the one hand came as a rude shock to the Rani and she had to face the enemy with her own resources, while on the other hand it encouraged and raised the morale of the soldiers in Rose's camp. The fire was resumed again on 31st April 1858. "Her men hurled at the stormers all sorts of missiles, earthen pots filled with powder, logs of wood and whatever came handy. For a time it appeared like a sheet of fire out of which burst a storm of bullets, round shots and rockets destined for our annihilation. Every inch of ground was contested till the palace was reached. Jhansi was a slaughterhouse reeking under the eastern sky."[130]

The British soldiers were determined to punish the Rani on whose head they thought rested the blood of slain. She was well aware of the punishment, "Not one iota undaunted," writes Lowe, "prepared a commensurate resistance such as one indeed as would have shed honour and fame upon the name of any princess, whose hands were unstained by the blood of the innocent and unoffending."[131]

When the Rani realised her weak position she cleverly escaped with her adopted son under cover of darkness and in the garb of a man. She travelled a distance of twenty-one miles in the company of Afghans who formed her escort. In the morning the flight was made known in the English Camp and a pursuit was ordered. Captain Forbes and Lt. Dowker followed with 3rd Light Cavalry and 14 Light Dragon. Fight ensued between the two rival forces. Some forty men of the Rani's troops were slain. Lt. Dowker got severe injuries and had to give up the pursuit. The Rani escaped with four attendants. Lt. Dowker writes: "The Maratha Queen was as much at ease galloping a horse as in the zenana listening to her favourite minstrel and stern chase ensued."[132]

The Rani of Jhansi with sixteen horsemen and one female attendant reached Bhandair[133] on 5th April 1858 and was put up at the Kutchery. She had been fasting for the last three days. Here as they were about to cook meals, information came that the British troops were in pursuit. The Rani and her followers after taking milk started for Koonch[134] and joined Tantia Tope and other rebel leaders.

Jhansi fell but Kalpi[135] became the meeting place of all the rebels. Rao Saheb, the Nawab of Banda, Tantia Tope and the Rani of Jhansi all combined advanced to Koonch, a strategic town on the Jhansi Road, to give fight to the British. During the battle the Rani dressed in a man's attire and armed with a sword and a dagger rode at the head of 50 sawars and 100 matchlockmen.

After a series of hard battles the rebels had to evacuate on 23rd May 1858. Hugh Rose writes: "While so many drawbacks weakened me, the enemy physically speaking, was unusually strong. They were under three rebel leaders of considerable influence, Rao Sahib, a nephew of Nana Sahib, the Nawab of Banda and the Rani of Jhansi. The high descent of the Rani, her unbound liberality to her troops, and retainers and her fortitude which no reverses could shake rendered her an influential and dangerous adversary."[136]

There were plans of capturing the Rani and for this purpose the Governor-General authorised Hamilton to offer twenty thousand rupees as reward.[137] The English General thought the work was over, but the Rani would not let him be in peace as long as she lived. Gwalior became the next rebel centre. "The Rani desperate and daring then conceived the plan of marching to Scindia's capital and taking possession of that stronghold."[138]

"The Rani was a resolute and intrepid woman who infected her troops with her own fearlessness, hardihood and carried on the struggle against the English with a coolness and capacity that exhorted full and frank admiration from our Generals. She it was, who in the darkest hour of her side's defeat made the astounding proposition that once more threatened the progress of our arms in India."[139]

This move came as a surprise and the idea, observes Holmes, was "as original and as daring as that which prompted the memorable seizure of Arcot."[140]

Gwalior fell to the rebels without a blow on June 4th and troops joined the rebels.

Friend of India of June 10th, 1858, wrote: "Tantia Tope has been proclaimed Nana, Rao Sahib has acquired some other dignity and the Rani of Jhansi retains all her importance. Thus the Marathas hope to recover their lost glory by eliciting an imposter for a Peshwa and by submitting to a woman stained with every crime."[141]

Rose retraced his steps on hearing the news. General Napier joined him. On June 16th, both after a hard battle were able to defeat the rebels under Tantia Tope of Morar. Next morning General Smith also came for their help. He attacked the city and met the force led by Rani at Kotah-ki-Sarai. The British forces were able to clear the place of the rebels. The Rani took interest in almost all the phases of the battle. "It is the characteristic of the Rani's thoroughness and capacity that she went out in person to supervise this important work. Disguised as a man she passed rapidly from post to post until the persistent and deadly fire of Smith's guns drove in her own artillery."[142]

Col. Sir R.C. Shakespeare, Agent to the Governor-General wrote, what seems to be a reliable account of the death of the Rani which was told by Damodar Rao and the people. The rebels were in possession of Gwalior for eighteen days. The Rani, hearing of the British troops advancing, went on the top of the house where she was living and seeing the British troops she descended and mounted her horse to start, but European soldiers surrounded her and she received a cut on the left eyebrow, another on the left hand and a bulllet pierced her right side. The guns of the fort having opened fire, the Rani returned. She fell from her horse as did a female attendant, named Moondar, who had also been wounded near her stomach.

After the English troops returned some of the Rani's soldiers attended on her and gave her water to drink. However, she could not survive the bullet wound and thus died "the bravest and best military leader of the rebels."[143] Her corpse was taken to a garden under the fort. Damodar Rao performed some ceremonies and burned the body in a stack of grass.[144]

The Rani's determined fight and death in the battlefield is an inspiration for all times to come. Malleson records: "Whatever her faults in British eyes may have been, her countrymen will ever remember that she was driven by ill-treatment into rebellion, she lived and died for her country."[145]

Rani of Ramgarh

The Rani of Ramgarh was another woman who participated in the outbreak of the 1857-58 war.

Ramgarh is a small village in Dinderi Tehsil of Mandala District in Madhya Pradesh. Raja Lachman Singh, the last ruler, died in 1850 leaving his only son Vikramjit as heir. The latter had not ruled the state for more than a few days when it was discovered that he was mentally unsound.

The British authorities, true to their policy of increasing their territorial limits took over the management of the estate and appointed their own Tehsildar. A pension was, however, fixed for the Raja and his family. The Rani protested against this measure, but it was in vain.

The outbreak in Central India was a signal for the Rani to rise to the occasion and redress her grievances. Ramgarh became the fountainhead of the revolt in Mandala District in July 1857, and the Rani of Ramgarh its originator.[146]

She removed the Tehsildar and took over the administration. When the Commissioner at Jabalpur came to know about the state of affairs in this area, he ordered her on August 26th, to see the Deputy Collector of Mandala District. She ignored the order and started preparations to face the British.[147] The Rani fortified Ramgarh by erecting barricades and increased her army strength. The Rani also contacted the neighbouring chiefs and zamindars with a view to obtaining help from them.

On April 1, 1858, the British forces advanced towards Ramgarh. She left the fort and led her troops to the battlefield. In an encounter with English troops in front of the town she had to bear a heavy loss. Her small force was defeated and she fled from the town. The Rani, however, did not lose courage and retired to the nearby jungles, from where she kept raiding the British camp. The Rani expected help from the Rewah rebels who joined the English.[148] Her position became precarious and her capture became certain. She did not want to be a prisoner of the British and hence borrowed a sword from her companion and plunged it into her own body. On her death-bed she revealed that she had stirred the people to rebellion.[149] The admission on her part showed her honesty and conviction in the sanctity of her cause.

Rani Tace Bai

Tace Bai also followed the example of her sisters in Central India and castigated her allegiance to the British authorities during the outbreak of 1857-58 war. She, however, did not have the same courage as the Rani of Jhansi and the Rani of Ramgarh. She was the daughter of Gopal Rao, a direct descendant of Gangadhar Govind, a former Raja of Jaloun. In 1842, the State had lapsed to the British Government and Rani Tace Bai, a claimant to the State was sanctioned a pension of twelve thousand rupees per annum.

After the revolt of 1857-58 Gursari chief established himself as the undisputed master of Jaloun District with the exception of parganas Kachhewagarh and Duboh with headquarters at Jaloun. Tantia Tope heading the Scindia's troops who revolted on September 22nd after the fall of Delhi, reached this place on October 29, 1857. Gursari chief was unable to face Tantia Tope and agreed to surrender. However, another claimant, Tace Bai, put forward her claim. Tantia Tope favoured her and put her son on the Gaddi with the condition that she acknowledge the Nana and pay a sum of three lakh rupees. Thus she transferred her allegiance.

On April 12, 1858, it was reported that when Tace Bai heard that Jhansi had fallen, she did not stay back to face the English instead, packed up her goods and left Jaloun for Ingumpur advising her followers to go wherever they thought it safe to retire.[150] She is reported to have rendered submission to the British.[151]

Hamilton, the Agent to the Governor-General, reported that there was no charge against Tace Bai of ill-treatment of any Europeans or having been guilty of any atrocity. "There is no doubt that she joined the rebel party, set aside the authority of the British Government and cast off her allegiance."[152]

As a consequence of her actions the British authorities decided to deport Tace Bai, her son Govind Rao and her husband beyond the territorial limits of Central India. She was also deprived of her pension of twelve thousand rupees. Her jewels worth thirty thousand rupees were sold and the money was credited to the Government treasury.[153]

Tace Bai was deported to Monghyr. The order of the Government of India was conveyed in a letter to the Secretary to the Government of Bengal regarding the nature of surveillance to be exercised on her: "She is to be treated with consideration and respect, the surveillance over her is to be sufficiently strict to prevent all hope of escape to check all correspondence with her own country and obviate all chance of successful intrigue."[154] She remained a prisoner for twelve long years before she was released by the British.

There were several other women in different parts of the country who lent their support to the cause. Their role may not have been significant, yet their contribution to the cause of freedom was of considerable help. For instance, the Thakurani of Budri contributed to the rebels funds, Rani Digambar Koer joined the rebels at Gorakhpur, and Rani of Tikari[155] (Gaya) added to the fortification of Tikari.

Former Rani of Jyetpore also took advantage of the opportunity afforded by this uprising. In defiance of the prohibition order issued by the Magistrate, she proceeded to Jyetpore with an armed force and established herself there. The Rani was again addressed by the Magistrate and he informed her that unless she vacated Jyetpore quietly she would not receive her pension of two thousand rupees. Various efforts were made to enable her to leave Jyetpore voluntarily. But she did not pay any heed to those offers. She was warned that the alternative would be forcible ejection.[156] She was later expelled from Jyetpore.

Rani Jindan,[157] who was in Nepal during the disturbances of 1857-58, took advantage of the opportunity and wrote letters in cypher to the Maharaja of Kashmir, which were intercepted and were believed to be genuine.[158] In these letters the Maharaja of Kashmir was exhorted to initiate an attack on British territory when Jung Bahadur would simultaneously descend from Nepal and attack Gorakhpur. Rani Jindan also informed the Maharaja of Kashmir of the arrival of Nana Sahib, Begum Hazrat Mahal, Banee Mahadeo and Hindustani sepoys, pleading with and encouraging him to do whatever was possible.

In 1850, Temple, then Commissioner of Lahore, discovered that Megh Singh and Kishan Singh, in Gurdaspur district, usually visited the Maharani in Nepal and had lately used seditious language against the Government. These people were punished. Another person named Jowahar Singh, a relative of the Rani Kulwallee, widow of Maharaja Kharak Singh, was also found out to have met the Maharani at Nepal.

He was ordered to furnish security by the British Government.[159] Rani Jindan was kept under strict surveillance and was neither allowed to come to India nor communicate with anybody in India or with her son in England.

Writing in 1862, Mr. Davies, Secretary to the Punjab Government, informed that the national feelings of the Sikhs, though repressed and extinguished, were likely to be excited by nothing more than the return of the Rani to the Punjab.[160] She was, however, later permitted to write to her son in England. Her son, Maharaja Dalip Singh, was allowed to visit her in Nepal. He took her to England where she died in 1863.

Notes and References

1. Holmes, T.R., *History of the Indian Mutiny*, London, 1898, p. 97
2. Gough, General Sir H., *Old Memories*, Edinburgh, 1897, p. 19.
3. J.C. Wilson's *Moradabad Narrative of Events* (Official), dated December 24, 1858.
4. ibid.
5. W. and R. Chambers, *The History of Indian Revolt*, 1857-58, London, 1859, p. 88.
6. ibid., p. 89.
7. Russell, Sir W.H., *My Diary in India in the Year 1858-59*, London, 1860, pp. 274-75.
8. Innes, Lieut-General J.J. Mcleod, *Lucknow and Oudh in Mutiny*, London, 1896, p. 117; *India Gazette*, Thursday, April 15, 1858, p. 355.
9. Outram succeeded Sleeman as Resident in Lucknow in 1854. He became Chief Commissioner of Oudh, and later was appointed to command Danpur and Kanpur Divisions.
10. Major-General Sir Henry Havelock had been in the Army for 42 years. He had earlier served in Afghanistan, Punjab and Persia. In the crisis of 1857 he was called upon to relieve Kanpur and Lucknow.
11. It is a garden in the suburb of Lucknow. Literally it means "The garden of the world". Within an enclosure of 500 yards, there is a building in the garden having a number of rooms.
12. Ball, Charles, *History of the Indian Mutiny*, Vol. I, London and New York, p. 246.
13. Commonwealth Relations Office, Vol. 163, pp. 443-445, quoted in *Civil Rebellion in the Indian Mutinies 1857-59*, Calcutta, 1957.
14. Malleson, G.B., *History of the Indian Mutiny, 1857-58*, Second edition, 1879, Vol. II, pp. 356-57.
15. Ahmedula Shah was a Muslim priest in Fyzabad. He preached Jehad or religious war in various places. He was a famous rebel leader of Oudh and took a prominent part in this uprising. When British took over

Lucknow, he fled to Shahjahanpur and kept on attacking the British forces till he died.

16. Forbes, Mitchell, *Reminiscences of the Great Mutiny,1857-59*, London, 1910, p. 173.
17. Russell, Sir W.H., op. cit., pp. 274-75.
18. Ball, Charles, op. cit., p. 246
19. ibid.
20. *Foreign Political Secret, A Consultation,* No. 34-38 of November 26, 1858, (N.A.I).
21. Mufti Intazamula Sahibi (edited), *Begumat Oudh ke Khatut* (Urdu), Delhi, p. 51.
22. ibid., p. 55.
23. There were a few Begums who along with their female attendants were taken prisoners by the British. Thus these women who once adorned the palace were reduced to pitiable plight. Russell who visited some of them, says: "We found them all in one large, low, dark and dirty room, without windows on the ground floor, and Bruce's entrance was the signal for shrill uplifting of voices and passionate exclamations from the ladies who were crouched down all around the wall." Russell, Sir W.H., op.cit., p. 357.
24. *Foreign Political Consultation* No. 413L, July 15, 1859.
25. ibid., No. 183/4, August 19, 1859, (N.A.I.).
26. ibid.
27. ibid.
28. *Foreign Political Consultation* No. 413/C, July 15, 1859 (N.A.I).
29. ibid. No, 183/4, August 19, 1859 (N.A.I).
30. The Chief Commissioner reporting about her complicity in the murder of Europeans wrote, "There is evidence to show that the heads of Europeans killed in different combats were exhibited to her and in particular there is strong testimony to the fact that the head of Mr. Deverive, a telegraph employee murdered at Bunnee in the extension of his duty while the Commander-in-Chief was in Lucknow in November 1857, was sent on to the Begum's private apartment, that she might feast her eyes on the sight and the bearer of the Trophy was rewarded with a dress of honour." *Foreign Political Consultation* No. 324, July 29, 1859.
31. *Foreign Political Consultation* No. 183/4. August 19, 1859. (N.A.I).
32. *Foreign Political Consultation* No. 3022, December 31, 1858 (N.A.I).
33. Maharaja Duleep Singh who was not able to come back to India.
34. *Foreign Political Consultation* No. 3022, December 31, 1858 (N.A.I).
35. *Foreign Political Consultation* No. 360, October 1877.
36. ibid.
37. *Foreign Political Consultation* No. 264, October 1879 (N.A.I).

38. Gordon, Alexandra, Lt. Col. W., *Recollections of a Highland Subaltern During the Campaign*, London, 1898, p. 104.
39. Forbes, Mitchell, W., op. cit., p, 57-58.
40. Russell, Sir W.H., op. cit., p. 357.
41. *Saddiq-Uli Akhbar*, Vol. 4, No. 3, July 20, 1857.
42. Jhansi had been virtually passed on to the British government during the misrule of Raja Raghunath Rao. It was handed over to Gangadhar Rao, brother of the late Raja in 1843.
43. *Sangharsh Kalin Netaon Ki Jiwanian* (Hindi) published under the auspices of History of the Freedom Movement Board, Uttar Pradesh, 1957, p. 148.
44. John Lang writes: "She was a woman of about the middle size—rather stout, but not too stout. Her face must have been very handsome when she was younger, and even now it had many charms—though according to my idea of beauty it was too round. The expression also was very good, and very intelligent. The eyes were particularly fine and the nose very delicately shaped. She was not very fair, though she was far from black. She had no ornaments, strange to say, upon her person except a pair of gold earrings. Her dress was plain white muslin, so fine in texture, that the outline of her figure was plainly discernible and a remarkable fine figure she had. What spoilt was her voice." Lang. J., *Wanderings in India and Other Sketches of Life in Hindustan*, pp. 93-94.
45. He was sixth in descent from the common ancestor Raghunath Rao, I.
46. Gangadhar Rao died in 1853.
47. *Foreign Political Consultation* No. 153-183, July 31, 1854 (N.A.I).
48. ibid.
49. Arnold, Edwin, *The Marquis of Dalhousie's Administration of British India*, Vol. II (London), 1865, p.151.
50. *Foreign Political Consultation* No. 153-183, July 31, 1854 (N.A.I).
51. *Foreign Political Consultation* No. 75 and K.W. March 2, 1 55, (N.A.I).
52. Dr. Surendra Nath Sen in his book *Eighteen Fifty Seven*, p. 270, writes that there was no resistance made by the Rani. It is true that she did not take up arms against the decision of the government, but the Rani certainly did not hesitate to represent her case to the Governor- General and then to the Court of Directors.
53. *Foreign Political Consultation* No. 75. and K.W., March 2, 1855.
54. Major Evans Bell in his *The Empire in India Letters*, London, p. 210, expressed his opinion thus: "The hereditary rights of the Raja of Jhansi were guaranteed by the treaty of 1817 without reference or their titles or insignia and that treaty contained no clauses or expression restricting the ordinary operation of Hindu Law."

55. *Foreign Political Consultation* No. 75 and K.W., March 2, 1855 (N.A.I.).

56. ibid.

57. ibid.

58. Forest, G.W., *Selections from the Letters, Despatches and Other State Papers, 1857-58,* Vol. IV, pp. 2-3

59. *Foreign Political Consultation* No. 26-31 and K.W., July 31, 1857 (N.A.I.).

60. Similar opinion has been expressed by Kaye: "Her resentment grew stronger and stronger. A woman of masculine energy and feminine vindictiveness, she eagerly awaited the rising of storm, well assured that her time would come." Kaye, J. W., *History of the Sepoy War,* London, 1876, Vol. III, p. 361.

61. *The Revolt in Central India, 1857-59,* Compiled in the Intelligence Branch, Division of Chief of Staff, Army Headquarters India, Shimla, 1908 (C.S.L.)

62. Kaye, J.W., op. cit., Vol. III, p. 360.

63. Forest, G.W., op. cit., Vol. IV, p. 3.

64. *Narrative of Events Mutiny in India, 1857-58,* Calcutta, 1881, Vol. I, p. 550.

65. This statement was made by Sepoy Aman Khan of 12 Native Infantry and was considered trustworthy by Sir R. Hamilton. *Foreign Political Supplementary Consultation* No. 283 of December 30, 1859.

66. *Narrative of Events Mutiny in India, 1857-58,* op. cit., Vol. I, p 550.

67. *The Revolt in Central India, 1857-59,* op. cit., p. 20

68. About 55 in number.

69. *Narrative of Events Mutiny in India, 1857-58,* op. cit., vol. I, p. 555.

70. ibid.

71. Reference to this fact is also made by (Captain) P.G. Scott in his report thus: "Some days before it (Mutiny) occurred, Captain Dunlop commanding the Left Wing of the 12th Native Infantry and the station of Jhansi too, sent over to Major Kirkee letters from Major Skene, the Superintendent and Captain Gordon, Deputy Superintendent of Jhansi, informing him that they had learnt from separate sources that one Luckmen Rao, the servant of the Rani of Jhansi, was doing his best to induce the men of 12th to Mutiny. It was not known whether the Rani authorised these proceedings." Forest, G.W., op. cit., Vol. IV, p. 1.

72. *The Revolt in Central India, 1857-59,* op. cit., p. 16; *Narrative of Events Mutiny in India,* op. cit., Vol. I, p. 550.

73. Kaye, Sir, J. W., op. cit., Vol. III, p. 364.

74. *Narrative of Events Mutiny in India,* op. cit., p. 550; Kaye, Sir, J.W., op. cit., Vol. III, p. 362.

75. *Foreign Political Consultation* No 75 and K.W., 2 March, 1855 (N.A.I.).

76. Martin, R.M., *Indian Empire (1858-61)*. Vol. II, p. 485, quoted in *Civil Rebellion in the Indian Mutinies, 1857-59*, Calcutta, p. 58.

77. *Foreign Political Supplement Proceeding* No. 280, December, 30, 1859; Forest, G.W., op. cit. The fact that Rani's father was actively associated with the rebellion is also acknowledged by Sen, Surendra Nath, op, cit., p. 274. He writes: "Rani's men had no reason to sympathise with the English in their difficulties and it may be assumed that Nana Sahib definitely identified himself with their enemies."

78. Majumdar, R.C., *The Sepoy Mutiny and the Revolt of 1857*, Calcutta, 1957, p. 155.

79. Further Papers Relative to the Mutinies in the East Indies-Presented to both the Houses of Parliament by Command of Her Majesty, 1857, enclosure 166, p. 75.

80. Majumdar, R.C., op., cit., pp. 144-145 examines various evidence available and comes to the conclusion that the Rani's guilt was more of her inference from the conduct of her servants and followers than based on any positive evidence. This finding is supported by him by quoting the first part of the report dated August 18, 1857 which reads: "It is the general impression that the sepoys were instigated by the Rani to attack the fort." But Majumdar does not take into account the second part of the report which categorically holds the Rani responsible for rebellious acts.

81. W. and R, Chambers, op. cit., p. 88.

82. *Foreign Political Consultation* No. 355-362. April 30, 1858 (N.A.I.).

83. Lowe, Thomas, *Central India During the Rebellion of 1857-58*, London, 1860, p. 264.

84. *Foreign Political Consultation* No. 46/7, July 16, 1858 (N.A.I.)

85. *Foreign Political Supplement* (Madar Bakhsh), 287, December 30, 1859, (N.A.I.),

86. *Foreign Political Supplement* No. 284, December 30, 1859.

87. *Foreign Political Supplement* No. 286, December 30, 1859.

88. His name is not given in the contemporary records.

89. Forest, G.W., op. cit., Vol. IV, p. vii.

90. Kaye, W., op. cit., Vol. VIII, p. 396.

91. *Foreign Political Consultation* No.46/7, July 16, 1858.

92. Majumdar, R.C., op. cit., p. 144.

93. Details of this letter are in Appendix B.

94. Parasnis, *Jhansi Sansthanchya Maharani Lakshmi Bai Sahen Hyanchen Charita*, p. 125, quoted in Sen, Surendra Nath. op. cit., p. 279.

95. *Foreign Secret Consultations*, A, No. 304, dated July 31, 1857.

96. *Foreign Political Supplement* No. 280, December 30, 1859.

97. *Foreign Political Supplement Consultation* No. 280, December 30, 1859.

98. Malleson, G.B., *History of the Indian Mutiny, 1857-58*, London, 1858, Vol. I, p. 93; Forest G.W., op. cit., Vol. III, p. 5.

99. *Foreign Political Supplement* No. 280, December 30, 1859.

100. *Foreign Political Supplement* No. 286, December 30, 1859, p. 465.

101. *Foreign Political Secret Consultation* No. 34, July 31, 1857 (N.A.I.).

102. ibid.

103. Details of these letters are given in Appendix C.

104. Both Majumdar, R.C., op. cit., p. 147 and Sen, Surendra Nath, op. cit., p. 279 taking this proclamation into consideration have come to the conclusion that the Rani assumed the administration of her husband's principality at the direction of the constituted authority. The letter from the Commissioner authorising the Rani to look after the administration of Jhansi is dated July 2, 1857. But the Rani had long before this as is clear from the 'perwanah' issued by her on 10th June had taken over the administration of Jhansi independent of the British Government.

105. *Foreign Political Secret Consultation* No. 355, July 31, 1857. For details see Appendix D, Part II.

106. ibid.

107. *Foreign Political Supplement* No. 288, December 30, 1859, p. 471. (N.A.I.)

108. ibid.

109. *Narrative of Events*, op., cit., p. 555.

110. *Foreign Political Supplement Consultation* No. 266, December 30, 1859 (N.A.I.).

111. *Foreign Political Supplement* No. 265, December 30, 1859, p. 405.

112. *Sangharash Kalin Netaon Ke Jiwanian (Hindi)*, op., cit., p. 162.

113. *Foreign Political Consultation* No. 61754 and K.W., December 30, 1859, Details in Appendix E. Majumdar, R.C., op., cit., p. 147, writes: "Reference to the Rani's sending agents to the Nana in June must be a matter of inference or hearsay report...."That it was not a matter of inference or hearsay is proved by this letter.

114. Nana Sahib Dhondu Pant was son of Mahadev Madho Narain and was born in 1824. He was one of the three adopted sons of Baji Rao, the last Peshwa. The Peshwa left his title and estate to Nana in 1839. He was one of the prominent leaders of rebels. Nana assumed the government during the rebellion at Kanpur. Later when the British forces took over Kanpur, he made his way to Oudh and escaped to Nepal.

115. Malleson, G.B., op. cit., Vol. I, p. 191.

116. *Foreign Political Supplement* No. 1764, December 30, 1859.

117. ibid., No. 1765, December 30, 1859.

118. *Foreign Political Consultation* No. 144-5, April 30, 1859.

119. *Foreign Political Supplement* No. 1765, December 30, 1859.

120. ibid.

121. ibid.

122. *Foreign Political Supplement* No. 1765, December 30, 1859.
123. *Foreign Political Proceeding* No. 127, May 28, 1858.
124. Ball, Charles, op. cit., Vol. II, p. 290.
125. Hugh Rose joined the army in 1820. He took part in the Turco-Egyptian War and was later appointed Consul General there. He came to India in 1857 and assumed the command of the Poona Division. Later he was appointed Commander of the Central India Force and fought against Rani Jhansi and other rebel leaders.
126. *Foreign Political Consultation* No. 3572-3575, December 29, 1858.
127. Malleson, G.W., op. cit., 1906 (Ninth edition), pp. 387-88.
128. Forest, G.W., op. cit., Vol. IV, p. 114.
129. Tantia Tope was born in 1814. His father was in the service of Peshwa Baji Rao II. Tantia was a prominent rebel leader and took part in almost all the stages of rebellion. Ultimately he was taken prisoner on April 7, 1859. He was court martialled and a death sentence was passed on him.
130. Forest, G.W., op. cit., Vol. IV, p. 120-124.
131. Lowe, Thomas, op. cit., p. 226.
132. *Foreign Secret Consultation* No. 73 of May 28, 1858; Forest, G.W, op. cit., p. 126.
133. Bhandair is a town 21 miles from Jhansi.
134. A town 40 miles from Kalpi.
135. A town in Jaloun District, on the right bank of Jamuna.
136. Forest, G.W., op. cit., Vol. IV, p. 81.
137. *Foreign Political Supplement* No. 1500 of December 30, 1859.
138. Lowe, T., op. cit., p. 147.
139. *The Indian World*, Vol. VIII, July-December, 1900, p. 14
140. Holmes, T.R., op. cit., Quoted in Sen, Surendra Nath, 1857 p. 293.
141. *Friend of India*, Vol. I, June 10, 1858, p. 533.
142. *Indian World*, Vol. VIII, 1908, p. 14 Arnold Edwin, op. cit., p. 152.
143. Forest, G.W., op. cit., Vol. IV, p. 139.
144. *Foreign Politics—A Proceeding* No. 395, April 1860.
145. Malleson, G.B., op. cit., Vol. III, p. 221.
146. Rudman, F.R.R., *Central Provinces, District Gazetteer, Mandala District*, Vol. A, p. 255.
147. Government of Madhya Pradesh, *The History of the Freedom Movement*, (1956), p. 80.
148. ibid., pp. 80-81.
149. Rudman F.R.R., op. cit., Vol. A., p. 255.
150. *Foreign Political Consultation*, No., 133, May 28, 1858.
151. *Foreign Political Consultation*, No., 139/47, August 13, 1858.
152. ibid.
153. *Foreign Political Proceeding* No. 43, February, 1860.
154. *Foreign Political Consultation*, No. 8/12 and K.W., September 3, 1858.

155. Further papers relative to the Mutinies in the East Indies presented to both the Houses of Parliament, Vol. VII, p. 212 (N.L.C.).

156. *Foreign Political Secret Consultation* No. 138, December 18, 1857 (N.A.I.).

157. Rani Jindan was daughter of Munna Singh of village Chachar in Gujranwala district. She was the youngest wife of Maharaja Ranjit Singh and became by the recognition of her son Duleep Singh and Sher Singh the most influential personage in the Punjab. When the English gained power in Punjab, she was imprisoned. Rani Jindan, however, escaped and took asylum in Nepal.

158. *Foreign Political Secret Proceedings* No. 1052, February 12, 1859. For details of her letters, see Appendix F.

159. *Foreign Political Secret Proceeding*, Vol. II, 1862, p. 101 (N.A.I.).

160. ibid.

3

THE POLITICAL AWAKENING: 1857-1900

A healthy nation is as unconscious of its nationality as a healthy man
of his bones. But if you break a nation's nationality it will think of
nothing else but get it set again. It will listen to no reformer, to no
philosopher, to no preacher, until the demand of the nationalist is
granted. It will attend to no business, however vital, except the
business of unification and liberation.

—*Bernard Shaw*[1]

The assumption of power by the Crown in 1858 helped in the political
and administrative unification of the country. India came to be
governed by one unified system of law. No doubt there were a number
of autonomous States, but their independence was in name only, for
their interests were subservient to the paramount power. "The Indian
people," observes Desai, "found substantial sector of their economic
and social life coming under the government of a universal and equally
operating system of law."[2]

The unification of the country was further promoted and
strengthened by the modern means of communication and transport.
Railways brought the people from different parts of the country closer,
thus enabling them to have an organisation of an all-India nature.

Western education which was an established feature of this time
afforded opportunities to the people to study the contemporary events in
Europe and works of political philosophers of that continent with a good
deal of interest. The French Revolution inspired the people in this land
with liberal and democratic ideas. The philosophies of Rousseau,
Voltaire and Mazzini influenced the mind of the educated Indians.

In fact, western education had produced a class of western educated intelligentsia. It was this class which was responsible for awakening the country both for social and political reforms. The Indian youth was face to face with ideas like freedom of speech and the pen, criticism of authority, the questioning of accepted dogmas, the insistence on the rights of man as opposed to his duties. "The growing familiarity with these," observes O'Malley, "has brought a new spirit into Indian life, the stirring of scepticism instead of a stagnant authoritarianism, a glimmering if not the forerunner of what we in Europe call democracy."[3]

When the western educated class measured the conditions prevailing in India against the yardstick of liberty and nationalism set by the European countries, they came to realise the apathy of the foreign rule. The Indian intelligentsia was thus challenged to remove the handicaps and barriers created in the way of progress of their country. Equally challenging to this section of the people was the rigid administrative system under which the country was being governed and which laid emphasis more on daily routine and departmentalisation [4] than on anything else, thereby widening the space between the ruler and the ruled.

The British bureaucracy was not concerned with the ultimate goal of the British Raj, i.e., they did not think it necessary to prepare the people for self-government. In fact, demands pertaining to any advance in the social and political fields were viewed with suspicion. "In India, during the greater part of this period, they are merely governing. Their rule is superbly incorruptible and highly efficient and it achieves many prodigious results, yet does not seem to contain within it... the impulse of organic growth."[5]

Moreover, the passage to the higher administrative posts was blocked for the people of India. There was no improvement upon the conditions prevailing as far back as 1818, described by Thomas Munro. He observed: "Foreign conquerors have treated the natives with violence and often with great cruelty but none has treated with so much scorn as we, none has stigmatised the whole people as unworthy of trust, as incapable of honesty, and as fit to be employed only where we cannot do without them."[6] Even the proclamation of 1858[7] had recognised the right of Indians to the covenant posts, but nothing substantial had been done in this regard.

These drawbacks in the foreign rule resulted in mounting resentment against the British regime and supremacy. As a reaction to the indifference exhibited by the English people towards the aspiration of the people of this country, came the Hindu revivalism which set in motion a number of reforms in the society. Organisations like the Brahmo Samaj, Arya Samaj, Theosophical Society and many others were, no doubt, religious institutions. But religion is so linked in this country with other aspects of society and such a thin wall separates the two that their intimate relationship could not be ignored. These religious movements worked for social reforms in the land and made India politically conscious as well. These institutions were also responsible in detecting the defects of the foreign government in meeting the social evils by pressing for social legislations.

The people felt that to have quick and effective social reforms, India must be able to decide things for herself instead of going to White Hall, London. If the country was politically free, social reforms would be easier to secure. Social freedom is interlinked with political freedom and for the progress of the country both are necessary pillars.

Brahmo Samaj

The first reformist movement was the Brahmo Samaj founded by Raja Rammohun Roy in 1828 at Calcutta. This organisation was given an all-India form by Keshub Chandra Sen who strengthened and popularised the institution. He toured the country and established branches of this organisation. The Ved Samaj, Madras (1864), and Prarthana Samaj, Bombay (1867), were started under the parentage of Brahmo Samaj and had for their aim the same reforms as advocated by the parent body. Women were encouraged to attend the meetings; but later separate branches of the Brahmo Samaj had their weekly meetings with a view to restoring "Hindu worship to its pristine purity."

The members of the Samaj were the pioneers of the social reform movements. "The Brahmo Samaj did what orthodox Hinduism was powerless to do; providing a half-way house where men could worship without idolatory. But for seventy years its influence was all pervading in every higher walk of Bengali life and it provided a succession of men for whom the only adequate adjective is noble."[9]

Leaders of the Brahmo Samaj were amongst the first reformers who were able to get laws enacted against Widow Burning (1829) and Brahmo Marriage Act, 1872, which aimed at abolition of child marriage. They also raised their voice in favour of widow remarriage. Schools for the education of girls were set up by the Samaj. Eradication of polygamy and purdah received their attention as well. Thus, this was the first organisation which treated women as individuals and also paved the way for their life outside the home.

The Brahmo Samaj aimed at reducing "ideals of freedom and democracy into a new law of life and a new code of domestic relations and social ethics. It repudiated the law of caste, thereby not only proclaiming the equality of all human beings but seeking to build up a society where this equality will be established upon a religious basis."[10]

Arya Samaj

The second great movement was the Arya Samaj founded by Swami Dayanand[11] on April 7, 1875, in Bombay. The teachings of the Samaj were summed up by Annie Besant thus: "The repudiation of the authority of the Brahmin, the denouncing of the infinite number of meaningless rites and the worship of image of different gods and goddesses which split the people into numerous belligerent sects and crusade against the mass of religious superstitions which kept for many centuries, the Hindu mind in a state of mental befogging and spiritual degradation—these were the progressive elements in the Arya Samaj."[12]

Dayanand observed that the causes of foreign rule in India were: "Mutual feud, difference in religion, want of purity in life, lack of education, child marriage in which the contracting parties have no voice in the selection of their life partners, indulgence in carnal gratification, untruthfulness and other evil habits, the neglect of the study of the Vedas and other malpractices. It is only when brothers fight among themselves that an outsider poses as a judge.... It is only when men remain honourable, just and true that they are politically great; when they become wicked and unjust, they are absolutely ruined."[13]

The Arya Samaj true to its creed started its crusade against ignorance. It also advocated the equality of sexes by opening schools for the education of both girls and boys. Co-education did not find favour with the Arya Samaj. Gurukuls were opened for the girls. The curriculum of the educational institutions was based on the vedic culture. Girls were given training in domestic science. Instructions in religious ceremonies also formed a part of their educational programme thereby enabling the women to take part in the religious rites on equal terms with men. The education for the major part was given in Indian languages so that it reached the common people. English was also taught as a subject.

The leaders of the Arya Samaj were opposed to the caste system. They said that birth should not determine the caste of an individual. The real Brahmin was one who was a Brahmin at heart and practice. A Brahmin's son could be Khatri, Vaish or Shudra according to his merit. The study of Vedas could not be confined to one caste or class and that all were equal before God.[14]

The Arya Samajists advocated against child marriage. They also insisted that marriage ceremonies should be simple and less expensive.

Widow re-marriage was not encouraged.[15] But to improve their lot widows' homes were opened where they could take vocational training and be economically independent. Orphanages were also founded by this organisation.

The Samaj raised its voice against the purdah-system. Its constitution made provision that the women could be on any administrative or general body of this organisation. This was a great step towards the emancipation of women. By condemning these customs the Arya Samaj paved the way for women's participation in the social and political life of the country.

The watchword of the Arya Samaj was 'back to the Vedas'. It taught the people to search their great past for inspiration, for it was the root of all civilisations. Thus the organisation was to establish the Hindu supremacy thereby inculcating in the youth of the land the spirit of patriotism and nationalism. Chirol observes: "The Arya Samaj which is spreading all over the Punjab and in the United Provinces, represents in one of its aspects a revolt against Hindu orthodoxy, but in another it represents equally a revolt against western ideals, for, in the teachings of its founder, Dayanand, it has found an aggressive gospel which bases the claims of Aryan, i.e., Hindu supremacy of the Vedas, as the one ultimate source of human and divine wisdom."[16]

Though it was not a political body yet a number of members of this society were politicians of high order and took a leading part in the political life of the country. "The freedom of thought and action in the domain of religion and social life for which they and the Samaj stood, was bound to lead to political aspirations of the most advanced type."[17]

During the early years of the 20th century this organisation was the target of political repression. It was regarded "as a society which had some occult creed and pursuits."[18]

Theosophical Society

The Theosophical Society was organised by Madam Blavatsky and Colonel Olcott in New York in 1875. It came to India in 1879 and established its headquarters at Adyar (Madras).

The Society's objectives were:

(i) To form a nucleus of the universal brotherhood of humanity, without distinction of race, creed, sex, caste or colour.

(ii) To encourage the study of comparative religion, philosophy, and science.

(iii) To investigate the unexplained laws of nature and the powers latent in man.[19]

The most prominent leader of this society was Mrs. Annie Besant. She openly proclaimed the superiority of the Hindu system. "Through its efforts regenerating Hindu society, it infused a spirit of devotion to Hindu ideals, readiness for sacrifice, a burning passion of patriotism; and of devotion to motherland."[20]

The society stood for the equality of sexes. For the education of girls, a number of schools were set up under the auspices of this organisation.

Besant was against child marriage. With a view to eradicating this custom she discouraged the admission of married students to the Hindu College, Banares. She said: "The future of India depends on the abolition of child marriage amongst the people, that as long as that persists, there are certain inevitable consequences, of lowered vitality, of the spread of nervous diseases, of premature old age, all of which you can see in India of today standing in the way of her taking her place among the physically stronger nations of the world."[21]

Annie Besant condemned the seclusion of women and remarked, "For India's uplift, the women must have an open field, unfettered hands, and unimpeded activity. The two sexes were not evolved that one should enslave the other, but that they should utilise the fuller life, the differences which pertain to sex. Womanhood as well as manhood must be consecrated to the motherland, for in their union lie the strength, the stability, the freedom of India."[22]

Besant discouraged widow remarriage in case of elderly widows and encouraged child widows to re-marry. She said: "It makes marriage a commercial contract of a union of bodies only as well as disintegrating the sacred life of the family which is the dearest pride of the Hindu."[23] Her's was a call to the women. "The woman sage is wanted as well as the woman saint, and women's wisdom as well as men's is needed to dig deeply and build strongly the foundation of the New India, the India of the free."[24] This call of Besant was acknowledged by her sisters in the country who slowly took up the challenge.

Namdhari Sect

The Namdharies, popularly known as Kookas, was a sect in the Punjab which, though not very influential, yet tried to raise the status of women in society. It was an offshoot of Sikhism and was founded by Baluk Singh, an Udasi Arora, in the year 1847 in the district of Rawalpindi.

Ram Singh[25] was one of the prominent leaders and assumed the title of 'Bhai' or head of the brotherhood in 1860.[26]

In the official records Ram Singh's mission is described thus: "He abolishes all distinctions of caste among Sikhs; advocates indiscriminate intermarriage of all classes, enjoins the marriages of widows, abstinence from liquor and drugs...exhorts his disciples to be clean and truth telling."[27]

It was reported: "Men and women rave together at his meetings and thousands of women and young girls have joined his sect."[28]

Smt. Hookmee, daughter of Ratan Singh, cultivator, resident of village Darya, District Amritsar, was an important person. She visited other districts and preached the doctrine of this sect with great success.[29]

In the political field it disliked the English regime and everything connected with it was shunned. "English education, law courts, mill-made cloth and other imported goods were boycotted."[30]

The Kookas also avoided the use of the Post Offices and depended upon their own system which was remarkably efficient.[31]

The Maharaja of Patiala wrote to Griffin, the officiating Secretary to Government of Punjab: "In the light of these facts (their well-organised postal system etc.) it was certain that Ram Singh's real motive and ambition was to reign and acquire dominion, upon a religious pretext. But the Kooka rising of Malerkotla[32] having been suppressed, the Lt. Governor of Punjab definitely declared that the Government was too strong, for the movement to succeed in its ambitions."[33]

The sect did not seem to gain much strength. In 1891, Kookas numbered 10,541 throughout the province.[34]

Ramakrishna Mission

The Ramakrishna Mission was founded by Swami Vivekananda[35] in 1897 to preach the universal ideas of the 'Vedanta' and to give practical expression to those ideas through philanthropic activities. The message of the Mission was divinity of men, and the fundamental unity of all systems of thought.

Vivekananda kept away from politics. He raised the stature of Indian civilisation in the eyes of the West and through his message of fearlessness he restored the confidence in the people of India once again. "The call to reform, restore and revive India, to help India in every way possible for human efforts was, essentially Vivekananda's call and of all the makers of modern India, his was the most classless and purely patriotic voice."[36]

Swami enjoined the Ramakrishna Mission to bring development all around the country by fighting poverty, starvation and social injustice and by spreading education. It was not possible for the ignorant and starved people to achieve the higher goal. The help given was not to be out of pity; the work of developing people should be done from the desire to serve others and this service was regarded as worship of God since God is one with creation.[37]

The Ramakrishna Mission opened a number of hospitals which had maternity centres. Schools were also opened for both boys and girls. Swami Vivekananda had charged his disciple Nivedita[38] with the education of girls and the improvement in their conditions. Initially her efforts met with failure, however, later she was able to start a school for girls in Calcutta, known as the Nivedita Girls School.

Branches of Ramakrishna Mission were founded all over the country. These centres made women not only socially aware of their importance but also politically conscious of the slavery of their motherland. Thus, women free from ignorance and superstitions realised their responsibilities and became builders of future national leaders and infused them with the spirit of dedication and sacrifice.

Indian National Congress

During this period when reforms were being piloted the extremists in the social reform movements experienced difficulties in making the foreign government enact the necessary social legislation. The experience thus gained in this field turned them into moderates in the political field. Leaders started thinking in terms of larger share in the government. To represent the aspirations of the people the Indian Association was started by Surendranath Banerjee in 1876. Even before this association came into existence political activities in each of the provinces had become important. For instance, there was the British Indian Association in Bengal, the Bombay Association in Bombay. The East Indian Association followed in the seventies of the last century. Madras had the Hindu Sahba and in Poona the Sarvajanik Sabha came to be founded.

These organisations, however, did not have a common platform and their activities were not coordinated. Thus they were largely ineffective.

The Indian Association tried to fill this gap. These were stirring times. The Illbert Bill[39] controversy in 1883 further aroused the national feelings. Sir Allan Octavian Hume[40] with the help of the leading people of the time founded the Indian National Congress in 1885 in Bombay.

At the very first session Hume warned the people thus: "Political reformers of all shades of opinion should never forget that unless the elevation of female elements of the nation proceeds *Pari Passu* (with equal pace) with the work, all their labour for the political enfranchisement will prove vain."[41] Soon women attended the annual sessions as delegates.[42] Mrs. K. Ganguli was the first woman to speak from the Congress platform in 1900. From then onwards increased number of women took part in the political field.

The Indian National Congress though remained a loyal organisation of the crown and contented itself with requests and petitions in its early years, yet it was able to arouse public opinion on an all-India basis.

Notes and References

1. Shaw, G.B., *John Bull's Other Island*, London, 1907, pp. XXXIV-XXXV.
2. Desai, A.R., *Social Background of Indian Nationalism*, Bombay, 1948, p. 154.
3. O'Malley, *Modern India and the West*, op. cit., p. VI
4. Ramsay Muir observes thus: "For these reasons the system of Indian Government was becoming not merely efficient, mechanical, more formal and more impersonal." (*A Short History of British Commonwealth*, New York, 1923, Vol. II, p. 557.)
5. Lord Elton, G., *Imperial Commonwealth*, New York, p. 439, quoted in *Short History of India and Pakistan* by Watter Wallabank, New York, p. 81.
6. Glein, G.R., *The Life of Sir Thomas Munro*, Vol. I, pp. 518-519.
7. This proclamation promised "that as far as may be, our subjects of whatever race or creed, be freely and impartially admitted to office in our own service." (A Collection of Extracts from Royal Proclamation, *Official Reports and Speeches*, New Delhi, Government of India Printing Office, p. 7).
8. Farquahar, J.N., *Modern Religious Movements*, New York, 1924, p. 34.
9. Thompson, E., and Garret G., *Rise and Fulfilment of British Rule in India*, 1936, p. 310.
10. Pal, B.C., *Brahmo Samaj and the Battle to Swaraj in India*, Calcutta 1929, p. 26.
11. Swami Dayanand was born in 1835 at Tankar in Morvi (Gujarat). Dayanand was taught in his very childhood the worship of Lord Shiva. When he grew a little older, he went from place to place and visited sadhus to find means of realising God. Ultimately he met Virjanand, an old sadhu, who was a great Sanskrit scholar. Dayanand's association with him (sadhu) opened his eyes. He learned many things from him (sadhu). He became a great scholar and his best work is *Satyarth Prakash*. He exerted a profound influence on Indian nationalism. According to Mrs. Besant, he was the first man to proclaim 'India for the Indians'.
12. Besant, Annie, *India A Nation*, p. 79.
13. *Light of Truth* (English Translation of Satyarth Prakash) Edited by Dr. Bhardwaja, 1927, p. 303 quoted in *Indian Journal of Political Science*, Vol, XIX, No. 1, January-March, 1968, p. 27.
14. *Census of Punjab*, 1891, Vol, XIX, Part I, p. 176
15. Desai, Neera, *Women in Modern India*, Bombay, 1957, p. 107.
16. Chirol Valentine, *Indian Unrest*, p. 27.
17. Lajpat Rai, *The Arya Samaj, An Account of its Aims, Doctrines and Activities with a Biographical Sketch of the Leader* (Lahore), 1932.

18. Macdonald, Ramsay, *The Awakening of India*, London, 1918. pp. 35-36.

19. Edger, Lilian, *Elements of Theosophy*, (1903), p. 16.

20. Besant, Annie, op. cit., p. 89.

21. Besant, Annie, *Wake Up India*, Madras, 1913, p. 30

22. Theosophical Publishing House, *The Besant Spirit*, Vol. 3 (Madras), 1939, p. 118.

23. Theosophical Publishing House, *Annie Besant Builder of New India*, p. 424.

24. Theosophical Publishing House, *The Besant Spirit*, Vol. 3, p. 116.

25. Ram Singh was a son of Jassa Singh, a carpenter of Bhaini village in Ludhiana District. He was born in 1815. In the year 1844 he joined the Sikh Army. Ram Singh fought against the British at Mudki (Ferozepore) in 1845. He left the army after the British occupied Lahore.

26. *Foreign Political Proceedings A*, March 1867, No. III/112.

27. ibid.

28. ibid.

29. *Foreign Political Proceedings A*, February 1868, No. 202/203, Appendix II.

30. *The Hindustan Times*, Republic Day Supplement, Thursday, January 26, 1954.

31. ibid.

32. In January 1872, some 100 Kookas attacked the treasury of Malerkotla with a view to obtain arms. In an encounter with the police, they killed eight policemen. Seven Kookas were also killed. The rest of the Kookas were imprisoned. Forty-nine of them were blown from the guns in a single day. Two women were also taken prisoners alongwith these Kookas and handed over to the Commanding Officer, Patiala troops. Ram Singh was deported.

33. *Census Report Punjab*, 1881, Part I, p. 38.

34. *Census Report Punjab*, 1891, Part II.

35. Swami Vivekananda was born on January 12, 1863, in a famous Dutta family of Bengal. He received good education. Vivekananda became interested in spiritual problems. He had his first lesson from his teacher Ramakrishna, a famous ascetic. He went to America to attend Parliament of Religions at Chicago and raised the prestige of Hinduism. After his return from the West, he founded the Ramakrishna Mission in memory of his Guru.

36. Vincent Sheen, *Lead Kindly Light*, New York, 1949, p. 354.

37. *Swami Pavitranand*, Ramakrishna Mission, Almora, p. 12.

38. For details see Chapter V.

39. This bill intended to remove the privilege granted to Europeans of being tried by British Judges in case of trial. The bill was distasteful to

the Europeans and a violent propaganda was started and the Defence Association was formed. Consequently, the European Community won its point.

40. Hume, Allan Octavian, was the son of Joseph Hume and was born in 1829. He entered the Bengal Civil Service in 1849 and served in the N.W.P. as Commissioner of the Indian Customs, Secretary to Government of India in the Revenue and Agriculture Deptt., member of the Board of Revenue, N.W.P., 1879. In the Uprising of 1857-58 war, he was a Magistrate of Etawah, N.W.P. He retired in 1882.

41. Murdoch, John, *Twelve Years of Indian Progress*, p. 36

42. Smt. Swarn Kumari Debi and K. Ganguli were the first two delegates. Their details are given in the following pages.

4

WOMEN SOCIAL REFORMERS: 1859-1900

Women social reformers were inspired mainly by the urge for the social uplift of their fellow sisters, but they also made a distinct contribution to the cause of Indian freedom. Prominent amongst them were: Sunanda also known as Maharani Tapasvini and popularly called 'Mataji,' Pandita Ramabai, Swarn Kumari Debi, Rani Shurnomoyee, Ramabai Ranade, Francina Sorabji and Rani Lady Harnam Singh.

Maharani Tapasvini

Maharani Tapasvini was the daughter of Narayan Rao, a feudal lord of the fort of Belur (Arcot, South India). She was the niece of Rani Lakshmi Bai of Jhansi. Tapasvini is reported to have taken part in the revolt of 1857 for which act she was interned in Trichinopally (South India). After her release she devoted her time to the study of Sanskrit and the practice of yoga. She went to Nepal where she was able to establish cordial relations with the royal household.[1] Later she came to Bengal and opened a Sanskrit Pathshala known as Maha Kali Sanskrit Pathshala. She took interest in the education of girls and is reported to have been one of the prominent persons who furthered the cause of women's education in Bengal.

Bal Gangadhar Tilak met Tapasvini in 1901 at Calcutta. It is understood that she advised Tilak to establish contacts with the royal house of Nepal. Emissaries were sent by Tilak seemingly with a purpose to open a tile factory there, but the real purpose of this mission was to start an ammunition factory in Nepal. Tapasvini helped Tilak's agents to get permission to start the factory. The British discovered the plot with the result that the work had to be given up.[2] She continued her work in Calcutta till she died in 1907.

Pandita Ramabai

Pandita Ramabai was born in an orthodox Brahmin family in a forest village of the western ghats in the year 1855. Her father was an honoured Shastri and had by his association with the Peshwa's family become interested in women's education.

Ramabai was educated by her mother. She was a clever girl and by the age of 12 she knew twenty thousand Sanskrit verses by heart.

After her parents' death in 1876, years of hardship followed and she had to go from place to place along with her brother. This nomadic life gave her an opportunity to have a first-hand knowledge of the conditions in the country. Describing her visits to various places she observed: "We travelled for six years in various parts of India. In our travels we were obliged to go on foot not having the means to afford conveyance. In this way we went a distance of two thousand miles. Thus we had a good opportunity of seeing the sufferings of Hindu women. We saw it not only in one part of India but it was the same in the Madras Presidency, Bombay Presidency, Punjab, the North-West Provinces, Bengal and Assam. This made us think much of how it was possible to improve the conditions of women. We were able to do nothing directly to help them but in the towns and cities we often addressed large audience of people and urged upon them the need for the education of women and children."[3]

Ramabai's brother died in the year 1880 in Dhaka. Six months later she met a sudra pleader, a Bengali gentleman, and married him, thereby setting an example of inter-caste and inter-provincial marriage. Her marriage in the low caste, however, was not appreciated by the orthodox Hindus. She had hardly settled down when her husband died after two years of their marriage.

After her husband's death Ramabai left Bengal to settle down in Pune. She came in contact with the social reformers and her desire to do something to ameliorate the conditions of her sisters increased. In Pune she founded the Arya Mahila Samaj, branches of which came to be found all over the Maratha country.[4]

In 1882, a commission was appointed by the Government of India to enquire into the question of education in India. It also included women's education as one of its special agenda. This commission was given a pleasant reception by three hundred women of the Arya Mahila Samaj.[5]

Ramabai was asked to give evidence before the commission. She suggested the training of men teachers and women inspectresses, and further requested that since in India the conditions were such that proper medical treatment could only reach the sick women of India through the women themselves, the study of medicine should be thrown open to Indian women. Ramabai's evidence created a great sensation and reached Queen Victoria. It bore fruit later in the starting of Women's Medical Movement by Lady Dufferin.[6] Now that Ramabai had started taking interest in the public work, she felt that her lack of knowledge of the English language was a handicap in her work. She tried to learn English and also made friends with Miss Henford who was at the time Superintendent of the Girls School, Pune. This friendship enabled her to go to London to study the education system there where she became a Christian.[7]

On the invitation of her cousin Mrs. Anandibai Joshi[8] who was in America doing her medical course, Ramabai left for that country in 1885. She spent three years in America studying the public school system and also took training in the Kindergarten system of imparting training to children. Ramabai acquainted herself with the methods of agriculture, weaving, printing, etc.

In 1858 a Ramabai Association was organised with headquarters in Boston and it had circles all over the country and its members agreed to contribute a certain sum for ten years to support a High Caste Widows Home in India.[9]

On her return to India she started the Sharda Sadan in Bombay in 1889. The object of this institution was to provide an asylum to the 'destitute high-caste widows.' Many high caste girls and persecuted young widows joined the Sadan for education. Ramabai had embraced Christianity but to avoid any misunderstanding she made it clear at the very start that the "school would not actively preach Christianity or try to make converts."[10]

The Sadan received generous financial help from missionary societies and so was obliged to do some Christian work. The whole atmosphere was in the grip of typical missionary spirit and as such it was bound to make impressions on the inmates.[11] Ramabai's work began to be watched with interest. Tilak was among the doubters that the school might be used to gain Christian converts. In December 1889, the *Christian Weekly* published a report on the progress of the Sadan stating that "at present there are seven young widows in the Sharda Sadan, two of whom have expressed their love of Christianity...."[12]

Tilak in his *Kesari* drew attention to this report and voiced a strong protest against Ramabai's activities.[13] The public storm became so great that persons like Dr. Bhandarkar and Justice Ranade had to severe their connection with the Sadan. The case was taken up by these people with the American sponsors who supported Ramabai's viewpoint. As a result Ramabai's institution lost its popularity as far as the Hindu community was concerned.

Ramabai shifted the centre of her activities from Bombay and a Mukti Sadan or House of Salvation was organised at Khedgaon. This implied a complete retirement. A third department was also opened and was called the Rescue Home.

In 1900 there was a severe famine in Gujarat and Ramabai came out in the field again. Twenty of her helpers went out to the area, eight were those women who had been starving in 1896. In 1896 she had resources for only 50 girls but she had to admit three hundred. Now she had resources for five to six hundred and she admitted 1,300, thus bringing the population of Mukti Sadan to 1,900. A school was organised which had 50 classes. Four hundred children were accommodated in the Kingdergarten. A training school for teachers was also opened and an Industrial School with garden, fields, oil press, dairy, laundry, bakery, sewing, weaving and embroidery was opened. For those who could do hard work there was grain parching and cleaning of utensils, etc.[14]

She remained an ardent supporter of the women's cause till her demise in 1922.

Swarn Kumari Debi

Swarn Kumari Debi was a famous social reformer of Bengal. She came from the famous Tagore family and was the sister of Rabindranath Tagore, the renowned poet. She was married at the age of 11 years in 1867. With the help of her husband she was able to discard purdah and took over the famous Bengali Journal *Bamabhadini Patrika* in 1884. She, thus, had the distinction of being the first Indian woman editor. Later, in the year 1886 she started a Ladies Association. The work of this Association was:

(i)   To promote friendly intercourse among Indian women and foster in them the growth of an active and enlightened interest in the welfare of the country.

(ii)   To provide a home for the education of poor girls to enable them to become useful members of the society.

(iii) To prepare them for employment and to help the spread of women's education by sending them out as zenana teachers.[15]

She was also the President of the ladies section of the Theosophical Society of Bengal in 1885-86. Swarn Kumari attended the Indian National Congress as a delegate from Bengal in its session held in Calcutta in 1900. This was the first time that a woman had attended the session as a delegate. Talking about her public service Amiya Bhusan Basu said in the *Calcutta Municipal Gazette*, "Her early efforts in improving the conditions of womenfolk in Bengal when the outlook was gloomy and opposition was so strong remind us of what Emerson said: 'There is always room for a man of force and he makes room for many'."[16]

The fiery spirit of Swarn Kumari found support in her daughter Sarla Devi who was not only a social reformer and educationist but also a politician of good standing.

Rani Shurnomoyee

She was the widow of late Raja Krishna Nath Kumar Rai Bahadur of Cassimbazar in Murshidabad. The Raja died at an early age leaving her in debt. With the able and honest services of her council she was able to bring the State back on a sound footing.[17] The Rani was an uneducated lady but her financial help without distinction of caste, creed or religion,[18] encouraged spread of education.

In Rajshahi she maintained an Anglo-Vernacular School for the education of her tenantry. She gave five hundred rupees for the erection of a house for the London Missionary School at Khangra close to Behrampore. The Rani also gave help to many schools on monthly basis.[19] Poor students, widows and orphans received her special care. In the famine of 1866, it was reported that about seventy to eighty maunds of rice was distributed by her amongst seven to eight thousand people.[20] A sum of two hundred rupees was paid by her for the building fund of the Indian Association which was established in 1876.[21]

A hostel was opened by her for the women students of the Grant Medical College, Calcutta. There were fifteen girls in it in 1886.

Ramabai Ranade

Ramabai Ranade was born in the year 1862 in Satara district. She was not even eleven years old when she was married to Justice Ranade who later won fame as a social reformer.

She met Pandita Ramabai in the year 1882 and under her influence became an active member of the Arya Mahila Samaj. The meetings of this Samaj were conducted at the house of Ramabai Ranade.

It was in the year 1884 that she made her first speech before Sir James Ferguson, the Governor of Bombay, at the Town Hall in Pune and asked for the establishment of a Girls High School in the city. She had to suffer opposition for this speech from the orthodox old women in her own house.

She started a Hindu Ladies Club which met at her house and later opened classes for illiterate women and widows. Thus a body of women was organised to render help in an emergency. So when plague and famine ravaged this city, these women were in the forefront.

She gathered women and lectured to them on first aid and social work. Gradually she formulated plans for the House of Service and finally started the Poona Seva Sadan with branches all over the Bombay Presidency.[22]

Mrs. Ranade's principal objects in starting the home were to teach and educate women through regular classes, to widen their range of knowledge with the help of libraries and lectures, to enable women to participate intelligently in all domestic affairs, social and national responsibilities.[23]

Mrs. Ranade also established the Seva Sadan Nursing and Medical Association in which high caste widows and girls volunteered to work and she was the one who took the first batch of probationers to the Sasoon Hospital, Pune.[24]

She was the leader of the agitation for compulsory primary education for girls. Her reputation as a writer was established by the production of her book *Reminiscences* now regarded as a Marathi classic.

Then came the suffrage movement in India. She supported the cause and presided over meetings demanding the right to vote. Sir H. Lawrence, a member of the Executive Council who supported the granting of voting rights to women said, "There is no council which would not be honoured, graced and helped by the presence of such a woman as one who is known to us all, Mrs. Ramabai Ranade."[25]

She was requested by the Pune Municipality to undertake care of thousands of women pilgrims and their little children who attended the annual fair at Alandi. Ramabai, along with her band of workers, "set forth for the sacred place and there in the temple courtyard, day and night she and her co-workers stood organising the women's visits to the temple taking charge of the infants."[26] Since then Seva Sadan had been called upon to work in cooperation with various social work undertakings.

Francina Sorabji

Francina Sorabji was another important personage of this time. Her main interest was education and she wanted to bring the children of all classes and communities into common schools. She started her social service in the villages.[27]

Rani Lady Harnam Singh

Rani Lady Harnam Singh was from the royal household of Kapurthala State in Punjab. She was the pioneer woman in the Punjab in the field of social reforms. Her enthusiasm for the emancipation of women was great. Writing to one of her friends she says: "India's greatest need is the proper education of our women." She further states: "What social reforms can we expect if the women are not educated and enlightened? What good are all the doctors if the mothers and wives are not able to carry out their instructions? What good are all the scientific sanitary rules if the ladies of our household do not understand the principles of hygiene and the benefits of sanitation? Therefore, something should be done to carry on our girls education even after they are married or put behind purdah."[28]

She started an Infant Welfare Centre at Jalandhar and also started sewing and knitting classes for women. She founded a ladies club in Shimla.[29]

Towards the close of the century, many more ladies took up the cause of women's education in particular and also contributed to the literature of the land. To mention a few: in Maharashtra there were, Miss Bhor, Mrs. Samaskar, Godavaibai, and in Gujarat Miss Patrick, a Parsi lady who conducted the Stri Mitra, Mrs. Putlibai, and in Bengal Mrs. R.N.Rai, Grindra Mohni, Pranila Nag and many others.

Notes and References

1. Shastri, Hardass Bal, *Armed Struggle for Freedom*, rendered into English by S.S. Apte, Poona, 1958, p. 159.
2. ibid.
3. Gedge E.C. and Choksi M., *Women in Modern India*, 1929, p. 17.
4. *The Indian Ladies Magazine*, November, 1909, p. 167.
5. *The Indian Review*, December 1929, Vol. 26, p. 311.
6. ibid., pp. 811-813.
7. Tahmankar, D.V., *Lokmanya Tilak*, London, 1956, p. 42.
8. Anandibai was born in 1865. She was the daughter of Ganpat Rao Amritaswar Joshi of Kalyan (Bombay). She was married in 1874 to Gopal Vinayak Joshi working in the Postal Department. She took to the study of medicine and went to England and America in 1883.
9. *Indian Review*, December 1929, Vol. 26, p. 813.
10. Tahmankar, D.V., op. cit., p. 43.
11. ibid.
12. ibid., p. 44.
13. Parvate, T.V., *Bal Gangadhar Tilak*, Ahmedabad, 1958, pp. 42-43.
14. Gedge, E.C. and Choksi, M. op. cit., p. 21.
15. *Modern Review*, Vol. 52, 1932, p. 242.
16. Quoted in Sen Gupta, Padmini, *Pioneer Women of India*, p. 90.
17. *Hindoo Patriot*, Vol, XVIII, May 1871, p. 150.
18. ibid.
19. ibid.
20. *Report on Native Papers* (Bengal) for the week ending October 6, 1866, p. 9.
21. Bagal, J.C., *History of Indian Association*, p. 57.
22. Sen Gupta, Padmini, op. cit., p. 39.
23. ibid.
24. Gedge, E.C. and Choksi, M., op. cit., p. 226.
25. Quoted in Cousins, M.E., *The Awakening of Asian Womanhood*, 1922, p. 115.
26. ibid.
27. Sorabji, Cornella, *The Position of Hindu Women Fifty Years Ago*, p. 10.
28. Sen Gupta, Padmini, op. cit., p. 69.
29. ibid.

5

EXTREMIST WOMEN IN INDIAN POLITICS: 1900-1913

The spirit of violent opposition which had been suppressed with British success in 1857 had not died out; in fact, it smouldered in the hearts of many a people waiting for an opportunity to spread out like wild fire. The Presidency of Bombay was prepared to give a lead and this province was conspicuous for its political activities in the ensuing period. General criticism of the British rule and against its imperial aspects occupied much more attention in western India—more particularly at Pune, the old capital of the Peshwas.

The closing years of the century were in particular a period of grim tribulations for the Indians. The last decade saw the passing of Indian Council Act of 1892 which was far from satisfactory for the people of the land. Lajpat Rai observed: "After more than twenty years of more or less public agitation for concessions and redress of grievances they had received stones instead of bread."[1] This period also witnessed a disastrous famine in 1896-97 attended with intense economic depression, manifestation of bubonic plague, the sentence of death passed on Chaupekar brothers[2] on account of the murder of two Englishmen (Mr. Rand and Lt. Ayest). To all these troubles was added the arrest for sedition of Lokmanya Bal Gangadhar Tilak in 1895. At the end of an exciting trial he was convicted for 18 months which inflamed the passions throughout the subcontinent.

These sufferings exposed not only the unpopularity of the alien rule in India but its failure in creating or maintaining conditions of contentment or satisfaction among the Indian people. The dissatisfied and disaffected among the educated had hoped for and now demanded a share in the administration. The British Government, instead of sending a Viceroy who could reconcile the ruler and the ruled and bring them closer to each other, sent a bureaucrat par-excellence in Lord Curzon with the ultimate consequence that the gulf between the two seriously widened and grew almost unbridgeable.

Curzon's curtailment of the powers of the Calcutta Corporation and his official Secrets Act which was condemned as a gagging measure tended to put back the hands of political progress to a great extent. His explanation was "freedom is granted to the press provided you refrain from writing."[3] The official takeover of the universities which made education expensive and finally the partition of Bengal smothered the aspirations of loyal people.

The people were further enraged by the convocation speech made by Curzon at the Calcutta University on February 11, 1905, wherein he remarked, "Truth took high place in the moral codes of the West before it had been similarly honoured in the East."[4] These remarks were condemned by the nationalists both in press and on platform. Curzon went still further and said that Indians were not fit to take up high offices. "Even more galling to our sense of self-respect than his speech in Calcutta regarding untruthfulness," writes Dr. Sitaramayya, "was his sweeping charge that we Indians by our environment, our heritage and upbringing are unequal to the responsibilities of high offices under the British rule."[5]

During this period Japan's amazing performance in the Russo-Japanese War and China's successful boycott of American goods gave high hope to our people. By and large the educated element felt that the British imperialism could be shaken off with the will of the people of the land. The Land Alienation Act Amendment Bill and the increase of water rates in the Bari Doab Canal caused visible commotion in the Punjab. This was followed by the arrest of Lala Lajpat Rai and Sardar Ajit Singh[6] which in turn found expression in the extremist activities. Grady exclaimed in the British Parliament that Lajpat Rai's arrest "had justified every tyranny committed by Dublin Castle or Russian autocracy."[7]

Curzon's parting gift—the partition of Bengal—became the focus of political agitation and the revolutionary element which first saw the light of day in Western India flourished in Bengal during this period. The rank and file in this Presidency (Bengal) were one in denouncing the decision which they felt was aimed at curbing their national unity and efforts towards progress. "The request of the people," observed Hardy, member of Parliament, was that "even if you cannot give us back Bengal, give us some modification of the present position of affairs so that we may not be a country cut in half."[8] Partition day was a day of mourning for the people of this region.[9]

Women in Bengal and Punjab

'Swaraj', 'Swadeshi' and 'National Education' became the slogans of the nationalists. Women who had begun to participate in the deliberations of the Indian National Congress now further took up the responsibility to share the national efforts through the press and the platform. There was no mass awakening amongst the women at this time but there was some sort of movement spreading slowly in them.[10]

Some five hundred women met at Jenokand village in the district of Murshidabad to protest against Government's decision and to urge the need of using the country-made goods.[11] Meetings were arranged by the ladies in their streets and spinning wheels were introduced in the zenana.[12]

Women contributed their bangles, nose rings, and bracelets to the national fund. In villages they had started putting away a handful of grain daily for such purpose. During the Provincial Conference of 1906 Smt. Sarojini Bose, wife of Tara Prasanna Bose, pledged that she would not wear gold bangles till the "Bande Matram" circular prohibiting the use of this slogan was cancelled.[13] Mrs. J.K. Ganguli gave her bracelet as a contribution towards paying off the fine of Shri Durga Mohan Sen,[14] who was convicted for seditious activities. Women outside India also did whatever they could to further the national cause.

Prosecutions and convictions became widespread. When Bhupendra Nath[15] was convicted on July 24, 1907, some two hundred women presented an address of appreciation to his mother.

Kumudini Mitter,[16] daughter of Kristo Mitter, a renowned nationalist, was very active during this period. She organised a group of educated Brahmin ladies for maintaining an illegal liaison between the different revolutionary leaders who were watched by the police. This organisation also helped in the circulation of revolutionary leaflets and literature. She preached the cause of the extremists through *Suprabhat*, a Bengali Magazine. It propagated the cult of revolution.[17]

Another lady, Smt. Bhag Bati of Noakhali (Eastern Bengal), wrote a song describing the wretched state of Indian people. She concluded with the following sinister prayer: "Kali! If you are under the influence of an evil planet, please save us, we will sacrifice white goats in Ganges if Bengal prospers."

While the women in Bengal were busy promoting the cause of freedom, women in Punjab also stepped into the political arena. Smt. Sushila Devi of Sialkot[19] delivered a series of lectures in which she attacked the government and exhorted women to rise to the occasion.[20]

Har Devi, wife of Roshan Lal, a Barrister of Lahore, who was a great social reformer and editor of a Hindi magazine, *The Bharat Bhagni,* also joined the ranks of the political workers. During this period she arranged meetings and collected funds for the purpose of assisting anarchists under trial.[21]

The women workers of the Arya Samaj were also responsible for arousing national spirit among the people. Smt. Purani who was working for the Arya Samaj at Hissar, was a prominent worker of the time. She toured the various districts of the Punjab and advocated the cause of swadeshi. Speaking to the women at Hissar, Smt. Purani criticised the caste restrictions, undue observance of which, she said, "prevented women from bringing up their sons as was done by the women of old, to be warriors and great men." She exhorted them "to bring up their sons, not with a view to joining government service, but to an independent participation in trade especially the manufacture and sale of swadeshi."[22]

Agyavati in Delhi was another person who took interest in the movement. She addressed both men and women and described the part played by the women in the management of the affairs of their own country in former times and she urged that until women were educated and took interest in the welfare of the country there was little chance of India making any real progress. She was reported to be a "very bold woman."[23] Agyavati started a Vidhawa Ashram where widows and other women, without distinction of caste or creed, received political training and were taught to spread the same.[24]

Sister Nivedita

Margaret Noble, known as Sister Nivedita, the daughter of Rev. S.R. Noble, was born at Dunganonco, Tyrone, on October 28, 1867. She was interested in education and became a trained teacher. She opened a school at Wimbledon with a broad and lively conception of education for girls.[25] Nivedita was very active at this time and was also instrumental in the establishment of Sesame Club (social centre for women and men).

In the year 1895, she came in contact with Swami Vivekananda. She came under his influence and came to India at his suggestion. By 1898 Nivedita was in India. The centre of her efforts was now shifted from London to Calcutta and India became her adopted motherland. She took strenuous tours of the north-west region along with Swami Vivekananda and three other western women. These tours were to serve as a guide in her future activities.[26]

The conditions prevailing at that time were painful to Nivedita. She expressed her feeling in a letter written in 1901 which indicated the interest she had developed in Indian affairs. The letter reads: "Only your friend is right about India's requiring foreign rule. Does the history of India bear the statement out? Of course, not. Even as written by her enemies it shows that India as large as western Europe, never suffered from such disorder. Think of wars between France and England alone, between England and Spain, between Germany and France, of the French Revolution.... Nothing is so extraordinary in India as the combination of intense religious conviction with marvellous political peacefulness, when one takes a large enough view of the situation to get the facts at a true focus. The only thing that never is written is good history, at least about India that I do understand."[27]

Sister Nivedita met Sarla Devi and acquainted herself with her work. But somehow she found a more congenial comrade in Sri Aurobindo who was striving to organise western India for revolutionary work. She is reported to have had affiliations with the Irish Revolutionary party.[28]

Her visit to Baroda in 1902[29] enabled her to have an insight into Sri Aurobindo's work at close quarters. When she returned to Calcutta she gave away her library of valuable books on the revolutionary and nationalist movements of different countries to the centre of revolutionary activities in Calcutta. It was at this place that she addressed the young men on the nationalist movements of other countries. She is reported to have been a member of the National Revolutionary Council along with Sri Aurobindo.[30]

Nivedita was present in the University Hall when Curzon made his convocation speech in 1905. She took the lead in condemning Curzon's observations. It was on account of her efforts that an article under the caption 'Lord Curzon in various capacities' appeared in the *Amrita Bazar Patrika* of February 13, 1905. This article was mainly written to prove that there was no truth in the statement made by Lord Curzon.

The leadership of the revolution which swept Bengal following the partition of the province was assumed by Rabindranath Tagore who fostered it and kept up its fire by his great literary creation of national songs, a unique poetry of patriotism. These patriotic poems were set to music with Ajit Chakravorty every evening in the hall of the Metropolitan Institution where the Dawn Society [31] was located. His close associate in this work was Hirendranath Dutta, and behind them was Sister Nivedita, and a more passionate patriot the country had yet to see. [32]

The famine and flood in East Bengal in 1906 was disastrous and Sister Nivedita was an eyewitness to the troubles of the peasants. She went from one farm house to another helping, healing and consoling the weak and the miserable. She addressed women's meetings and preached the use of swadeshi goods. Nivedita also emphasised the need to take to Charkha and other useful crafts. [33] Writing about the famine in Bengal in 1906 she observed: "Under western imperialism the methods of exploitation are different from those of the past. The subjection has become financial and growing exploitation proceeds along building of rail-roads, the destruction of native industries and the creation of widespread famine—there are so many landmarks, as it were, in a single process of subordination and exploitation." [34]

She believed that it was the school and not the parliament which was to be the cradle of new social combination. Her opinion was that the schools in British India had long stood without any morals, because there was no central ethical imperative round which could gather the new morality of the new era. Every student of every race and every province had caught the word of command "Arise and become a nation! Be the servant of your people! Be a man of your own land!" [35]

While referring to the peasants Nivedita observed that they had enough common sense to take the affairs of their country in their own hands. She further said that those who paid the revenue also had the right to control the expenditure. This fact could not be denied by Englishmen. "As long as India is contented to sit and argue the question," remarks Nivedita, "he is perhaps but wordly wise to take what he can and refuse concession. Argument is never dangerous. But if a day should come when she ceased to argue, if she suddenly declared that she cared nothing about theory, for three hundred millions of human beings had determined on a new arrangement? Not our right but our will. If this cry were heard throughout the land what could be said by the tax gatherers then? What then? What then?"[36]

Besides being a revolutionary of a high order, Nivedita took up the pen to arouse the zeal for the cultivation of national art, architecture, literature and history, education and culture. Though she did not join the political movement or any political party she advocated the revolution.[37] "The promotion of the cause of Indian nationality was with her a mission and a passion, as was women's education."[38] Nivedita dreamt of a unified India and desired that all should join together to achieve success in this great work. Talking about the unity of India she writes: "Side by side must work brothers of all shades of opinion, of all forms of energy, for the recreating of the Dharma, for the building anew in the modern world, of Mahabharata, Heroic India."[39]

Nivedita went to the court in 1907 to stand surety for Bhupendranath Dutta, youngest brother of Swami Vivekananda, who was arrested for sedition as editor of *Yugantar* and subsequently convicted to one year's rigorous imprisonment.[40]

Hard work had its effect on Sister Nivedita's health and she breathed her last in 1911. Speaking on her memorial meeting, Rashbehary Ghose said: "If the dry bones are beginning to stir, it is because Sister Nivedita breathed the breath of life into them. If our young men are now inspired with a burning passion for a new, a higher, a truer and noble life the credit is in no small measure due to the lady who has been so prematurely called away from us."[41] He further said, "If we are conscious of a budding national life at the present day it is in no small measure due to the teaching of Sister Nivedita."[42]

Sarla Devi

Sarla Devi was one of the prominent personages of this period. She formed the link between Punjab and Bengal revolutionaries. She was the niece of the great poet, Rabindranath Tagore, and was born in the year 1872. Her mother, Swarn Kumari, was an ardent worker for the swadeshi cause.

The spirit of patriotism was imbibed in Sarla Devi by her mother. Her work from the year 1897, when she took over the editorship of

Bharati,[43] which she edited till 1899, is of great significance. Through the pages of *Bharati*, she advocated the Hindu-Muslim unity as unity alone could oust the foreigners. At the seventeenth session of the National Congress a song composed by Sarla Devi invoking the people of different provinces of the country to join hands in the national struggle was sung in chorus.

Sarla Devi's impressionable years were spent in western India with her uncle, Satyendranath Tagore, where she witnessed the revival of Ganapati Festival, Shivaji coronation festival and the organisation of the society of physical and military training by Damodar and Balkrishna Chaupekar, who were Chitpavan Brahmins. She felt so inspired that she wanted to introduce similar activities in Bengal to revive the heroic spirit among the people. She established a centre for physical culture at her home in Calcutta and suggested to the congress to organise an exhibition of physical feats. In the year 1903 she organised the celebration of Birastni Brata and Pratapaditya Brata[44] modelled on the lines of Shivaji 'Utsav' of young Marathas who followed Tilak. Just as the Marathas celebrated the Puja of Bhabai, tutelary deity of Shivaji, so Sarla Devi celebrated the Kali Puja, tutelary goddess of Pratapaditya. Referring to this move of Sarla Devi, Bipin Chandra Pal[45] wrote in *New India*, "as the necessity is the mother of invention, Sarla Devi is the mother of Pratapaditya to meet the necessity of a hero for Bengal."[46]

Sarla Devi opened 'Lakshmi Bhandar' for popularising swadeshi goods. In 1904 she won the gold *medal* for exhibiting improved varieties of textures of fabrics.[47]

Sarla Devi was married to a popular Arya Samajist and a well-known nationalist leader, Rambhoj Dutt Chaudhery of Lahore, in 1905 and her centre of activities then shifted from Bengal to Punjab. She continued to direct her activities from Punjab and maintained the link between the two provinces.[48]

Sarla Devi gave a new life to the Suhrid Samiti in 1905. The Suhrid Samiti was started in 1901 as a benevolent institution in Mymensingh district of Bengal. It became a political organisation and its changed creed was due to the trend of the time in general and the two special causes in particular. The first was the visit of Aurobindo Ghose, Subodh Mullick and Bipin Chandra Pal to Mymensingh district in 1905 and the second special cause was the predominant influence of Mrs. Rambhoj Dutt (Sarla Devi) She attended the provincial conference and then organised the Suhrid Samiti as an instrument for political work and tried to infuse a martial spirit into the members by introducing religious rituals. The association had its headquarters in Mymensingh and they aimed at starting new centres for propagating their ideas. In 1908 it had six branches in Mymensingh, four in Dhaka and six in Sylhet and one each in Noakhali and Chandanpur. The Brati Samiti and Sakti Samiti of Calcutta and Sevak Samiti of Dhaka were also branches of the same society. It was reported in 1908 that Mrs. Rambhoj Dutt "maintains a fairly brisk correspondence with the leading members of this Samiti."[49]

She had organised agricultural farms[50] to propagate her work. One such farm was started in Sylhet district under the charge of Kedar Nath. The ostensible object of the farm was to teach the arts of agriculture to 'bhadralog youth'. But in reality the agricultural aspect of the farm was if "not a mere pretext than at any rate a subsidiary object."[51] It was found that the youth on the farm were in closest touch with the authorities of the 'Suhrid Samiti'. The members of the Suhrid Samiti figured in numerous political demonstrations.[52]

The minds of the 'Suhrid Samiti' members were well trained by religious ceremonies, inflammatory speeches, songs and literature and by participation in political meetings and demonstrations. They were subjected to physical training designed to develop muscles and arouse martial spirit. Boxing, wrestling, drill, lathi exercises, sword and dagger exercises, were among the items of this training. Most of the volunteers possessed daggers and sword sticks. Many had unlicensed revolvers. The members of the Samiti looked up to Sarla Devi as their leader and she continued to "exert powerful influence from Lahore."[53]

Sarla Devi went from Lahore to preside over the New Year's Day 1909 and Pratapaditya Anniversary. It was during this meeting that an attempt was made for the first time to use the word "Bande Mataram" as a national slogan. "Each member of this Samiti after nestling to mother country mine," exhorted Sarla Devi, "should consider every act beneficial to the mother country as my work, my duties and try to accomplish it without waiting for the other with the motto to accomplish by witchcraft or to die, to guide you in life, carry through whatever you feel to be my work."[54]

Sarla Devi toured extensively, more especially the Punjab. She opened the Arya Samaj branches for women. Addressing a meeting at the Arya Samaj Girls School, Saharanpur, she said, "Knowledge is the great remedy for fear. Give knowledge to your womenfolk. Get them rid of fear and they will transmit fearlessness to your veins. Do not let all this remain mere talk, a theme for day's platform speaking clapping only but be sincere, be alert, arise, awake and having achieved the goal, rest."[55]

She also condemned the police officer of the Criminal Intelligence Department, who had followed her to keep a watch over her activities. She said, "Here was a stripling, a boy of my own race and blood corrupt to the core, treacherous to a degree, trying in the meanest cowardly fashion to frighten a lady supposed to be partial to the motherland out of wits to get lift in Criminal Intelligence Department."[56]

Addressing a meeting on May 1, 1908, at Lahore,[57] she said that it was required of every true and loyal son of the soil to take an oath of allegiance to the country, to revere the past, to preserve relics of the past, to study history and science, to have thorough mastery of the language, to strive for their own rights and privileges and on behalf of others.[58]

Sarla Devi supervised the work of the Hindustan Press. She regularly attended the office and skilfully divided the press into two parts, setting aside three machines for jobbing and three for regular work of the paper. The object of this decision was to save three machines if they were ever ordered to be confiscated.[59]

To provide immediate incentive to the people to take interest in the affairs of their country, Sarla Devi arranged competitions and her favourite subjects were: (i) Welcome to hardships, (ii) Knowledge, and (iii) Patriotism, as also for the best essay in Punjabi language and Hindu-Muslim unity.[60] Meetings were also arranged by her in which she encouraged discussions on topics like women's education and patriotism.[61]

Sarla Devi took steps to organise women's movement. The nucleus of this movement was formed at Lahore in 1910. She was the tireless Secretary of the Bharat Stri Maha Mandal which was organised in the teeth of opposition. Branches of Stri Maha Mandal were also instituted at Allahabad and Calcutta. The object of this society was to bring together the women of all castes and creeds on the basis of their common interest in the moral and material progress of women in India.[62] The government could not ignore the activities and the lead given by Sarla Devi and so she was put under surveillance. She was told that if she objected to being watched she should restrict her activities.[63]

Sarla Devi came under the influence of Gandhiji in the year 1919. She was one of the few women in Punjab who raised their voices against the tyranny of General Dyer. She also took part in the franchise movement set in motion by Mrs. Cousins. In Bengal it was she who was instrumental in securing a voting right for women. Sarla Devi remained an ardent Congress worker till her death in 1945[64] and participated in the various campaigns launched to achieve freedom.

Indian women outside India also did their best to make this cause a success. Most important of those who worked for the revolutionary activities were Mrs. Shyamji Krishna Verma, Miss P. Naoroji, granddaughter of Dadabhai Naoroji, Miss M. Chattopadhya, sister of Nirendranath Chattopadhya and Madam B.K. Cama. The last named was amongst the top ranking leaders of the revolutionary party in Europe.

Madam Bhikaji Rustum K.R. Cama

Madam Cama was born on 24th September, 1861. She was the daughter of Sorabji Framji Patel. Her education was completed in Bombay at the Alexandra Parsi Girls School. After leaving the school she devoted herself to the mastery of some foreign languages which was useful to her in later life. She was married to the son of K. Rustum Cama, a Parsi reformer, who made a name in the Presidency.

She went to Europe in 1902. Madam K.R. Cama spent a year in Germany, Scotland and Paris before settling down in London in 1906. These wanderings were perhaps a prelude to her political career. By the time she was back in London the seed of Revolutionary Party had already been sown by patriots like Shyamji Krishna Verma.[65] But it was left to Madam Cama to nourish this tender sapling into a vigorous tree.

Bhikaji Cama came in contact with Shyamji Krishna Verma who inspired her to join the revolutionary movement wholeheartedly. She had, perhaps, already made up her mind to dedicate her life to the cause of her motherland and started the work in a systematic manner. She took immediate steps to establish contacts with nationalists of Ireland, Russia, Egypt and Germany. She was mindful of the handicaps of the extremists at home and supplied them revolvers concealed in toys ostensibly sent as Christmas presents.[66]

When it was announced that the International Socialist Congress was to meet in Stuttgart (Germany) in August 1907, Madam Cama was quick to grab this opportunity to acquaint the cosmopolitan gathering with the conditions prevailing in India. Her speech on that memorable occasion dealt with the lives of the dumb millions of Hindustan "who are undergoing terrible tyrannies under the English Capitalism and British Government."[67] She said that 35 million pounds were taken annually from India and consequently people, in India died of poverty. At the end of the speech she unfolded the Indian National Flag, a tricolour in green, yellow and red, with the words 'Bande Mataram' on the middle band. Thus Bhikaji Cama was the first Indian who unfolded the Indian National Flag in a foreign country before an international gathering. Subsequently she made it customary to unfurl the national flag before addressing any meeting because she said "she was in the habit of speaking under the flag."[68]

Madam Cama did a yeoman's task for the election of Dababhai Naoroji to the Parliament, he being the first Indian to sit in the House of Commons.[69]

Immediately after the conference in Germany she left for America where she was to launch a vigorous campaign to win the sympathy of the people of that great republic for her just and sacred cause. She was interviewed by the pressmen at New York. She boldly replied that "Swaraj and Self-Government" was her goal. She told the interviewer that "starved and uneducated as we are, the past few years have shown an increase of millions of patriots. We shall have liberty, fraternity and equality some day. We hope for freedom within ten years."[70]

On October 28, 1907, Madam Cama addressed the members of the Minerva Club at the Waldorff Astoria Hotel in New York and asked their help for political enfranchisement of India. She said: "The people here know about the conditions in Russia but I do not think that they know anything about the conditions in India under the English Government. Our best men are deported or sent to prison like criminals, and there they are flogged so that they have to go to the prison hospitals. We are peaceful, we do not want a bloody revolution, but we do want to teach the people their rights and throw off despotism."[71] She addressed meetings at several places. She was the first Indian (woman) unofficial ambassador of the people of India to the United States.

In November 1908, Madam Cama was back in London and addressed the gathering at India House. Her speech was printed in a leaflet, copies of which were afterwards sent to India in large numbers. This leaflet became the manifesto of the revolutionary creed. She justified the use of force when one was forced to use force. She explained that tyranny is tyranny and torture is torture wherever applied and that success justified any action. She said that the struggle for freedom called for exceptional measures and that successful revolution against the foreign rule was patriotism. In a message to the youth of the country she said: "March forward friend! and lead our helpless, dying, downtrodden children of motherland to the goal of Swaraj in its right sense. Let our motto be, 'we are all for India for the Indians'."[72]

It may be mentioned that Madam Cama was not a born revolutionary. As she said at a meeting of the India House in 1908, "Three years ago it was repugnant to me even to talk of violence as a subject of discussion but owing to the heartlessness, the hypocrisy and the rascality of the liberals that feeling is gone."[73]

Madam Cama was an apostle of unity—whether she addressed the Muslims, the Hindus or the Sikhs—her watchword was that they should fasten the ties of brotherhood—that relation between the countrymen should be firm and resolute without bringing in the question of religion.[74]

She preached the sermon of non-cooperation in a far off land and exhorted the Indians not to accept any office however high it might be under the British Government. They ought to serve themselves, improve trade, industry and art and then the country would be their own.

By now Madam Cama's activities were widely known and the British Government began to look upon her as a dangerous revolutionary whose aim was to overthrow the British rule in India. The detectives were set to follow her like a shadow. She decided to move to Paris and left London in May 1909. Here she associated with S.R. Rana,[75] Shyamji Krishna Verma and other revolutionary leaders. Madam Cama interested herself chiefly in the business of preparing and forwarding to India seditious literature in the form of leaflets and generally in assisting with advice and what was probably more important with her money. She was at this time the recognised leader of the revolutionary movement and was said to be regarded by the people as a reincarnation of goddess Kali.[76]

In 1907 when the renowned Indian journalist and revolutionary, B.C. Pal, editor of *Swaraja*, was prosecuted for his seditious writings, Madam Cama felt the need of having a press of her own away from the clutches of the British Government. This dream materialised in 1909 when she shifted to Paris. To carry on the required propaganda work she started the well-known monthly journal *The Bande Mataram.*[77] This journal was supported by voluntary contributions and there was no fixed subscription. The famous Press Act was imported to India by the bureaucratic government in 1910. By virtue of this Act several editors were sent to jails and the presses were closed down. Madam Cama was not to be defeated by this high handed measure. She encouraged her countrymen and wrote in Vol. I, March 1910, of her journal that Press Act was a confession of the defeat on the part of the Indian Government and attributed to the efficiency of the revolutionary party. It was emphasised that the Act would not affect the future of the cause since revolutionary journals and books were printed abroad. The writer added: "We must recognise that importation of revolutionary literature into India from foreign countries is the sheet anchor of the party and the centre of gravity of political work has shifted from Calcutta, Poona and Lahore to Paris, Geneva, Berlin, London and New York."[78]

In another article in 1911, Madam Cama appealed to the Indians in Europe to make the best of their stay in the West, by taking all kinds of physical training. Above all she asked them to "learn to shoot straight because the day is not far when coming into the inheritance of Swaraj and Swadeshi, you will be called upon to shoot the English out of the land which we all love so passionately."[79] Copies of this journal found their way to America, Egypt and many parts of Europe and India. At one time nothing less than 426 copies were intercepted at the Oxford Post Office.[80]

The cause of women was dear to her. She wanted the women to share the responsibilities, sufferings and sorrows of their countrymen. In 1912 in an open letter to Young Orients on the subject of foreign wives, she advised them to marry Oriental girls for all their weaknesses and for all their goodness and improve them and make them progressive. By doing so the young men would be improving the conditions of the country and strengthening it at the same time. She said: "You should rather suffer everyday in your life in teaching the progressive ways to an Oriental little wife than getting a readymade article and live an easy home-life, by marrying an Occidental woman."[81]

At the meeting of the Egyptian National Congress at Brussells in 1910 she remarked: "I see here the representatives of only half the population of Egypt. May I ask where is the other half? Sons of Egypt, where are the daughters of Egypt? Where are your mothers and sisters, your wives and daughters?"[82] She further remarked that they should "remember that the hand that rocks the cradle is the hand that moulds the character. That soft hand is the chief factor in the national life. So do not neglect that powerful hand."[83]

It would be wrong to say that she had anything against the women of other countries. In fact, she stressed: "I have nothing against American or English sisters."[84] She said that she was an internationalist in her feeling and that it will be a day rejoicing when she could say that "the world is my country, every human being is my relation. But to establish internationalism in the world there must be nations first."[85]

Madam Cama was so popular in Socialist circles in Paris that when V.D. Savarkar's[86] arrest and recapture became known she used her influence with such effect that the 'affair Savarkar' was at once taken up in the *Socialist Paper*. Madam Cama engaged Socialist *advocate* Jean Longueat to watch the proceedings of the Hague Tribunal on Savarkar's behalf and represent him there.[87]

Besides contribution to the National Fund of which she was the treasurer, Madam Cama also contributed liberally to the Abhinav Bharat Society.[88] This society was started by V.D. Savarkar in India and in London which was responsible for the murder of Jackson, at Nasik and later through V.V.S. Aiyer in Pondicherry of Ashe in the Tiruneveli District.[89]

The British Government was alarmed and the Governor-General issued orders for the interception of Madam Cama's mail. A thorough check was made on all the seaports. But Mrs. Cama was not defeated by these moves. Her leaflets and parcels reached India via Pondicherry.

The British Government thought of another device to put a check on her activities in 1910 by depriving her of her material resources. She was declared an absconder from justice under Section 88 Criminal Procedure Code on non-execution of warrants. Her property worth one lakh of rupees was attached.[90]

The following year partition of Bengal was annulled. The year 1914 witnessed the beginning of the First World War. Thus the activities of the revolutionaries were circumscribed. After the outbreak of war no foreigner was allowed to remain in Paris without licence. When she received her licence in which she was described as a British subject, she was indignant, and exclaimed that she was not so, but was a free Hindu.[91] However, when she was told that if she did not produce the licence she would be locked up at once, she had to make use of it. The French Government also yielded to pressure from the British and on 1 November, 1914, an undertaking was taken from her to cease seditious activities during the war and report herself to the police authorities once a week. She wanted to visit the war prisoners at Geneva but was disallowed by the French government.

Madam Cama fell seriously ill in 1914, but the moment she recovered, she set about her work again with the same old vigour and enthusiasm. At this time she helped in distributing copies of the *Gujarati Ghadar* and carried on copious correspondence with the Indian revolutionaries in all parts of the world. The Director, Criminal Investigation Department, reported that Indian nationalism is not a wide enough field for her energies and that her war cry was "the Orient for Orientals."[92] Even the Egyptians, the Turks, the Persians and the Chinese visited her for help and sympathy.[93]

Indian ladies, at the instance of Madam Cama, introduced a lecturership of the value of one thousand rupees for Indian women in connection with the society of political missionaries. The only condition was that the candidate had to be in sympathy with the objects of the society.[94]

Madam Cama continued her work in the face of all these difficulties till the toil of years rendered her invalid.

Pandit Jawaharlal Nehru who visited her during his European tour in 1926, wrote in his *Autobiography:* "We saw Madam Cama, rather fierce and terrifying, as she came up to you and peered into your face and pointing at you asked abruptly who you were. The answer made no difference (probably she was too deaf to hear) for she formed her own impressions and stuck to them, despite facts to the contrary."[95]

She died on 13 August 1936 at Bombay. This brave lady who sacrificed her all for the liberation of her motherland and spent practically her whole life in exile in a far off land, was amongst the pioneers of the freedom struggle.

Indian Women in South Africa

While Indian women in India and Europe were fighting for freedom, the women in South Africa were setting examples by exhibiting the strength of the passive resistance movement. They were taking training in the Satyagraha Army of Mahatma Gandhi. This training proved useful for many of them who came back to India to take their place amongst the freedom fighters.

The judgement given in a case on 14 March, 1913, by Justice Searle of the Cape Supreme Court (South Africa), whereby all the marriages were declared illegal except those celebrated according to Christian rites and registered by the Registrar of Marriages, was a challenge to the Indian womanhood. This decision could not be accepted at any cost. Mahatma Gandhi rose to the occasion and took up leadership of the Satyagraha army which included both men and women.

Mahatma Gandhi explained to women the difficulties which might follow the observance of Satyagraha. He told them that they might have to go to jail, or starve and do hard work. "But these sisters," remarked Mahatma Gandhi, "were all brave and feared none of these things, one of them was in an interesting condition while six of them had young babies in arms. But one and all were eager to join and I simply could not come in their way."[96] A batch of eleven women (all Tamilians, except one) principal among whom were: Mrs. Tambi Naidu, Mrs. N. Pillay, Mrs. K.M. Pillay, Mrs. A. Perumal Naidu, and many others entered Transvaal without permits but the police did not arrest them.[97]

The women in the Phoenix Farm[98] could not stay back. They joined the struggle. Mahatma Gandhi did not tell his wife Kasturba Gandhi[99] about this programme, but she overheard the conversation and came to Gandhiji and said: "I am sorry that you are not telling me about this. What defect is there in me which disqualifies me for the jail? I also wish to take the path to which you are inviting others."[100] Gandhiji replied thus: "There is no question of my distrust in you. I would be only too glad if you went to jail but it should not appear at all as if you went at my instance."[101] She assured her husband: "You may have nothing to do with me if being unable to stand jail I secure my release by an apology. If you can endure hardships and so can my boys, why can't I? I am bound to join the struggle."[102]

Kasturba Gandhi joined the struggle and hereafter she was always beside her husband and shared his responsibilities.

The second batch of sixteen women, principal among whom were: Mrs. Kasturba Gandhi, Mrs. J.K. Doctor, Mrs. Kashi Chagan Lal Gandhi, and Mrs. S. Magan Lal Gandhi, crossed the border and entered Transvaal without permits. They were arrested and sentenced to three months' imprisonment with hard labour.

The first batch of women from Tolstoy Farm was not arrested for entry into Transvaal without permits. So they took the next step of influencing the labourers to raise their voice against the indentured labour and for this they went to New Castle.[103] The Government could not tolerate any more and arrested them.

Another famous lady who had to go to jail was, Mrs. Rambhabai Sodha, wife of a passive resister. She was prosecuted for entry into Transvaal, was tried and sentenced to imprisonment. She appealed but the decision was not changed. She had a small baby in her arms and another three-year-old by her side.[104] In jail they were treated harshly and were not even provided with wholesome food. As a result, several of them, on release, were found to have been reduced to a skeleton. A sixteen-year-old girl, Valliamma R. Munuswami Mudaliar, came out of the jail with a fatal fever and died.[105]

Bai Fatma was another person who refused to give her finger impressions and was arrested along with her mother and daughter.[106]

During this period women had started taking interest in civil and political matters concerning India. There were women's societies working for the uplift of their kind. One such society was in Kanchi known as Kanchi Mahila Parishad and was started by Smt. Parvati Devi who was the headmistress of Hindu Girls School at Kanjeevaram. The aim of this women's association was "to equip the ladies of Kanchi with general information and to create public opinion among them regarding matters national.[107] Another society knowr as Gujarati Hindu Stri Maha Mandal was started in 1904. Mrs. Jamnabai Nagin Das Sakki was instrumental in "infusing a new and vigorous spirit into the lives of the women of Bombay."[108]

During this period two other ladies, Annie Besant and Sarojini Naidu, came on the political scene. They were later to rank amongst the topmost leaders of India.

Notes and References

1. Lajpat Rai, *Young India*, Lahore, 1916, p. 158.

2. Damodhar and Balkrishna Chaupekar were two brothers from a Brahmin family.

3. *Hindoo Patriot*, January 3, 1905.

4. *University of Calcutta, Convocation Address, Vol. III, 1889-1906*, Calcutta, 1914, p. 981.

5. Sitaramayya, Dr. P., *History of the Indian National Congress*, Vol I, p. 67.

6. Ajit Singh belonged to Jalandhar district. He was one of the first men to raise his voice against the British rule in Punjab. His revolutionary songs became very popular.

7. *Parliamentary Debates* (House of Commons), 1907, Vol. 175, p. 922.

8. ibid.

9. On this day hundreds and thousands went in mourning. No fire was kindled, no shoes or stockings were worn and only a loin-cloth was wrapped around the body. The constitutional party held over a thousand meetings to protest against the partition. [*Parliamentary Debates*, House of Commons, 1907, Vol. 175, p. 922.]

10. Mrs. Macdonald, wife of Ramsay Macdonald, who visited India during this period, observed that there was a "tremendous movement going on amongst the women. We are fond of labelling the Indian aspirations as sedition when if they were amongst ourselves we should call them patriotic. This movement seems to be spreading as much amongst women as amongst men." (*Modern Review*, August 1910, p. 124).

11. The Theosophical Publishing House, Adyar, *The Besant Spirit*, Vol. 4, p. 74.

12. Chirol writes: "The revolt seems to have obtained a firm hold of the zenana and the Hindu woman behind the purdah often exercises a greater influence upon her husband and her sons than the English woman who moves freely about the world.... In Bengal even small boys of so tender an age as still to have the run of zenana have I am told been taught the whole pattern of sedition and go about from house to house dressed up as little Sanyasis in little yellow robes preaching hatred of the English."(*Indian Unrest*, p. 103).

13. *Home Political (Confidential) Proceeding*, No. 13, July 1909.

14. ibid.

15. He was brother of Vivekananda, the saint patriot.

16. She belonged to Bengal.

17. The tone of the propaganda can be judged from a poem which appeared in its column:
    The mother can no longer be worshipped with fruits and flowers;
    The mother's hunger can no longer be appeased with words;
    Blood is wanted;
    Bands of followers are wanted with firm resolves.
    [*Home Political (Confidential) Proceeding,* No. 7-10, December, 1910].

18. *Home Political Secret*, No. 48, March, 1908.

19. Sialkot is on the border of Jammu in West Punjab.

20. *Home Political A Confidential* No. 18-25, August, 1910.

21. *Home Political A Confidential* No. 161-168 of May 25, 1908.

22. *Home Political Secret* No. 48, March, 1908.

23. *Home Political Proceeding* No. 18, October, 1908.

24. ibid.
25. *Studies From An Eastern Home by Sister Nivedita*, 1913, p. viii.
26. She then started a school for girls in Calcutta, but this experiment was unsuccessful and she had to abandon the idea. Attempt was again made in 1902 and she was able to start a school in Bosepara Lane, Bagh Bazar, Calcutta.
27. 'Prabudha Bharata', November 1936 Bengali, quoted in *Indian Review*, Vol. 32, January, 1937, p. 58.
28. *Modern Review*, Vol. I, July-December, 1907, p. 615
29. Immediately after the death of Swami Vivekananda in 1902, she severed her connections with the Ramakrishna Mission.
30. *Modern Review*, Vol. 8, July-December, 1910, p. 615.
31. Dawn Society was started in 1902. The society trained the youth of the country for political responsibilities. It also prepared them for the freedom fight. During this period it became an active propaganda organ for the Swadeshi cause. (Quoted in *India's Fight for Freedom, 1905-1906*, op. cit., p, 56).
32. ibid.
33. *Modern Review*, Vol. I, January-June, 1907, pp. 232-34.
34. ibid., p. 433.
35. ibid., p. 433.
36. *Modern Review*, Vol. I, January-June, 1907, p. 433.
37. *Modern Review*, June 1953, p. 470. (Article written by J.C. Bagal)
38. *Modern Review*, 1911, Vol. 10, p. 344.
39. Nivedita, Sister, *Selected Essays of Sister Nivedita*, 3rd Edition, Madras, Ganesh and Co., p. 152.
40. *Modern Review*, June 1953, op., cit., p. 470.
41. ibid., April 1912, Vol. II, P. 450.
42. ibid.
43. Bengali journal edited by Sarla Devi.
44. Religious ceremonies to honour the departed heroes.
45. Bipin Chandra Pal was the editor of the *New India*, and opposed the partition through its column. He was a renowned orator. He was associated with the Congress from its early stage. He was prosecuted in 1907 for writing an article on 'Actinology of the Bomb'.
46. *Modern Review*, Article by Bagal, J.C., June 1953. p. 469.
47. *Modern Review*, June 1953, p. 469.
48. *Home Political A Confidential* No. 135, May 1909.
49. *Home Political Secret* No. 111, February, 1908; *Home Political Secret*, No. 135, May, 1909.
50. *Home Political Proceeding* No. 2, April 1909.
51. *Home Political A Confidential* No. 135, May 1909
52. ibid.
53. *Home Political A Confidential*, No. 135, May 1909

54. *Home Political Proceeding*, No. I, October 1909.
55. *Home Political Confidential Proceeding* No. 46-52, January 1910.
56. ibid., No. 63-70, November, 1908.
57. This meeting, besides, 3000 people, was attended by high dignitaries like Lajpat Rai, Rambhoj Dutt, Duni Chand Barrister and others.
58. She also referred to the good turn done by Jahangir to Sir Thomas Roe. "Sir Thomas Roe, the Ambassador, came to India and rendered good services to Emperor Jahangir. He was given in return, the trading rights and from this gift have sprung these cancers which are now feeding on the flesh and blood of the people of India." (*Home Political Confidential Proceeding*, No. 161-168, May, 1908).
59. *Home Political Confidential*, 63-70, November, 1908.
60. *Home Political Confidential B Proceeding* 41-49A, April 1908.
61. *Home Political Confidential*, August 2, 1908.
62. *Modern Review*, October 1911, p. 344.
63. *Home Political Confidential*, No. 1—4, July 1911.
64. Taliwar, D.R. *Bharatvarsh Ki Vibhutian* (in Hindi), p. 167
65. Verma, Shyamji Krishna, was born at Mandvi in Kutch State. In 1879 he went to England. After being called to the Bar he came to India in 1885, the year A.O. Hume founded the Indian National Congress. He went to England in 1897 but came to prominence only when he started his paper *Sociologist* in 1905 and then the 'India House' and has "good claim to be regarded as the founder of Indian Revolutionary Movement abroad." (*Home Political Confidential Proceeding* No. 169, December 1914).
66. *Home Political B Secret Proceeding* No. 18, January 1911.
67. *Home' Political Confidential Proceeding* No. 1 of July 1913.
68. ibid.
69. ibid.
70. ibid.
71. ibid.
72. ibid.
73. ibid.
74. ibid.
75. Rana was a Parsi gentleman from Bombay. He was engaged in pearl business in Paris. Rana was one of the active revolutionaries of this period in Europe, and was one of the organisers of India House, London.
76. *Home Political Confidential Proceeding*, No. 1, July 1913.
77. ibid.
78. ibid.
79. ibid.
80. ibid.
81. *Home Political Confidential Proceeding*, No. 37-39, August 1913.

82. ibid.
83. ibid.
84. ibid.
85. ibid.
86. Vinayak Damodar Savarkar was born on May 28, 1883, in Maharashtra. After his early education he proceeded to England in 1906. He had won the Shyamji Krishna Verma Endowment Scholarship. He was arrested in London in 1910 and as no charge was proved against him he was sent to India. He tried to escape as his boat was passing by the shores of France.
87. *Home Political Confidential Proceeding* No 1, July, 1913.
88. The society was revolutionary in its creed and had members in the various parts of the Western India.
89. *Home Political Confidential Proceeding* No. 1, July 1913.
90. *Home Political Confidential B Proceeding* No. 9-16, June 1910.
91. *Home Political Confidential Proceeding* No. 215-217, December 1914.
92. ibid. No. 227-228. December 1914.
93. ibid. No. 623-625, 1914.
94. ibid. No. 1, July 1913.
95. Nehru, Jawaharlal, *An Autobiography* (1935), p. 111.
96. Gandhi, M.K., *Satyagraha in South Africa* (1928), p. 421.
97. ibid.
98. Phoenix Farm—A settlement started in 1904 by Gandhiji. It was about 14 miles from Durban and about 3 miles from Phoenix.
99. Kasturba Gandhi was born in 1869 and was married to Mahatma Gandhi in 1882.
100. Gandhi, M.K., op. cit., p. 432.
101. ibid.
102. Gandhi, M.K., *Satyagraha in South Africa*, 1928, p. 422
103. ibid.
104. *Modern Review,* Vol. 9, January to June 1911, p. 313 and 544.
105. Gandhi, M.K., op. cit., p. 430.
106. ibid.
107. *Modern Review,* Vol. 13, 1931, p. 160.
108. ibid., Vol. 19, January-June, 1916, p. 581.

6

ANNIE BESANT AND THE HOME RULE AGITATION: 1914-1918

Keep the Flag of Freedom flying
To your latest breath;
If you cannot win Her living
Conquer Her by death.

—*Annie Besant*[1]

This period is of great significance in the history of the national struggle for it was for the first time that a woman, Annie Besant, led the national movement and "she wrenched Indian politics out of its automatic and placid theorising, made it a living and vital issue before the country and the whole Empire..."[2]

These years were equally important on account of the First World War, a crisis which threatened the integrity and stability of the British Empire. The Indian people helped the British war efforts with men, money and material and thus saved the English from disaster. The political parties, for once, decided unanimously to suspend political activities to help the British in their perilous hour.

The period also witnessed the birth of few major national events, i.e., reunion of the Moderates and the Extremists in the Indian National Congress in 1916,[3] an alliance between the Muslim League and the Congress, the outcome, of which was the Congress-League Scheme[4] (Lucknow Pact, 1916), and above all the inauguration of the Home Rule League and the Home Rule Agitation which shook the nation from its deep slumber and increased the tempo of national life.

These years are of far greater importance in the history of the women's movement. It was due to the lead given by Annie Besant that an organised movement[5] for the emancipation of women and to put forward the demand for political rights for women came to be established. Her leadership gave strength, encouragement and inspired the women of the land to participate in the national life of the country and to join the national movement in increased numbers. C.M. Reddi observed, "Dr. A. Besant prepared the ground for the Gandhian freedom movement in which women have played a prominent part."[6]

Early Life and Marriage

Annie Besant, the daughter of Dr. William Page Wood,[7] was born on October 1, 1847, in London. Following her father's death in 1852, when she was just five years old, the family faced great difficulties. So she had to leave home at the age of thirteen in 1861. She came to stay with Miss Maryat in Paris who was stern and religious. Besant did not spend all her time in religious activities and found time to read translations of Plato, Dante and the Iliad. These readings, perhaps, laid the foundation for her political career.

The two main tragedies of her early life were her rejection of Christianity and her marriage. She was married in 1867 to Frank Besant, a clergyman, but the marriage proved to be a failure.[8] Mrs. Besant had to seek divorce. Separation meant the end of family life. As a consequence she had to come out into the world. This gave her the opportunity to gain experience in the varied professions which she had to adopt to earn her living. She worked as a cook, a nurse and did needlework to support herself.

Beginning of a Public Career

Mrs. Besant came under the influence of Charles Bradlaugh[9] in 1847 and joined his *National Reformer*. In 1881, she became its co-editor with Bradlaugh. Mrs. Besant made her first speech at the Cooperative Institute in Castle Street, London, and demanded political status for women and equality in all spheres on the basis that if they were inferior they would not be able to withstand open competition.[10] Mrs. Besant frequently spoke about land system, cost of Royalty, the obstructive power of the House of Lords and also demanded justice for the weaker nations. She condemned the aggressive and oppressive policy of England in Ireland, Transvaal, Afghanistan, Burma and Egypt. Later she became ill. This illness perhaps gave her required leisure to plan her future line of action. She decided, as she said, "to give myself wholly to propagandist work as a free thinker and a social reformer, and to use my tongue as well as my pen in the struggle. The desire to spread liberty and truer thought among men, to war against bigotry and superstition, to make the world freer and better than I found it—all this impelled me with a force that would not be denied."[11]

As soon as she recovered she undertook strenuous tours and sometimes she visited as many as twenty towns in a month.

She joined the Theosophical Society under the influence of Madam Blavatsky.[12] In 1892 Madam Blavatsky died and Mrs. Besant along with Mr. W.O. Judge became the joint head of the Esoteric Section of the Society. In a letter sent to Adyar[13] the next year she declared that even in England, India and Indians were nearer to her than her fellow countrymen. "In heart I am one with you and to you by my past I belong. Born last time under the Western skies for work that needs to be done, I do not forget my true motherland and my true nature turns eastward even with filial longing. When Karma opens the door I will walk through it and we will meet in mind."[14] Annie Besant's desire was to be fulfilled within the next two years and she came to India in 1893.

Work in India

From this time onwards she busied herself with the uplift of Indians and her work can distinctly be divided into four divisions each pertaining to a different period, involving different procedure and a different subject. Her first interest was religion and this work occupied her up to 1893 when she took up the cause of education. In 1903 she stepped from the field of education to that of social reforms—the cause she held dear till 1913, the year she turned to politics. It goes without saying that even though the subject, the problem and the period differed from each other, each overlapped the other.

The closing years of the nineteenth century was a period when the western education and the western domination were manifest. A section of the people felt proud in imitating western mode of life and culture while the conservative section of the society was reactionary to this newly developed Anglicised section of the society. Mrs. Besant realised the gulf in these two sections and formed a link between them. She acquainted herself with the religion philosophy, manners and customs of the land. She toured the country and visited various provinces and towns reminding of the glorious past of India.

Mrs. Besant dealt with the conservative element amongst the people by opening schools and colleges. She also spoke of theosophy and Hinduism and associated herself with Sanatan Dharm Paliani Sabha, Banares, founded by Colonel Olcott (one of the founders of the Theosophical Society) with the object of "improving the morals of Hindu students and of engendering a love for Aryan simplicity and Aryan spirituality."[15] She also associated herself with the *Arya Bala Bodhini*, a monthly journal in English, issued at the nominal rate of one rupee per annum, the aim being, through "the agency of rising generation" to "restore to India her past greatness in her religion which is her only life and strength."[16]

Mrs. Besant raised her voice against the caste system. Her interpretation of the East was not very tasteful to the people with the result she had to face a certain amount of opposition, but this opposition was insignificant, because the majority were appreciative of her services to Hinduism. She also raised her voice against child marriage and untouchability. Speaking about untouchability she said: "You complain, and justly, of the harsh and rude manners often shown to you by your English rulers, but are they one-hundredth part as insolent to you as you are insolent to this race whom you in the past have brought under your yoke?"[17]

Mrs. Besant began her crusade for education, with the declared ideal that it was to be "an education founded on Indian ideals and enriched not dominated by thought and culture of the West."[18] In 1897 she started working for the Hindu College at Banares and was able to build a full-fledged college in the next two years. Under its auspices she helped in bringing out publications on Hinduism better known as the *Sanatan Dharm Series*, the like of which had not been published until then. Later she opened schools and colleges for girls as well. Among such institutions are: Central Hindu Girls School, Banares, Madanapalla High School and College and Adyar National College. Mrs. Besant who had championed equality for women in 1885 in England had by now changed her views on the subject. She did not seek absolute equality for girls and felt that they had a different role to play. The girl "must be educated as the wife and mother, not as the rival competitor of man in all forms of outside and public employment."[19]

In 1906 Mrs. Besant organised within the Theosophical Society the 'Sons of India' and the 'Daughters of India' to work for social reforms. Later in 1913 a new body, the Theosophical Stalwarts appeared, each member taking a pledge to disociate himself from certain customs. The next year it developed into an order of the 'Brothers of Service' who pledged to disregard all caste restrictions.

Mrs. Besant preached the use of swadeshi from an economic stand-point. "The Intelligence Department labelled this as political propaganda." Her tone of lectures throughout the year 1909 was moderate and she advised the students not to meddle with politics. She was in favour of gradual reforms and was of the opinion that India was not fit for self-government and universal suffrage must only be applied in municipal matters.[20]

In 1911 Mrs. Besant organised the "Order of the Rising Star". This organisation was "for the protection of the good, for the destruction of evil doers, for the sake of firmly establishing righteousness."[21] In 1913 a junior branch of the "Order of the Rising Star" entitled "The Servants of the Star" was established. It consisted of people below twenty-one years of age. Its membership was open to those who wished to be trained in the special kind of service which the spirit of the new age demanded. The membership of the Order up to 31st March 1916, was 5,547 and that of the Servants 1,400. The total membership of Brothers of the Stars in May 1917 was 16,476 including the Servants 8,999.[22]

Political Conditions

Political conditions in the country at this juncture remained disturbed. The partition of Bengal, a 'settled fact', was unsettled in 1911 after a great deal of agitation. In the same year Lord Hardinge, a moderate Viceroy, sent his famous Despatch[23] of 25 August 1911, to the Home Government supporting the aspirations of Indians for provincial autonomy. The indentured labour was also abolished.

These gestures on the part of the authorities were able to quieten the atmosphere to a certain extent but hidden behind them were the Press Act, Sedition Act and the Criminal Law Amendment Act. The age-old regulation III on 1819 was still at work. It was quite apparent from the excise duties on cotton manufactured in India that the Government was not interested in India's industrial development. This period also witnessed Gokhale's Education Bill under discussion with very little chance of its going through successfully.

The Indian intelligentsia could not appreciate the smaller things with all these restrictions. The Partition of Bengal was annulled, but it came too late and thus could not be much appreciated. The

Revolutionary element was still active and a proof of this was given by throwing a bomb of Lord Hardinge on the occasion of his State entry into Delhi (1911). Consequently, the Government tightened the provisions regarding the press. The Minto-Morley Reforms which were announced in 1910 by granting separate representation to the Muslims, widened the gulf between the two major communities and weakened the national front against the Imperial Government. The Ghadar Conspiracy was unearthed[24] and the people involved were prosecuted. Bhai Parmanand was convicted and sentenced to transportation for life.

Mrs. Besant's Political Activities

Mrs. Besant who had by now come to be well-known both in India and Europe for her social, educational and theosophical work entered the political arena. She had a large number of followers with the result that her success in political work became easy. She took up political work not by choice. She was forced by circumstances to take interest in this field. She herself observes thus: "It is possible that I should have never jumped into political work, had not increasing repression by the authority, narrowing of liberty, the ill-treatment of students, and the danger of revolution forced me into the field."[25]

The country was in need of a General. During this period the veterans of Indian freedom of the standing of Gopal Krishna Gokhale and Sri Pherozeshah Mehta were no more. Dinshaw Edulji Wacha was too old to do any active work; S.N. Banerjee was not in line with the latest thought, and M.K. Gandhi had not yet taken the rein of political work in his hands. Lala Lajpat Rai was virtually exiled in America. Bal Gangadhar Tilak was released in 1914 after a long term of imprisonment, but he was in shattered health and thus unable to carry on the work— "a circumstance which stood in the way of his undertaking energetic propaganda throughout India, moving on the wings of time and electrifying the people by an appeal to their emotions. This was left to be done by one older than himself in age, frail in sex, but enjoying a better start in life, not being under a cloud in the scene of her operations, better known to the world and endowed with that dynamic energy which knows no fatigue and seeks no rest."[26]

Thus, India in 1915 was a leaderless country whose cause went unheard. Mrs. Besant sensed the need of the time and jumped from theosophy to politics bringing along with her a new zeal, a vigorous demand and an unyielding determination. Her interest in political condition of India can be traced to the year 1878 when she published a pamphlet on England, India and Afghanistan. In this little pamphlet she condemned the invasion on the last named country. As early as 1902 while in London, she challenged the people of England for the conditions in India for whose good government they were responsible. "I ask you," she had said, "whether you have a right to rule 30,00,00,000 people in name and not understand the alphabet of Indian question very largely in your Imperial Parliament."[27] She blamed England for ruling India on western lines. Mrs. Besant observed: "India is not ruled for the prospering of her people but rather for the profit of her conquerors and her sons are being treated as the conquered race."[28] She attributed the famines to the financial drain of the "Home Charges" and the huge bureaucracy and partly the destruction of the manufactured goods of India for the profit of Lancashire.[29] "India", she said, "must be governed on the basis of Indian feelings, Indian traditions, Indian thought and Indian ideas."[30] To achieve this end she started working for the revival of village councils as a necessary unit of Local Self-Government.

In 1912, Mrs. Besant organised a band of public workers, namely, The Brothers of Service' with a view to promote union amongst the workers in the spiritual, educational, and political fields under the parentage of Indian National Congress. During the same year—October and November—Mrs. Besant gave a series of lectures, as she said, "to mark the beginning of an earnest and concerted movement for the uplifting of India."[31] Hereafter she took active interest in politics of the country. She made a demand at a public meeting called by the Madras Congress Committee, that a standing Committee of the British House of Commons for consideration of Indian affairs be established.[32] She also suggested at the Congress Session of 1913 to sponsor a national movement embodying religious, educational, social as well as political reforms. She brought out a weekly paper the *Commonweal* to do the required propaganda.[33]

Mrs. Besant opened her political campaign by giving a political lecture in January 1914 at Madurai (South India) which was presided over by the municipal chairman. The year also witnessed the beginning of the First World War. She supported the war efforts and advocated the cause of the Allies. Mrs. Besant urged others to support the war loan and herself raised six hundred recruits for the defence force.[34] Later she herself was the first one to break the political truce and wanted to have a definite promise with regard to self-government before the War ended.

Mrs. Besant joined the Congress in 1914 and she "brought new ideas, new talents, new resources and altogether a new method of organisation and a new outlook into the field of Congress."[35]

The same year she was elected as a delegate for the Congress session and spoke for the first time moving a resolution which was carried asking for reciprocity between India and the colonies in the matter of emigration. Political equality with the other citizens of the Empire was also demanded.[36] Mrs. Besant went a step further and asked for self-government not as a reward but as a right. She said that "there had been talk of a reward due to India's loyalty, but India does not chaffer with the blood of her sons and proud tears of her daughters in exchange for so much liberty, so much right. India claims the right as a nation, to justice among the people of the Empire. India asked for this before the war, India asks for it during the war, India will ask for it after the war, but not as a reward but as a right does she ask for it, on that there must be no mistake."[37]

By this time Mrs. Besant had received her Marching Orders[38] from Bhagwan Sanat Kumar, who summoned her in Shamballa in the Gobi desert. These orders became her declared policy. India was to be free within the Empire like other dominions and that the freedom was to be achieved by peaceful means.

To educate the people and to make known the demand of a nation to the ruling power, Mrs. Besant felt the necessity of having a press of her own. She bought the *Madras Standard* in July 1914, and was registered its sole proprietor, publisher and printer. She was exempted from furnishing security. The title of the paper was later changed to *New India*. The *New India* was brought out with the sole object in view "to press forward the coming changes in India and to claim steadily India's place in the Empire."[39]

In her paper she wrote a series of articles of self-government and announced her intention to lead a political campaign in favour of 'Swaraj'. "Her methods", observes a Director of the Criminal Investigation Department, "were highly objectionable as they inevitably led to inflaming racial feelings."[40] Supporting the cause of India she said: "The fate of British Empire hangs on the fate of India and therefore it is but wisdom and prudence to keep India contented by granting Home Rule to her." India was "a tremendous reservoir of manpower, far greater than America and home ruled India was an asset to the Empire in the struggle against German militarism."[41]

In the first issue of the *Commonweal* she stated her political aims. "In political reforms we aim at the building up of complete self-government from village council through district and municipal boards and provincial legislative assemblies to a national parliament, equal in its powers by whatever name they may be called, also at the direct representation of Imperial Parliament, when that body shall contain representatives of the self-governing States of the Empire."[42]

Her writings and speeches during this period mainly dealt with arguments against the British rule, i.e., the poverty of India, the drain (Home Charges), employment of Indians in the public services, executive bias in the administration of justice, army commissions and railway policy. At the same time she paid glowing tributes to India's past greatness.

She attended the Muslim League and Congress sessions in 1915. At the conference of the All India Muslim League she criticised the Government. The Commissioner of Bombay Police ordered Mrs. Besant to leave the platform. She questioned his authority and asked if he had any warrants for arrest. The Commissioner replied: "I shall have to arrest you if you do not leave." Mrs. Besant rose from the chair and said: "Do it if you dare." The Commissioner, however, did not dare to step further.[43]

Formation of Home Rule League

The idea of starting a Home Rule League[44] was first mooted by Mrs. Besant at a private meeting, while the Congress was holding its session in 1915, in China Bagh, in Bombay, with Surendranath Banerjee in the chair. The need for starting such an organisation was felt. She herself explained that "it was because the Congress showed little activity between its annual sessions that the need for Home Rule League had arisen to be an active propagandist body and the words Home Rule were chosen as a short public cry, making the fact clear that the struggle was not against Great Britain, but for liberty within the Empire.[45]

Dr. Zacharia observed that Mrs. Besant's plan was to disentangle the nationalist extremists from their compromising aliens with the revolutionaries and to affect reconciliation between the moderates and the extremists.[46] She also wanted to bring India and Great Britain closer. Mrs. Besant declared: "One thing that lives very near to our heart is to draw Great Britain and India nearer to each other by making known in

Great Britain something of Indian Movements and of the men who will influence from here the destinies of the Empire."[47]

"Home Rule", explained Mrs. Besant, did not necessarily mean democratic government. "It is not the form of government that makes Home Rule. It is that a nation is governing itself. A nation which by its own free vote, voted an autocracy will still be a self-governing nation."[48]

Home Rule for India was essential firstly, because, "It is the birthright of every nation, and secondly, because, her most important interests are now made subservient to the interest of the British Empire without her consent and her resources are not utilized for her greater needs."[49] Moreover, "Self-government is necessary for the self-respect and dignity of a people, other government emasculates a nation, lowers its character and lessens its capacity."[50]

The objects of the League were:

(i) To secure self-government for India through law-abiding and constitutional activities, i.e., agitation and propaganda, the constitutional way being the best way to political evolution.

(ii) To maintain connection with Great Britain by becoming a free nation within the Empire under the Imperial Crown of His Majesty, the King Emperor George V, and his successor.

(iii) To support and strengthen the National Congress, which had laboured for thirty years, to lay the foundation of Indian self-government.

(iv) To carry out continuous educative propaganda on the necessity of Home Rule for India.[51]

The membership of the League was open to all men and women over eighteen years of age. School boys and students were not permitted to become members. Undergraduates could associate with the League and they could be enrolled full-fledged members on ceasing to be undergraduates. The members had to pay ten rupees entrance fee and a life subscription. They (members) in return received a small silver badge and ribbons.[52]

The badge for the Home Rule League was a pointed star of the Indian Empire with Home Rule in red engraved in the centre. The colours were red (Hindus), green (Muslims).

The organisation was simple. A few people who were interested to work for Home Rule formed themselves into a group and chose one of the members as their representative who communicated with the secretary of the Home Rule League. Copies of all the literature were sent to the chosen representatives who distributed it to the members to enable them to do the propaganda, by placing them in reading rooms, libraries and local clubs.[53]

The Home Rule League members were expected to open a Home Rule League Room in every town and village and to call meetings to strengthen the propaganda. These branches, so formed, were required to form joint local committees affiliated to the Provincial Congress Committees. This was with a view to sending as many delegates as possible to the Congress platform and to ensure that the Congress of 1916 declared that "Home Rule was the immediate necessity."[54]

The Home Rule League was to be a separate body from the Congress. While in no way supplanting it, it had to take up work which the Congress could not do with its annual sessions and the rare meetings of its committees. Mrs. Besant dissociated herself with all the reforms for which the Congress stood, save the one for self-government; and she worked continuously in press and platform for that one thing.[55]

The meeting convened by Mrs. Besant at Bombay in 1915 to elicit support from the national leaders to start Home Rule League was not very encouraging for her as the leaders were not in favour of starting a separate organisation. They, however, informed her that the Congress would take up the work outlined by the Home Rule League. In view of this promise Mrs. Besant agreed to wait till September 1916. However, Bal Gangadhar Tilak supported the idea and formed a Home League in Pune on 23 April 1916.

Mrs. Besant, however, gave shape to her ideas and decided to start the Home Rule League. The League was to consist of two divisions, one in India and the other in England.

The Home Rule for India League in England was started on June 7, 1916. It was to serve as an auxiliary body to the National Congress and the British Committee in England with Home Rule for India as its only object. The general aim was to educate the British Democracy in relation to India and place before them the demand of the Congress for self-government. This League printed and circulated large numbers of pamphlets to create a lively interest in India. Amongst the prominent members of the League were De La Warr, Miss Barbara Villars and John Lansbury.[56]

The Congress and the Muslim League which were supposed to consider the adoption of the Home Rule League programme at a joint meeting in August 1916 failed to do so. Mrs. Besant, therefore, set about her work regarding the establishment of the Home Rule League.

Before starting the Home Rule League in India she went on a lecture tour and delivered a series of lectures in Calcutta, Lucknow, and Allahabad. The Home Rule League was finally inaugurated in September 1916. It was started with a view to giving concrete shape to the 1914 Congress resolution of self-government. She felt that Indian National Congress of 1916 must be more definite and work for the achievement of self-government. Mrs. Besant believed that Swaraj could be obtained if the extremists and the moderates, and Hindus and Muslims together put forward their demand. She visited Pune a number of times with the aim of bringing Gokhale and Tilak together to present a united front.[57] She was able to influence Mohammed Ali Jinnah to become one of the secretaries of the Home Rule League so that the Hindus and Muslims could come closer.

Mrs. Besant felt that it was necessary to have a promise that when the war was over, India would have her place in the Council of the Empire and that Indians would be the masters of their own motherland. She remarked: "No good smith waits for the horseshoe to get cold before he strikes."[58]

Therefore, Mrs. Besant went all out to take the opportunity offered by the War and launched a vigorous propaganda. The two Leagues, i.e., the one started by Tilak and the other inaugurated by Besant, worked together and pushed forward a strong propaganda for Home Rule in the country. Tilak's daily *Kesari* and weekly *The Maratha* and Mrs. Besant's weekly *The Commonweal* and daily *New India* advocated the cause. In the press or on the platform, Mrs. Besant criticised the foreign policy, the policy in regard to Home Charges, the method of recruitment in the army, industries, the land tax and education.

Mrs. Besant said, addressing the students in the Hardinge Theatre at Calcutta, that in other countries the students were kept under discipline and they were encouraged to read the lives of great men thereby inculcating in them a spirit of patriotism and fostering in them a love of their country. When these students went into the world they were made to understand that the future of their country depended on their individual acts which identified them with their country. In India a student had to perform household work besides studies and when he left college he was a man, spiritless and often broken in health. "If the country has to progress," she said, "it is vital that the young of the country should be taught to appreciate their national greatness."[59]

Mrs. Besant felt that the whole system required a change, i.e., change in Local Self-Government, Provincial Government and in the Central Government. To make changes of this nature India must have her freedom and observed: "Who has the right to give to her or to withhold from her the freedom? She is no pauper begging for alms, for the crumbs of freedom, that fall from the tables of Western Liberty. She is discrowned queen claiming her heritage."[60] Mrs. Besant demanded self-government for it was better to have bullock carts and freedom than "a train deluxe with subjection."[61]

Mrs. Besant held that no nation gave liberty to another nation, and a nation was fit for liberty the moment she determined to have it.[62] However, Mrs. Besant could never dream of India severing relations with England. She wanted India to be a members of the Common-wealth like any other dominion.[63]

The propaganda carried out by Mrs. Besant had far-reaching effect. Her example led the programme she had adopted to being adopted by other political bodies.

The New India of October 11, 1916, announced that there were fifty branches of the Home Rule League in principal provinces of India except the Punjab and the League membership was between two thousand and eight thousand.

In November the same year a memorandum demanding political changes of a sweeping character was presented to the Government of India by nineteen members of the Viceroy's Council.[64]

Government Check on Mrs. Besant's Activities

The Government was not going to be a spectator to Mrs. Besant's activities. Lord Pentland, Government of Madras, issued her a warning, but it was of no avail. The *New India,* her daily paper, remained an organ of active propaganda. It was through its columns that she exposed the policy of the Government and the conditions of Indians in their own land.

The Press Act, a ready instrument in the hands of the Government was at once put into use in case of Mrs. Besant. Two thousand rupees were demanded as security in May 1916, (even before she started her

Home Rule League). This gave her another opportunity to criticise the Government and she embarked upon a rigorous campaign against the Press Act which led to her security being forfeited. At the same time five thousand rupees as security was demanded, from the Vasanta Press.[65] This press was also owned by Mrs. Besant.

The *New India* was allowed to continue on enhanced security of ten thousand rupees. She filed a petition in the High Court under Section 17 of the Press Act to have the forfeiture set aside but the application was dismissed. She contested in the Madras High Court the validity of such orders. The publicity of the proceedings which she conducted in person in the High Court intensified the agitation.

It was the first time that the Press Act was put to test in Madras Province. The feelings of the people ran high and an appeal was made to organise the 'New India Defence Fund.' The fund was organised to collect the sum demanded by the Government. "Let us show the Government that the security has been demanded from the nation and it will gladly pay the heavy toll which will fit her for the Home Rule she has been striving for."[66]

The Government of Madras was alarmed at Mrs. Besant's activity. The Bombay Government also shared the fear. So the Government of Bombay issued an order forbidding her to enter the Bombay Presidency.[67]

The example of Madras and Bombay was next followed by the Central Provinces. In November 1916, the Central Provinces Provincial Conference arranged a conference. At the same time the Theosophical Society also announced a meeting which was to be presided over by Annie Besant. The meeting could not be presided over by her as the Government of Central Provinces issued an order prohibiting her entry in the Central Provinces.[68] Thus the Government gave another weapon to her with which she intensified her propaganda. She said that religion was being interfered with. She wrote in her paper, "for the first time an Act professedly passed for the military purpose has been used to infringe the religious liberties of a section of His Majesty's subjects in India thus destroying the religious mentality of the Government and preventing the free enjoyment of its liberty for a religious purpose under the protection of religious liberty guaranteed to Indian subjects under the most sacred pledge.[69]

In addition to the Home Rule League Mrs. Besant founded the

Young Men's Association and Theosophical Educational Trust. The aim of the association as stipulated by her was to bring youngsters and elders together in the service of the country.[70]

Repressive steps taken by the Government, however, did not discourage Mrs. Besant. She kept the momentum of her work and tried to revive the Swadeshi movement and initiated a Swadeshi vow.[71]

Mrs. Besant did not spare the judges of the High Court, the civilian judges in particular. Her attack was pointedly on their character and independence and not on their capacity. "We doubt," Mrs. Besant said, "if, save in Calcutta, a judge would be found strong enough to resist such pressure, illegitimate as it is. The result is the confidence of Indian public in British justice is beginning to be shaken."[72]

Warnings were issued to Mrs. Besant by Lord Pentland, Governor of Madras, again to suspend her activities but she informed him that since she felt Home Rule was necessary for the maintenance of the Empire it was therefore not possible to change or modify the tone of *New India*. Mrs. Besant was undaunted. "I would indeed be guilty of sedition," she said, "if for cowardly fear of further punishment at the hands of the Government I shrank from urging the change which alone can prevent the disruption of the Empire."[73]

Mrs. Besant stood for the presidentship of the 1916 Congress but lost against Ambika Charan Majumdar, a veteran Congressman. However, she was able to influence the Congress Committee to approve a resolution urging local Congress Committees, Home Rule League and other political associations to carry on an agitation in support of the Congress Reforms Scheme.[74]

When the Government failed to persuade Mrs. Besant in regard to the suspension of the Home Rule propaganda being carried out during the war, it used the Defence of India Act and an order of internment was issued on June 16, 1917. The order was comprehensive. It forbade Annie Besant, Arundale and Wadia to attend meetings, to deliver lectures or speeches or to publish any of their writings. It also provided for censoring their correspondence. The order was later modified and they were allowed to carry on their work in connection with the Theosophical Society, subject to pre-censorship. All the three refused to dissociate political work from their religious work.[75]

Though Mrs. Besant was actually arrested in 1917 yet the plans to arrest her or to remove her from the Indian scene were being contemplated from 1915 itself. It was the Madras Government that suggested in 1915 that Mrs. Besant should be ordered to leave India under the Defence of India Rules because, "warnings are closely wasted on Mrs. Besant and I think the time has come to put an end to her mischievous writings and public utterances, more of which are promised."[76]

She had already clarified the position of the Theosophical Society and issued instructions on July 28, 1917, edition of *New India*, that no Theosophical Lodge should pass any resolution in connection with prohibitory orders issued by the Government of Bombay nor in support of me in my political difficulty with the Government. The Theosophical Society has no politics and a large number of followers are government servants. Any such resolution Mrs. Besant said "is unconstitutional and wholly against my wishes."[77] Even during her internment, Mrs. Besant wanted the Indian flag to fly. Mrs. Besant and her companions hoisted a Home Rule League Flag, red and green on their houses. At night they showed a red and green light. This could not be tolerated and the Magistrate issued an exparte order under Section 144 Criminal Procedure Code forbidding them to fly the flag or show the lights.

Release of Annie Besant

The immediate result of this internment was that an even more intensified campaign against the Government was set in motion. Montagu, while writing about Mrs. Besant, observes: "I particularly liked that Shiva who cut his wife into 52 pieces, only to discover that he had 52 wives," and, "this is really what happened to the Government of India when it interned Mrs. Besant."[78]

Protest meetings were held all over the country. On the 16th of every succeeding month large processions were taken out in all the important towns of the Province.[79] Her internment strengthened the movement for Home Rule not only in India but also in the United States and in the Dominions of the Commonwealth.

President Wilson of America made diplomatic representation to British Government against Mrs. Besant's internment under the pressure of public opinion.[80]

Passive resistance was planned in order to secure the release of internees. Subramaniam Aiyer renounced his Knighthood as a protest against the internment of Mrs. Besant and her co-workers. The first person who left the Medical College, an official institution was Mrs.

Shiva Kamu, later a sister-in-law of George S. Arundale. The Government of India was alarmed at the state of affairs and therefore directed the local Government to point out to all the Indians "who were likely to listen to reason" that men of importance who wield influence should dissociate themselves from the Home Rule Campaign and that students and schoolboys should be prohibited from attending meetings in pursuance of this campaign. A firm policy was to be followed to discourage the Home Rule Campaign by the Government.

The Madras Government was the first to put the order of the Government of India to test. General orders were issued on May 1, 1917, directing that no undergraduate student in any college and no pupil in any school should be permitted to take part in the political discussion, to attend political meetings, to join any political association or to take part in any movement.[81]

The aspirations of Indians for self-government failed to move the British authorities "until the Government of India implored it to put war maps aside for a moment and make some definite pronouncement that should stem the rising tide of political unrest in India."[82]

As a result of this agitation for Home Rule League the British Government was forced to take some immediate action, and thus further reforms were announced on August 17, 1917, to the effect that "the policy of his Majesty's Government with which the Government of India are in complete accord, is that of the increasing association of Indians in every branch of the administration and the gradual development of self-governing institutions with a view to the progressive realisation of responsible government as an integral part of the British Empire."[83]

This announcement of the Secretary of State paved the way for Mrs. Besant's release. He asked the Government of India to release the prisoners in view of the changed policy which would be followed in regard to India. Her release, however, was not considered advisable by the Government of Madras and the Secretary of State was informed accordingly.[84]

On August 31, 1917, the Secretary of State addressed the Government of India that the case of Mrs. Besant should be considered again as a strong agitation on her behalf had been started in England and she could not indefinitely be kept in prison. Some convincing excuse must eventually be found for releasing her.[55] He further advised the

Government of India that her release could be announced on the ground that "a cessation of agitation was hoped for now that the policy of the Government had been declared."[86]

The Madras Government was still hesitant to release Mrs. Besant. It felt that the influence both of the Home Rule League and Annie Besant had not weakened and the agitation might be encouraged by amnesty. The Madras Government was, however, willing to release her only on "consideration of policy other than local."[87]

Ultimately under the pressure of the Home Department the three internees Wadia, Arundale and Annie Besant were released on September 17, 1917. Mrs Besant's release was perhaps an example that the Government would yield to an organised opposition. After her release she engaged herself to bring every class of opinion into line so that a united front may be presented to the Secretary of State who was to arrive in India in November 1917. For this purpose she made triumphant tours of Madras, Calcutta, Banares, Allahabad and Bombay. A feature of the tour was the display of the Home Rule buntings. She issued an appeal in the light of the forthcoming changes that people must organise the work more effectively.

On November 26, 1917, Tilak and Mrs. Besant represented a joint deputation of the League and the Congress which presented a memorandum to Montagu. Mrs. Besant had no rest. The tireless solider's attention was now invited to 'Vote for Women'. Mrs. Cousins[88] was the first to raise this issue and it was decided to send a deputation[89] to the Secretary of State under the leadership of Mrs. Naidu.[90] The deputation was received by Montagu on December 18, 1917, a memorable day in the history of women's franchise movement. It was this step which later gave equal rights to women in the matter of political franchise.

It was under the presidentship of Mrs. Besant that in 1917 the Congress "expressed the opinion that same tests be applied to women as to men in regard to franchise and the eligibility to all elective bodies concerned with local government and education."[91] A women's Indian Association was established with the following aims:

(i)   To make women aware of their responsibility as daughters of India.

(ii)   To help them realise that the future of India lies in their hands, for as wives and mothers they have the task of training and guiding and forming the character of the future rulers of India.

(iii) To form women's groups for the purpose of self-development and education and for the indefinite service of others.

Mrs. Besant as President of the Congress

Mrs. Besant was elected president of the 1917 Congress. All the Provincial Congress Committees except Bengal voted in favour of Mrs. Besant. This was the highest honour India could bestow on anybody at that time. She was the first woman to occupy the Congress president's chair. For Mrs. Besant, her work did not end with presiding over the Congress, but the beginning of a whole year of strenuous work. Her presidential address was a charter of national liberty. She touched almost all subjects of national importance.

Speaking about the relations between England and India she said: "Today let me, Western born, but in spirit Eastern, cradled in England but Indian by choice and adoption, let me stand as the symbol of Union between Great Britain and India, a union of hearts and free choice, not of compulsion and therefore of a tie which cannot be broken, a tie of love and mutual helpfulness beneficient to both Nations and blessed by God."[92]

She exposed the policy of the Government in regard to the training of army officers which was an unwanted financial burden and was resented by Indians. She said if her own sons had profited by her being used as a training ground for the Empire, there would have been lesser degree of resentment. "But in this case as in many others," remarked Mrs. Besant, "India has shared Imperial burden while not sharing Imperial freedom and power."[93]

Mrs. Besant outlined the help given by India to England during the war and said that India's condition of helping the Empire is her freedom. She will tax herself willingly when her taxes remain in the country and *fertilise* it when they educate her people and thus increase their productive power, when they foster her trade and create for her new Industries.[94]

Annie Besant outlined the causes of the awakening of the New India spirit:[95]

(i) The awakening of Asia.
(ii) Discussion abroad on Alien rule and imperial reconstruction.
(iii) Loss of belief in the superiority of white races.
(iv) Awakening of merchants.

(v)   The awakening of women to claim their ancient position.
(vi) The awakening of masses.

English education was conducive to the progress of India and it evoked keenness among Indian mothers. Hinduism, an integral part of education was, perhaps, observed Mrs. Besant, "the first movement in modern days which aroused among them in all parts of India a keen and living interest."[96]

The treatment meted to Indians in South Africa, more especially with regard to the sacredness of Indian marriages, indentured labour etc. was degrading. "These were perhaps the other causes,"[97] observed Mrs. Besant, "but deep in the heart of India's daughter arose, to mother's voice calling on them, to help to arise and to be once more mistress in her own house."[98]

Indian women could not be indifferent to the great movement for India's freedom. The strength of the Home Rule movement said Mrs. Besant, "is rendered tenfold greater by the adhesion to it of large numbers of women, who bring to its help the uncalculating heroism, the endurance, the self-sacrifice, of the feminine nature. Our League's best recruiters and recruits are among the women of India."[99]

The Congress session of 1917 was important, for the question of national flag was formally raised. The Home Rule League had already adopted the tricolour. This Congress appointed a Committee which never met, and the Home Rule League's flag virtually became the Congress flag, with a 'Charkha' added to it later on. In 1931, the Flag Committee substituted saffron colour for red.

Before the year 1917 was out, Mrs. Besant started the Scout Movement as a part of the fight for India's rights. The Scouts Association with its headquarters at London refused to give affiliation. Mrs. Besant regarded it as an insult and founded the Indian Boy Scouts Association in the same year.

In the following year, the Montagu-Chelmsford Report was published and the same year saw the end of the First World War. The people of India had helped the British in their trying years and had faced hardships, the natural outcome of such a crisis. It was, therefore, in the fitness of things that they expected changes which would mean substantial steps towards the building of self-government. The reforms envisaged by this report were a half way house and the extremists like Tilak and Besant denounced them. She (Besant) went to the extent of saying that "the scheme is unworthy to be offered by England or to be accepted by India."[100] However the Moderates approved the reforms and were in favour of giving them a trial. Thus there was a split in the Congress ranks once again.

A special session of the Congress was convened in August 1918, in Bombay, to modify the Montagu-Chelmsford Scheme and to find a via media whereby both the sections of the Congress (Moderates and Extremists) could be brought closer. This Congress passed a resolution[101] that a fully responsible government should be introduced in the provinces.

Notes and References

1. The Theosophical Publishing House, *The Besant Spirit*, Vol. 3, *Indian Problems*, 1939, p. 19.
2. ibid., p. 11.
3. The Congress Session held in 1907 at Surat which was presided over by Rash Behari Bose, was interrupted by disturbances amongst the delegates themselves. One section was led by B.G. Tilak. The rift between the left and right wings of the Congress came to be known as Moderates and Extremists. The Moderates remained in command of the Congress.
4. According to this pact the Indian National Congress for the first time endorsed the principle of communal electorate. It not only agreed to give the Muslims separate representation but also weightage in representation.
5. She was the first President of Women's Association, founded in 1917.
6. Cousins, J.H., Ed., *The Annie Besant Centenary Book* (Article by C.M. Reddi, "The Religion and Social Reforms").
7. Mrs. Besant's mother was Irish and her father of mixed Irish and English descent.
8. She herself acknowledged, "He with very high ideas of husband's authority and wife's submission, holding strongly to the master in my own house theory. She accustomed to freedom, indifferent to home details, impulsive, very hot-tempered and proud and a Lucifer." (West Geoffry, *The Life of Annie Besant*, p. 38).
9. Charles Bradlaugh was a sympathiser of India's cause and was a free thinker and reformer. He was also President of the National Secular Society.
10. Besant remarked, "I would urge on those who believe in women's natural inferiority, why in the name of common sense are you so terribly afraid of putting your theory to the proof?" (West Geoffry, op. cit., p. 89).

11. ibid., p. 181.
12. Madam Blavatsky was one of the founders of Theosophical Society which was founded in New York in 1875.
13. Adyar is in Madras city. It is the head-quarters of the Theosophical Society.
14. West, Geoffry, op., cit., p. 121.
15. *Home Political Confidential Proceeding* No. 247 and K.W., March 1912.
16. ibid.
17. Besant, Annie, *Wake Up India*, Quoted in West, Geoffry, op. cit., p. 217.
18. West, Geoffry, op. cit., p. 212.
19. ibid., p. 214.
20. *Home Political Confidential Proceeding* No. 247 and K.W., March 1918.
21. ibid.
22. ibid.
23. In this Despatch Lord Hardinge recommended the reunion of Bengal as a presidency and Separate Lieut. Governorship for Bihar and Orissa, a chief commissionership for Assam, transfer of Imperial Capital from Calcutta to Delhi and acknowledged supreme claims of provincial autonomy in any scheme of national reconstruction.
24. Ghadar Conspiracy—it had two centres, one in Punjab and the second one in U.S.A and Canada. The founder of the Ghadar Party was Hardyal from Punjab who came in contact with Lajpat Rai and became an ardent advocate of independence. A newspaper by the name of *Ghadar*, was established in San Francisco in November 1913. He was in Berlin during the war years and tried to bring about revolution in India. During this period a lot of people returned to India indoctrined in Ghadar ideology. They launched a widespread movement that called for a revolt during February 1915.
25. *New India*, April 4, 1917.
26. Sitaramayya, Pattabhi, *The History of the Indian National Congress*, 1946, Vol. I, p. 125.
27. West, Geoffry, *The Life of Annie Besant*, 1929, p. 220.
28. ibid.
29. *Modern Review*, January to June, 1920, Vol. 27, p. 41
30. West, Geoffry, op. cit., p. 221.
31. Aiyer, A. Rangaswamy, *Dr. Annie Besant and Her Work for Swaraj*, p. 10.
32. ibid.
33. First number of this paper was brought out on January 2, 1914.
34. *Parliamentary Debates*, Vol. XCVL, 1917, p. 1219.
35. Sitaramayya, Pattabhi, *The History of Indian National Congress*, 1946, Vol. I, 119.

36. In view of profound and avowed loyalty, the people of India have manifested in the present crisis, this Congress appeals to the Government to deepen and perpetuate it and make it an enduring and valuable asset of the Empire, by removing all invidious distinctions here and abroad between His Majesty's Indians and other subjects, by redeeming the pledge of provincial autonomy contained in the despatch of 25th August 1911, and by taking such measure as may be necessary for the recognition of India as a component part of a Federated Empire in the full and free enjoyment of the right belonging to that status. (Proceedings of Indian National Congress, December 1914, Quoted in Andrews, C.F. and Mukerjee, G., *The Rise and Growth of Congress*, p. 244).

37. Sitaramayya Pattabhi, op. cit., p. 119.

38. Marching Orders were thus: "You will have your time of trouble and danger. I need not say, have not fear, but have no anxiety: Do not let opposition become angry. Be firm but not provocative. Press steadily the preparation for the coming changes, and claim India's place in the Empire. Do not let it be stained by excess. Remember that you represent in the Outer World the Regent who is my Agent. My hand will be over you and my peace with you." (*Theosophist*, November 1929, Vol. I, p. 151)

39. *Home Political Confidential Proceeding* No. 652/657, September 1916.

40. ibid., No. 652/657, September, 1915.

41. Besant, Annie, *Builder of India*, pp. 75-84.

42. It was in her speeches at Nagpur in 1915 that she explained as to what she meant by Self-Government: "that the country shall have a Government by the Councils, elected by all the people, with the power of the purse and the Government its responsible to the House. There should be elected element in the Imperial Council, the holders of portfolios should be responsible to the elected House. The Provincial Parliament shall also be elected with ministry responsible to the Parliament and that the Governor would act as the King acts in England. In the District Councils and Taluqas and in Municipalities and in Village Panchayats—the one need is elected element who shall be responsible to the electorate which places them where they are." (*Home Political Confidential Proceeding* No 652-656, September, 1915).

43. Cousins, J.H., op. cit., Article by S.N. Sharma.

44. The idea of having Home Rule League for India first occurred to Shyamji Krishna Verma long before Mrs. Besant brought home to the people of this land. However, the systematic and determined application of the term Home *Role* League we owe to Mrs. Besant.

45. Besant, Annie, *The Future of Indian Politics*, p. 91.

46. Zacharia, *Renascent India*, p. 165.
47. Besant, Annie, *India Bonded or Free*, p. 163.
48. *Home Political Proceeding* No. 652-656, September 1916.
49. Theosophical Publishing House, *Besant Spirit*, Vol. IV, p. 79.
50. *Home Political Proceeding* No. 166-168, November 1915.
51. *Home Political Confidential Proceeding* No. 652-656, September 1916.
52. ibid.
53. *Home Political B Confidential Proceeding*, No. 653-665, September 1916.
54. ibid., No. 652-656, September 1916, Extract No. 146.
55. *Home Political Proceeding* No. 166-168, Extract No. 28, November 1915.
56. Besant, Annie, *The Future of Indian Politics*, p. 144.
57. Annie Besant herself relates in her book, *The Future of Indian Politics*, how she brought about reconciliation between the Extremists and the Moderates. While staying in Poona in the autumn of 1914, she was asked by Gokhale "to go to Mr. Tilak, his old enemy, and see if a via media could be found for joining into one body all who desired India's freedom, so that the great split made at Surat might be healed." Ultimately at the Bombay Session in 1915 the Congress Constitution was so altered as to open the door for the entry of the Secessionists.
58. *Home Political Proceeding* No. 166-168, Extract No. 28, November 1915, (Mrs. Besant's address of 14 September 1915).
59. ibid., Extract No. 26, November 1915; Home Political Proceeding, No. 454-457 and K.W., February 1916.
60. ibid., November 1915.
61. Besant, Annie, *India Bonded or Free*, Great Britain, 1926, p. 4.
62. *Home Political Proceeding* No. 166-168, November 1915.
63. ibid.
64. ibid., No. 247 and K.W., March 1918.
65. ibid., No. 53 September 1916.
66. *Home Political Proceeding* No. 652-656, September 1916.
67. "...whereas in the opinion of the Governor in Council there are reasonable grounds for believing that Mrs. Besant has acted and is about to act in a manner prejudicial to the public safety.
"Now therefore the Governor in Council...is pleased to direct that the said Mrs. Besant shall not enter and shall not reside or remain in the Province of Bombay pending further orders of the Government. And, the said Mrs. Besant is hereby informed that if she knowingly disobeys this order she will be liable to imprisonment of either description for a term which may extend to three years and will also be liable to fine." (*Home Political Proceeding* No. 652-658., Serial No. 8154, September 1916).

68. *Home Political Confidential Proceeding* No. 347 and K.W., March 1918.

69. ibid.

70. *Home Political Confidential Proceeding* No. 347, and K.W., March 1916.

71. "Whereas the Press Act and the Defence of India Act are being used to cripple the liberty of the Indian Press and to deprive persons of their liberty against whom no evidence exists of disloyalty or intent to resort to violence," and

"Whereas it is necessary to draw the attention of the British public to the serious discontent arising from the widespread and illegitimate use of these measures, the power of the Supreme Government of India to enact", and

"Whereas the supreme and local governments are utterly indifferent to Indian opinion as proclaimed in hundreds to meetings and articles in Indian papers, it is therefore, necessary to take such peaceful but effective action as is open to us."

It is hereby resolved that "invoking the blessing of Almighty God and making an appeal to His Justice for the purpose of winning ourselves and for unborn generations, of the elementary rights of freedom of persons and security of property until deprived of them by judicial sentence after open trial, we make the solemn vow to purchase home-made goods in preference to foreign ones even at a sacrifice. And may Almighty God give us strength of will to carry out this our solemn vow until these rights are restored to the Indian Nation." (*Home Political Confidential Proceeding* No. 247 and K.W., March 1918).

72. *Home Political Confidential Memo*, on articles in *New India*, No. 247 and K.W., March 1916; *Home Political Confidential Proceeding* No. 166-168, November 1915.

73. *Home Political Proceeding* No. 652-655, Extract No. 102, September 1916.

74. This scheme demanded Self-Government within the British Empire. The British Government was to have control of military matters and foreign affairs. Indian members of the Government were expected to have a fairly complete control over legislation as far as the Central Government was concerned and full control in the provinces. The theory of special electorate was endorsed...

75. *Home Political Confidential Proceeding* No. 247, March 1918.

76. *Home Political A Confidential Proceeding* No. 166-168, November 1915.

77. *Home Political Confidential Proceeding* No. 247, K.W., March 1916.

78. Montagu, Edwin. S., *An Indian Diary*, 1930, p. 157.

79. Theosophical Publishing House, *Dr. Annie Besant and Her Work for Swaraj*, p. 16.

80. ibid., p. 26.
81. *Home Political Confidential Proceeding* No. 129-135.
82. Valentine, Chirol, *India*, 1926, London, p. 163.
83. Dodwell, H.H. (Ed.), *The Cambridge History of India*, Vol. VI, p. 589
84. *Home Political A Confidential Proceeding* No. 129-135, January 1918.
85. ibid.
86. ibid.
87. ibid.
88. Her account appears in the following chapter.
89. The deputation consisted of Mrs. Sarojini Naidu, Mrs. Besant, Lady Sadasiva Iyer, Mrs. Cousins, Mrs. Srirangamma, Mrs. Lazarus, Mrs. Chandrasekara Aiyar, Mrs. Dalvi, Mrs. Herabai Tata, Begum Hasrat Mohani, Mrs. Guruswami Chetty.
90. Her account appears in the following chapter.
91. Sitaramayya, Dr. P., *The History of the Indian National Congress*, Vol. I, p. 52.
92. Theosophical Publishing House, *The Besant Spirit*, being the Presidential Address to Indian National Congress, 1917, Vol. 4, p. 31.
93. ibid.
94. The Theosophical Publishing House, *The Besant Spirit*, Vol. 4, p. 31
95. ibid., p. 46.
96. Besant, Annie, *India Bonded or Free*, p. 205.
97. Theosophical Publishing House, *Besant Spirit*, Vol. 4, p. 74.
98. Besant, Annie, *India Bonded or Free*, p. 205
99. ibid.
100. Banerjee, Surendranath, op., cit., p. 305.
101. Some of the other resolutions passed by this Congress demanded declaration of rights of the people and abolition of corporal punishment.

7

THE CIVIL DISOBEDIENCE MOVEMENT: 1919-1929

To call woman the weaker sex is a libel; it is men's injustice to women. If by strength is meant moral power, then woman is immeasurably man's superior. Has she not greater intuition, is she not more self-sacrificing, has she not greater powers of endurance, has she not greater courage? Without her man could not be. If non-violence is the law of our being, the future is with woman. I have nursed this thought now for years.

—*Mahatma Gandhi[1]*

Political Conditions of the Period

In the preceding chapter, a reference has already been made to Gandhiji's emergence on the political scene of India in 1918. After closely watching the political situation and events in the country for nearly three years, he equipped the freedom fighters with a new weapon of passive resistance which came to be popularly known as Satyagraha (passive resistance movement), a technique he had earlier experimented in South Africa.

The years following the First World War are most outstanding in the annals of the freedom struggle for, during this period an organised and country-wide attempt to overthrow the foreign rule was begun by boycotting the Government on essential things and by launching Satyagraha. It was probably due to this technique that the freedom movement which was more or less a monopoly of the intellectuals found a fertile field amongst the masses of the country and invited interest of the rich and the poor, the old and the young, the educated and the uneducated, industrialists and labourers, merchants and customers, lawyers and doctors, teachers and social workers, and above all, of the women who now came forward to join the Satyagraha Army.

Lately, women had been taking increasing interest in socio-political affairs; fillip to this was given by the partition of Bengal, the treatment of Indians in South Africa, the Home Rule League of Annie Besant, the First World War and by the Women's India Association which came in existence in 1917. This organisation became the pivot around which women gathered to discuss and demand their rights. A decade later an all-India organisation, the All India Women's Conference, was founded and its political goal was self-government. The members emphasised the need for responsible government which could satisfy the aspirations of the people.

The question of suffrage for women brought them to a common platform. The silence maintained by the Montagu-Chelmsford Scheme on this subject, in spite of the representation made to the Secretary of State, accentuated the common feelings. Later the Southborough Committee was appointed to collect information and elicit opinion of the people of India on the projected reforms and on the question of franchise. This committee toured India. When it visited Bombay a requisition signed by eight hundred women of the Presidency was submitted to it.[2] In addition similar requisitions were sent by the Women Graduates Union Bombay, all the Branches of the Women's India Association which numbered about forty, the women's branch of the Home Rule League, the Bharat Stree Mandal and by the members of the All India Women's Deputation which had earlier met the Secretary of State on this subject.

Indian ladies also appeared personally as witnesses before the Southborough Committee to express their viewpoint. The South-borough Committee disfavoured the extending of franchise to women on the ground that the prevailing social conditions in the country did not warrant franchise for women. Margaret Cousins, on behalf of the Association, reiterated: "Is this handful of men better able to judge these conditions than were the thousands of Indian delegates to the Bombay and Delhi Congresses?[3] They urged the removal of disqualifications in all the terms of reforms."[4] Resolutions were passed in different parts of the country protesting against this decision.[5]

Mrs. Besant and Mrs. Naidu, who were in England as members of the deputation to give evidence before the Joint Parliamentary Committee, took up the case for women's franchise. Mrs. Hirabai Tata[6] and Mrs. Mithi Bai Tata[7] were sent to England by the Women's Committee to express strong feelings of Indian women on this issue. The Joint Select Committee, however, left the responsibility of deciding the question of franchise for women to be settled by the future Legislative Councils of India for each province.

Madras was the first province to remove the disqualification of sex for the legislative franchise on April 1, 1921 and other provinces followed in its wake.[8] Thus the women of India had begun to understand their rights and responsibilities. They were conscious of the help given to the British for successful completion of the war. Some of them had helped in collecting war funds while others in sewing clothes and doing other odd jobs. Many had suffered the loss of their brothers, fathers or husbands as soldiers who fought for the Allies.

India had helped the British Government with men, money and materials throughout the war. It was, therefore, natural that they should look for reward in the way of political progress of the country. But a vehement demand on the part of the leaders of the people fell on deaf ears for it led to the enactment of the Rowlatt Bills which aimed at curbing the existing modicum of liberties. Following the armistice it was hoped that there would be some relief but the condition remained unchanged. For instance, the transport facilities were disorganised, the cost of living was still high in 1919 "and the few cotton rungs which the poorest ryot wears became almost unpurchasable."[9]

Immediately after the publication of the proposed Rowlatt Bill in January 1919, a meeting was convened by the Indian National Congress in the Gandhi Ashram (Ahmedabad), wherein a resolution[10] was passed to disobey this Act, if passed.

One of the Bills was, however, passed in the teeth of opposition and it gave the Government powers in an emergency to judge cases without trial. The passing of the Bill came as a shock to the nation as a whole. Gandhiji, therefore, announced his intention of launching a Satyagraha movement on 30 March 1919. This date was later changed to 6 April, but unfortunately the news of this change did not reach in time to many places with the result that 30 March was observed as a day of *hartal* and inauguration of the disobedience movement. In the beginning the movement was non-violent, but slowly it became violent due to provocation by the police, and also, perhaps, because people were not trained enough to take part in such a mass movement non-violently. The events moved fast and the situation in the Punjab, as compared to other provinces, was serious. There was a considerable amount of fermentation in the districts of Lahore, Gurdaspur and Amritsar. People came out in mobs and the rowdy elements damaged the railway carriages, telegraph wires and the government buildings, the post offices and a few places were set on fire as well. The Government retaliated sternly. Martial Law was proclaimed; the Punjab witnessed a reign of terror which dragged on till 11 June 1919.[11]

This movement culminated in the firing which took place in Jallianwala Bagh at Amritsar. It was in this city that a peaceful assembly of twenty thousand people was fired upon on 13 April 1919, under the orders of General Dyer. According to the Hunter Enquiry Committee Report, four hundred people were shot dead and twelve hundred injured. Over and above this, people were humiliated in a variety of ways. The women had to suffer as well and there were instances of outraging of the modesty of women. In some villages women were called out from their houses and harassed. The faces of the women were forcibly uncovered and foul languages was used against them.[12] The whole country demanded redress of the Punjab atrocities and the All India Congress Committee endorsed these demands and asked for an impartial enquiry. Ultimately, forced by the circumstances the Government appointed an Enquiry Committee with Sir Hunter as Chairman. The Indian National Congress also appointed another committee for the same purpose.

The next year saw the Report of the Hunter Enquiry Committee. The recommendations and findings of this Committee were far from satisfactory. The Government's decision was "that Dyer's" action was dictated by a stern though misconceived sense of duty.[13] Following the government decision, Dyer was censured and was deprived of his command. The action was approved by the House of Commons but there was a furore in the House of Lords over the punishment inflicted on Dyer. Not only this, he was even hailed as a hero by certain sections of the people and a campaign in his favour was launched which included the sponsoring of a fund for him. He was also presented with twenty-three thousand pounds and a sword by the English ladies in India.[14]

This action fanned the fire of nationalism in India. Added to this was the unsettled state of Turkey, the 'Khilafat'[15] movement which greatly excited the feelings of the Muslims of India.

Turkey was considered the greatest Muslim power by the Muslims of this country. The Sultan of this Empire was 'Khalifa' of Islam and as such temporal head. During the war period Muslims were given assurance by the Prime Minister of England that the Turkish Empire would be preserved. A deputation of the Muslim Khilafat Conference also went to England to put forward their viewpoint as regards Turkey and the Khilafat. The Government did not pay any heed to these requests and the draft treaty called the Treaty of Severes published on May 14, 1920,[16] set aside all the promises made during the war and this disquietened the Muslims further.

Gandhiji felt that this was an opportunity to bring the two communities together. He, therefore, warned the Government that if justice was not done to the Muslims he would resume Satyagraha.[17] A special session of the Congress held in September 1920 in a resolution approved the resumption of policy of "progressive non-violence, non-cooperation until the said wrongs were righted and Swarajya established."[18] To achieve this end a nation-wide programme of boycotting titles and honours, elections and legislatures, schools and colleges, courts and tribunals was launched. The people were advised not to offer themselves for military service. The Government 'durbars', official and semi-official functions were boycotted. The sale and use of liquor and foreign cloth was prevented through peaceful picketing.

Mahatma Gandhi had faith in women. Writing in 1921 he said: "I expect great things from you, I expect the women to do their full share in the struggle. Let government capture everyone of our soldiers—I don't mind. Our work is so very easy that even our women can carry it out and without difficulty."[19] The Satyagraha movement which was inaugurated by Gandhiji was such that women could not sit and watch the battle between the Government and the people and so a quick response was made to the call of Mahatma Gandhi. They (women) took out processions, propagated the use of Khadi, and even courted jail. Though the number of women arrested was very small, yet a beginning was made and an example set that, if need be, women would not hesitate to face the most difficult situations.

Bengal had been in the vanguard of the freedom movement and women of this province did not lose any time and came out in the field.

They organised "Mahila Karma Samaj" or the Ladies Organisation Board of the Bengal Provincial Congress Committee,[20] to carry out propaganda and constructive work amongst the women of Bengal. The organisation had its own office and arrangements for the stay of the whole time workers also. Branches of this organisation were spread all over Calcutta. A group of twenty-five or thirty women workers were given a number of houses to carry out their work. The women members of the organisation addressed meetings as well. It was in one such meeting organised by Smt. Inder Prabha Majumdar and Smt. Radu Bibi that in response to the appeal made by these ladies many women present gave up their ornaments, broke their foreign 'churies' (bangles) and vowed that they would not wear these again.[21] Women volunteers were also enlisted at the meetings. In a single meeting at Guwahati (Assam) sixty women volunteers were enlisted. They (women) went about on foot carrying the message to the people to stop selling or wearing foreign cloth.[22]

Smt. Basanti Devi and Urmila Devi, wife and sister, of Desbandhu Das, were the leaders of the women's movement in Bengal. They went about the streets of Calcutta selling Khaddar and propagating against the use of foreign cloth and the habit of drinking. They were arrested while selling handloom cloth.[23] The others who were arrested with them were: Smt. Anukul Mitter, Smt. Surya Shome, Smt. Umashi Devi, Smt. Satya Devi, a few boys and eight Sikh ladies. They were, however, released in the evening.[24] But their arrest stirred the people of Bengal and further strengthened the movement. Later when Smt. Urmila Devi was interviewed in Ahmedabad and was asked why they had courted arrest, she replied, "We felt that although Bengal was sympathetic it was only a sort of passive sympathy. To make it most dynamic we thought Bengal must be appealed to in a special manner of involving, of course, a special measure of sacrifice and so, our arrest produced the desired effect."[25] Urmila Devi urged the women to join the ranks of volunteers. She said that women would be called upon to undertake responsibilities while men were being put behind bars.

Mrs. Basanti Devi also presided over the Bengal Provincial Congress Session in 1922 at Chittagong. She said, "Freedom will come as a matter of course to the extent we are able to do penance by our sacrifice, by our sorrows and sufferings, by our patience and by the strength of our character."[26]

In Bombay women also held protest meetings against His Royal Highnes, the Prince of Wales' visit and the municipal address which was to be presented to him on behalf of the citizens of Bombay. After the meeting, they went in a procession to a temple and offered prayers for the attainment of Swaraj.

Kasturba Gandhi, who had her first lesson in Satyagraha in South Africa, took her place here as well. She presided over meetings and also toured the various States propagating for the success of the movement. Presiding over the Gujarat Provincial Conference she condemned untouchability and preached Swadeshi. She appealed to the women to take to spinning and weaving of Khadi. "If we want to earn Swaraj," she said, "we shall have to fill the bowl of Goddess of Freedom."[27] When it was reported to her that her son Devdas Gandhi had been arrested, she took the news saying: "Only two sons of mine have gone to jail, but twenty thousand sons of mother Hind are in jail; how can I bemoan my lot! Young sons of mother Hind, prosecute the work of Khaddar with such zeal that you may either regain your brothers or join them in jail."[28]

In the Punjab the first ladies' meetings was held on the 6th and 7th of December 1922, which was presided over by Kasturba Gandhi. Radha Devi, wife of Lala Lajpat Rai, was the Chairman of the Reception Committee. In her address (this was read on her behalf by Smt. Parvati Devi) she declared that the object of the conference was to strike a note of warning to the idlers while the leaders were undergoing imprisonment.[29] She exhorted her country women to support the Swaraj movement with zeal and courage, characteristic of Punjabi ladies.

Parvati Devi

Parvati Devi,[30] an ardent worker of the Congress, was arrested in Meerut for the so-called inflaming speeches. She was taken to Agra Jail in jail-clothes. No one was allowed to be on the platform. As a mark of respect ladies took out a procession on December 16, 1922.[31] She was convicted and was sentenced to two years imprisonment. This was the highest sentence so far awarded to any lady.

Bai Amman (Abadi Bano Begum)

Bai Amman was one of the important personages at this time. She belonged to an aristocratic family of Muslims but threw off her veil when her sons[32] were deprived of their liberty. She went about addressing meetings all over India. She was invited to join the deputation for women's franchise. But she refused on the ground that she would rather influence her own countrymen than go to an Englishman with a petition.

Addressing a meeting at Lahore she said the Indians have committed two follies during the last 150 years; it was they who sided with the British which brought about the capture of their own King and secondly, they helped the English during the outbreak of 1857. If Indians had not done so there was no possibility of these "merchants" getting supremacy in India and shakling Indians in the fetters of serfdom. "Would they," she continued, "commit another folly and put their aged mother to shame?" "Be man," she added, "and carry out the determination you have formed."[33]

In an open letter Bai Amman thanked the people for their kind feelings towards her and her sons. She hoped that the Muslim women would rise to the occasion and help the national cause by putting every pice, and handful of grain that could be spared as duty to the motherland. She wrote, "We had been sacrificing ourselves for our fathers and husbands and sons, but so long as this spirit of Indian womanhood is not lost, I, for one, feel that nothing really matters is lost."[34]

Bai Amman advised the establishment of Panchayats throughout India. She ardently, advocated the use of Khaddar and the Hindu-Muslim unity.[35] Her services to the cause of the Khilafat, Swaraj and Hindu Muslim Unity, were invaluable. In this connection she visited Rawalpindi, Gujranwala and Kasur.[36] In a meeting at Simla in September 1922, she made a special appeal to women to take up Khaddar. She was keen to visit the Frontier Province, but orders were issued banning her entry into that region.[37]

In another meeting in the Punjab, Bai Amman said that some people left houses or ornaments to their children after their death, but she was of the opinion that there was nothing as good as freedom and asked women to leave Swaraj after their death for the children. Swaraj, she said, could not be had by asking, but was sure to come if people had courage and women a heart to make sacrifices for the cause.[38]

Bai Amman addressed another ladies' conference at Bombay which six thousand people attended. A resolution urging the women to enrol as members was passed at the gathering. At another meeting at Ahmedabad, she appealed to the people to unite, for, "without cooperation among the different communities we can't liberate our country or live peaceful and honourable lives."[39]

In February 1922, she went to Patna and Bhagalpur. At Bhagalpur she was not allowed to see the political prisoners and as a protest the prisoners and their relatives refused to see each other.[40] She collected sixty thousand rupees from Darbhanga (Bihar) for Khilafat Committee and she was presented with a purse of twenty thousand rupees at Mongyr[41] (Bihar).

The question of prosecuting Bai Amman for objectionable speeches also came up before the government. But her arrest was not considered advisable.[42]

Mahatma Gandhi sent a special message to Bai Amman on the eve of his arrest in March 1922. He said: "Tell Bai Amman to pray for me and for all of us and to carry on the work which we have left behind. Her prayers and work will be quite sufficient to ensure our quick release and success."[43]

Bai Amman continued the political work so dear to her till her death in 1924. Mahatma Gandhi paid a touching tribute to her. He said: "She realised that the freedom of India was impossible without Hindu-Muslim unity and Khaddar. She, therefore, ardently preached unity which had become an article of faith with her. She had discarded all her foreign or mill made clothing and taken to Khaddar..."[44]

Women in almost all the provinces were doing their best to encourage men to participate in the struggle and were helping to carry on the propaganda. Mrs. Motilal Nehru, when she heard of the conviction of her only son, Jawaharlal, said: "I am happy Jawaharlal has the courage and bravery to stand for his conviction for the cause of liberty and truth...." She appealed to her sisters to consider the touch of foreign cloth as polluting. "This cloth has blood of our brothers and sisters, how can we wear it?"[45] She said that the work for which Jawaharlal had gone to jail could not be stopped. If the men of India have lost courage she said, "we women will do it. Are the jails of mother India meant only for men?"[45]

Lucknow also was a centre of activity at this time. Meetings under Section 144 were prohibited but such weapons of the Government did not worry the people. They had their meetings in the Congress Committee's Office which were presided over by Mrs. Abdul Qadir. Women were urged to take to wearing Khaddar and to exhort men to join the national movement. A committee was formed, with Mrs. Abdul Qadir as president, to carry on the work among the women.[47]

Sindh was not to lag behind. Women of this province took out processions and moved through the main bazars and streets singing national songs and delivering inspiring lectures.[48]

The non-cooperation movement daily gained ground. The author of the Simon Commission observed that "Defiance of authority became widespread, an extraordinary development in Indian districts, where the power of Government had never been questioned within living memory."[49]

The Government on its part met this challenge by arresting people, by lathi charging on processions and by declaring the organisation as unlawful. When the Congress met in 1921 some thirty thousand Congress workers were in jail.[50]

The movement at this time was also becoming violent. There were riots in Bombay which resulted in fifty deaths and three hundred and seventy-nine wounded. The same year there was a Moplah outbreak[51] which was quietened with the timely action of the national leaders.

These riots were followed by a tragic action in Chauri Chaura in Gorakhpur district, United Provinces, where twenty-one police constables were murdered with revolting cruelty by a mob acting under the excitement of the anti-Government movement.

Gandhiji could not bear the movement changing its creed of non-violence and as a result suspended the movement. He was arrested and sentenced to six years' imprisonment.

Apparently the movement had failed; but it had awakened the interest of the masses and also imparted the first lesson in Satyagraha to the nation. Gandhiji gave a new foundation to the new movement. Emerson observes: "Gandhi has, I believe, done his work. He has made India self-conscious. He has given India a new sense of self-respect. His programme has been characterised by many negative features.... It has never put forward even a suggestive outline of the Government, it would substitute for the one, it would tear down.... But Gandhi has given a moral basis and a spiritual standing to India's revolution."[52]

Annie Besant

Mrs. Besant did not however view this policy of Gandhiji with favour from the beginning and felt that a reign of chaos would follow if his plans were given a concrete shape. She spoke vehemently against it. Speaking at a meeting of the National Liberal Federation held on 30 December 1920, she characterised non-cooperation as revolt.[53] Besant was so upset over the non-cooperation movement that she refused to pay her annual subscription to the Congress.[54]

By taking this stand against Gandhiji's line of action Mrs. Besant became unpopular.[55] Even her own Home Rule League members refused to elect her as president with the result she founded the National Home Rule League in April 1919. Later, as its representative, she gave evidence before the Enquiry Committee presided over by Lord Selborne and constituted by the Parliament.

While in England Mrs. Besant and other members of the deputation, i.e., B.P. Wadia, P.K. Talang, Jamna Das and Dwarka Das tried their best to educate the public opinion in favour of Indian reforms with Home Rule for India as the goal and an Indian Parliamentary Committee was formed in England with Mrs. Besant as chairman, and a council in which several members of Parliament were members through whom the League sent out literature and information relating to India. It had one hundred and eighty-eight members with nearly three hundred Labour Associations and Trade Unions affiliated to it.[56] She represented India with great "vigour and ability and demanded at least a partial liberation at the Centre."[57]

Mrs. Besant did not favour the setting up of a Council of State for the conservative elements were already in the country and to strengthen them by creating a second chamber would hamper the progress.[58] Besant was of the opinion that dyarchy as envisaged by the Act of 1919 should not be for more than five years.[59]

In India Annie Besant directed her energies to popularise the Reform Act of 1919. She issued pamphlets in different languages and exhorted the people to work for the success of these reforms.

After the 1919 Amritsar Congress Annie Besant made strenuous tours and was able to establish twenty-five branches of the National Home Rule League in Madras, forty-five in Andhra, nine in Malabar, thirteen in Bombay and two in Sindh. A few branches were also founded in Bengal, Bihar, U.P. and Delhi.

Immediately after the elections were over, in accordance with the Reform Scheme (Government of India Act, 1919), Besant set about her task of calling a national Convention with a view to frame a constitution best suited to the people of the country to be ratified by Parliament later.

Formation of a National Convention

The National Convention was formally inaugurated in 1922 and was supported by the liberals and the National Home Rule League. Besant who was instrumental in bringing about such an organisation was deputed to visit Simla to lay the scheme before the two Houses of Parliament which were in session then. An Executive Committee, from amongst the members of both the houses representing the various provinces, was formed. A conference was convened in Delhi in 1923 reasserting itself. Besant carried a vigorous agitation for the recognition of this body and also started a private company in England for the foundation of a weekly newspaper called *United India*. This was sent to the selected list of Peers of the House of Lords and also to the Indian newspapers.

A deputation on behalf of the National Convention also was sent to England under the leadership of Besant on 26 April 1924, for the furtherance of the cause of self-government for this country. Besant divided the activities of the deputation in England into three kinds: lectures and usual discussions, large demonstrations in Queen's Hall, London, and Free Trade Hall, Manchester, to influence public opinion in England and a special meeting with the Indian Parliamentary Committee through which the members of the House of Commons were to be addressed, and interviews with the members of the government. The deputation presented a memorandum signed by Dr. Besant and others, making a united demand for Dominion Home Rule for India.

The National Conference met in Delhi in the early part of 1924 immediately after the general elections at the end of 1923. Mrs. Besant was elected the General Secretary. Dr. H.S. Gour who proposed her name for this office said: "I am sure that when the work of the convention is fulfilled and achieved, she will live in our hearts as a lady who has done far more for the emancipation of the people of this country than any political thinker or statesman of our race and blood, who has striven and worked for the achievement of the Self-Government for India."[60]

The convention divided itself into seven committees to deal with different sections of the constitution to be prepared for the country. A draft was based on these reports and the convention sat in Bombay in December of the same year and considered and amended it. It printed the results and circulated them to political parties, inviting further amendments. Later the draft was submitted to a sub-committee appointed by a Committee of All Parties which was presided over by Mahatma Gandhi. Its sub-committee made a number of amendments and these with all the others were submitted to a Drafting Committee in Madras consisting of the Hon'ble C.P. Ramaswamy Aiyer, Mr. Shiva Rao, Sir Ram Yadunandan Prasad and Dr. Annie Besant with powers to correct any oversight in language where necessary and to see the Bill through the press and publish it in the name of the Convention.[61]

The Bill[62] was taken to England in July 1925, and was introduced in the House of Commons as a private member's measure in December 1925, and again in 1927. It received the active support of the Labour Party. For more than three years it stood as the first and only constitution for India drawn by responsible representatives in a National Convention and that it was in itself a sufficient answer to those who asserted that Indians lack national unity and that its leaders could produce no outline of an agreed constitution.

Even though Besant could not reconcile herself to the Non-Cooperation Movement of Gandhiji, yet she expressed her opinion at the All India Congress Committee meeting in May 1926, that she was ready to work with the Congress for Swaraj. She felt that the third party, i.e., the English, had taken advantage of these differences and factions. It was therefore in the interest of the country that all must unite. She again appealed in May 1927, in a cable sent from London to the Indian press: "Let us forget the recent past and unite for the coming future. If the Bill, now in the House of Commons, does not please you, make another and if that other gives you equal freedom with the Bill of 1925, I will be the first to tear up the old one and welcome the new."[63]

The Bill known as the Commonwealth of India Bill, however, was passed in its first reading. It could not become an Act as the Government of England was later approached by some leaders who were in disagreement with this Bill.

Mrs. Besant also disfavoured the setting up of the Simon Commission[64] with only Englishmen as its members.

While supporting the boycott resolution at the Indian National Congress on 26th December 1927 she said: "We want men who know India's needs and Indians' wrongs, men who can understand Indian problems. You have boycotted us, we boycott you. You have said no

Indian shall sit on the Commission, we say let no Englishman judge
India's fitness."

Throughout the next year Besant appealed for unity and appealed to
the nation for a single bill to be sent to Parliament as India's demand.
She attended the first meeting of the All Parties Conference (1928)
where she initiated discussion which led to the appointment in May
1928, following a motion by Mrs. Besant, of the Nehru Committee.

During this period the Government kept on intercepting her letters.
So, she challenged the Government to prosecute her if they had
evidence against her.[65]

In the same year (1928) while supporting the resolution on
Dominion Status in the All Parties Conference, Besant urged the
formation of a parallel government on Sein Fein[66] methods. She said:
"Make many Bardolis all over the country and I tell you that the English
people are very practical people and before many Bardolis are
established they will come to you for settlement. This is the kind of
agitation they understand."[67]

Besant was seventy-two years old at this time but perhaps not tired
as yet. She started her campaign in favour of the Nehru report and
visited Lucknow, Banaras, Bombay, Poona and many other cities. In
December the National Congress endorsed the report but she was up
against Gandhiji once again when he moved a resolution saying that if
the British Government failed to accept the report in its entirety by the
end of 1929, (the constitution drafted by the Nehru Committee), the
Congress would again organise Non-Cooperation.[68]

Mrs. Besant's health was becoming worse. Ceaseless public work
done by her for six decades effected the health of this tireless soldier. By
1933 she was no more, but her work in different fields lives in the hearts
of the people even today.

It was Mrs. Besant's work and efforts which led gradually to the
attainment of Swaraj. It is possible that the Commonwealth of India Bill
1925, if agreed upon by all the political leaders, would have brought
freedom to the country much earlier, and may be, without partition of
the country.

It was also Annie Besant's agitation and aspirations which led to
the non-cooperation movement of Mahatma Gandhi. It was at her
instance that the title of Knighthood[69] (mention of this has been made in

chapter VI) was denounced, and a beginning in dissociating from governmental educational institutions was made.[70] The National Education Trust was also founded by Annie Besant. Sri Prakasa rightly observed: "When we think of it, it might almost be said that Mahatma Gandhi who had been the undisputed leader of the Indian National Congress and as such of a major portion of political India since 1920 only intensified the programme that had been chalked out by Annie Besant in the days when she led the extreme wing of Indian Politics."[71]

Mrs. Besant had taken up subjects like untouchables, education on Indian lines and suited to the people of this land, Swadeshi from an economic point of view, women's participation in the struggle, and Hindu-Muslim unity; and these were the subjects on which Mahatma Gandhi laid stress later.

It must be admitted here that Mrs. Besant was a great person, who did many great things for this land and inspired the men and women of this country to realise their freedom.

Women Legislators

The years were of great significance because it was for the first time that women exercised their vote in the elections of 1926. The franchise granted to women was very restricted.[72]

During these elections 22 per cent women voted in Madras, 12 per cent in Bombay and in Punjab, 9.6 per cent in Bengal and 4.5 per cent in the U.P. The first woman to stand for elections was Kamala Devi Chattopadhyaya.[73] She polled 4,461 votes while her opponent polled 4,979, thus, losing her seat by a narrow margin.

Amongst the Indian States, Travancore was the first to give representation to women. Dr. Poonan Ducose was the first woman health minister in India in 1925. Smt. Madhavi Ammal was nominated to the Cochin Legislative Council.

In British India Madras led again by nominating Muthulakshmi Reddi to the Legislative Council. She was subsequently elected as Deputy President of the Madras Legislative Council. Muthulakshmi Reddi[74] was the first woman medical graduate of the Madras University. She associated herself with Women's India Association from its very inception, i.e., from 1917, and was one of the members of the deputation which met the Secretary of State in connection with the women's franchise.

Once Mrs. Reddi was in the Council, who was a staunch advocate of women's welfare, she saw to the enactment of the abolition of the Devdasi system; and for laws to close brothels and protect minor girls. She brought amendments to the Children's Act and worked for the creation of Health-Schools and Children's Wards. Reddi was also an active campaigner for the Sharda Act which was passed by the Central Legislature.

Reddi also became the first Alderwoman of the City Corporation, Madras, for two years during which she took interest in problems like the child education and child welfare and beggary.

In 1928, Muthulakshmi Reddi was in England as a member of the Hartog Committee appointed by the Secretary of State to study women's educational growth and problems in India. On her way back to India she represented the country at the Paris Congress of the Women's International Alliance as a delegate from India.

Absorbed as she was in the work for the uplift and education of women, the eradication of social ills and the reconstruction of Indian society on an equal and democratic basis—Mrs. Reddi could not fail to be drawn towards political activity. It was obvious that the emasculation of the nation and the economic exploitation to which it was being subjected were insuperable barriers in the way of efforts for a better society.

Mahatma Gandhi inaugurated another Civil Disobedience movement commonly known as the Salt-Satyagraha in 1930[75] resulting in his arrest. Mrs. Reddi resigned from her membership[76] of the Legislative Council in 1930 as a protest against the arrest of Gandhiji and devoted herself to the constructive programme launched by the Indian National Congress. The All Asian Women's Conference took place in Lahore in which Mrs. Reddi took a prominent part.

Mrs. Reddi visited America and attended the International Women's Council in Chicago in 1933. The same year she went to England to give evidence before the joint select committee in connection with women's franchise.

Mrs. Reddi was instrumental in bringing about the establishment of the Cancer Hospital in Madras. She was the first organiser and Chairman of the Madras State Social Welfare Advisory Board, a place she occupied till recently (1954-1957). Muthulakshmi Reddi was awarded Padma Bhushan in 1956 for her work. She continued to take active interest in various organisations.

It will not be out of place to make a reference to certain provincial movements for, these movements attracted country-wide attention.

Bardoli Satyagraha-1928

A no-tax campaign was launched in Bardoli[77] under the leadership of Sardar Patel. This campaign was undertaken in order to correct an economic injustice. The Government of Bombay, contrary to the advice of the Joint Parliamentary Committee and contrary to the resolution of the Bombay Legislative Council of the Bombay Presidency in 1924, considerably enhanced the rate of rural taxation which was nominally 20 per cent but in actual application, in some instances, over 60 per cent. The public felt that the increase was unwarranted and that an impartial committee to hold enquiry be constituted. The Government paid no heed.

The people refused to pay the taxes. The authorities, however, met this challenge with the usual lathi charge, imprisonment, fines, attachments and auctions of land. But none of these threats had much effect on the people. The women of Bardoli took part in this movement from its very inception but they lacked leadership. Smt. Mithuben Petit and Smt. Bhaktben Desai from Bombay greatly strengthened the movement amongst women. The women attended the meetings even if it meant covering long distances on foot. They had composed inspiring songs appropriate to the fight.

Sardar Patel arranged for Mithuben, Bhaktben, Maniben Patel[78] and other ladies to camp on those very lands which were to be sold by fixing their tents and huts on it. The women in the area helped in the collection of funds also. A lady, whose name still remains unknown, gave two hundred rupees and promised to send this amount regularly every month till the fight was over. The Bardoli Satyagraha, besides proving an eye opener to the people, displayed the large measure of strength among women. However, it served as a training ground for the women of Bombay and an inspiration for women all over the country. It was for the first time here that not only the literate but the illiterate and ignorant women participated in the movement. "The heroism of the simple unsophisticated women of Bardoli", observed Mr. Desai, "was an inspiration to all women outside Bardoli."[79]

The Bardoli Satyagraha was successfully completed in September 1928, after five and a half months of struggle. It made known to the Government the strength of an organised and combined effort.

Simon Commission

The Simon Commission arrived in India in 1928. Since no Indian was represented on the Commission, it was boycotted by the nationalist Indians. The Dominion State Constitution (popularly known as the Nehru Report) was adopted by the All-Parties Conference during the same year. The Calcutta Congress undertook to adopt this constitution if the British Parliament accepted it in its present form before December 31, 1929, failing which civil disobedience was to ensue.

Notes and References

1. Gandhi, M.K., *Women and Social Injustice*, Ahmedabad, 1945, p. 169.
2. *Mrs. M. Cousins and Her Work in India*, p. 14.
3. The Indian National Congress in its session held in December 1918 passed a resolution unanimously on the franchise of women, "that this Congress urges that women possessing the same qualifications as are laid down for men in any part of the scheme, shall not be disqualified on account of their sex." (Proceedings of the thirty-third session of the Indian National Congress held at Delhi in December 1918, p. 5, *Modern Review*, January to June 1919, p. 652).
4. *Modern Review*, ibid., p. 652
5. About 11 cablegrams were sent, giving the text of the resolutions passed at the public meetings to prominent people in England emphasising the need for women's franchise.
6. Mrs. Hirabai Tata was the General Secretary of Bombay Women's India Association. She organised a number of meetings in Bombay and popularised the women's suffrage movement.
7. Daughter of Hirabai Tata.
8. The reactionary element was however not in favour of granting the franchise right to women. The Women's Association busied itself in writing to the members of the Councils, appealing to them to accede this right to women. Its members also went from province to province to witness the debate on suffrage.
9. Chirol, Valentine, *India*, London, 1926, p. 183.
10. In part the resolution reads: "We shall refuse civilly to obey these laws and such other laws as a committee to be hereafter appointed may think fit, and we further affirm that in this struggle we will faithfully follow truth and refrain from violence to life, person or property." (Report of the Disorders Enquiry Commission, *The Hunter Report*, London, p. 61).

11. Sitaramayya, Dr. Pattabhi, *The History of the Indian National Congress*, Vol. I, p. 164.

12. For details see Appendix G.

13. *India in 1920* (Official Report published every year), p. 238.

14. Sitaramayya. Dr. Pattabhi, *The Nationalist Movement of India*. Bombay, 1950, p. 45.

15. The Khalifa is the spiritual head of the Muslims; Khilafat is that which pertains to him.

16. This draft treaty was in one way lenient. In fact no consideration was given to the feelings of the Muslims in this country. By virtue of this treaty the Straits were internationalised. Turkey was also deprived of her rights in Egypt, Tripolitania, Morocco and Tunisia and the territories of Arabia, Palestine, Mesopotamia and Syria were taken away. In addition, Greece was temporarily to administer Smyrna and South Western Asia Minor and add Eastern Thrace (predominantly Turkish) to her realm.

    However the treaty of Lausanne offered better peace terms to Turkey by 1922.

17. The first Satyagraha was suspended on 18 April 1919.

18. Proceedings of the Indian National Congress, 1920, Quoted in Post Wheeler, *India Against the Storm*, New York, p. 177.

19. *Independent*, December 22, 1921 (unregistered paper edited by Mahadev Desai, A.I.C.C. Library).

20. *Amrita Bazar Patrika*, July 7, 1922

21. ibid., July 9, 1922.

22. Independent (unregistered paper edited by Mahadev Desai) December 27, 1921.

23. *Amrita Bazar Patrika*, January 10, 1922.

24. ibid.

25. *Amria Bazar Patrika*, January 1, 1923.

26. ibid., April 16, 1922.

27. ibid., May 30, 1922.

28. ibid., May 20, 1922.

29. ibid., December 9, 1922.

30. She was the daughter of Lala Karam Chand of Lyallpur (West Punjab), a rich man of the area. She was born in April 1888. Parvati was educated in the Kanya Maha Vidyalaya, Jalandhar, from which institution she passed her middle class examination. It was her father who broke the caste barrier by marrying her in 1905, to Dr. Milkhi Ram Bhatia employed in the Railway Service, thus setting an example of an intercaste marriage, an unknown thing in those days. Her father also had two scheduled caste servants in the house who later took a prominent part in the Ghadar Party. The family therefore was far ahead of the times. Parvati was not fated to enjoy the married life for long as

her husband died after two and a half years of her marriage in an accident. She, therefore, came to live with her father and decided to devote her life, working for the country. She qualified in Sanskrit and became a teacher in Delhi. She later came to Amritsar as a teacher and was in this city at the time of the Rowlatt Act Agitation. (This information was supplied by Shri Chander, brother of Parvati Devi.)

31. *Amrita Bazar Patrika*, December 17, 1922.

32. Mohammed Ali and Shaukat Ali.

33. *Civil and Military Gazette*, August 31, 1922.

34. *Amrita Bazar Patrika*, January 9, 1920.

35. In fact "one noticeable feature of the general excitement" observed *India 1919*, "was the unprecedented fraternization between the Hindus and the Muslims. The union between the leaders had now for long been a fixed plan of the nationalist platform. In this time of public excitement even to lower classes agreed for once to forget their differences. Extraordinary scenes of fraternization occurred. Hindus publicly accepted water from the hands of Muslims and vice versa. Hindu-Muslim unity was the watchword of processions indicated both by cries and banners. Hindu leaders had actually been allowed to preach from the pulpit of a mosque."

36. A place near Lahore in West Punjab (Pakistan).

37. *Amrita Bazar Patrika*, September 2, 1922.

38. ibid., December 12, 1922.

39. ibid., January 5, 1922.

40. ibid., February 5, 1922.

41. ibid.

42. *Home Political Proceeding*, 1922, File No. 933, p. 1.

43. *Amrita Bazar Patrika*, March 21, 1922.

44. ibid., May 23, 1922.

45. ibid.

46. ibid., January 13, 1922.

47. ibid.

48. ibid., June 25, 1922.

49. An Indian Statutory Commission was appointed to go into the question of constitutional development of India under Sir John Simon, which is popularly known as Simon Commission.

50. *Report of the Indian Statutory Commission* (Simon Commission), 1930, Vol, I, p. 250

51. *Moplah* are Mohammedans living in Malabar on the West Coast of Madras Presidency. They are mainly the tenants of Hindu land owners. Following the propaganda of the non-cooperators and the Khilafat, they rose in rebellion and destroyed the official machinery of the Government in their area, and either killed or drove away the officials. Afterwards they turned to the Hindus and serious riots took place.

52. `Emerson, *Non-Violent Non-Cooperation in India,* Asia, August 1922, p. 674; quoted in Walterbank T. Walter, *A Short History of India and Pakistan,* p. 157.

53. *Bengalee,* January 1, 1921.

54. In a letter to the Secretary, Provincial Congress Committee, Madras, she explained her position thus: "I am a firm believer in the value of British connection and strong opponent of the programme of non-cooperation. I believe the Nagpur Congress has narrowed the basis of the former constitution and has thereby ceased to be national. It has rejected the former ideals of the Congress and has adopted a policy which must land the country in ruin if successful and almost surely in riot and bloodshed if it fails. It no longer permits freedom of opinion or of speech but imposes on the minority intolerable tyranny. I, therefore, can no longer adhere to it nor change with its changes. With deep regret for the destruction of once noble Institution." (*Bengalee,* January 1921, p. 5)

55. Sharp division had taken place between the Congress and Mrs. Besant at the Delhi Congress of 1918. This breach became complete at the 1919 Congress of Amritsar.

56. Aiyer, A. Rangaswami, op. cit., p. 37.

57. *Modern Review,* January-June 1920, p. 41.

58. ibid., p. 42

59. ibid.

60. Aiyer, A. Rangaswami, *Annie Besant—Her Work for Swaraj,* p. 48.

61. Besant, Annie, *India Bonded or Free,* Second Edition, 1930, p. 237.

62. For details of the Bill, see Appendix to *India Bonded or Free* by Annie Besant, p. 225.

63. West, Geoffry. op. cit., p. 245.

64. *Indian Quarterly Register,* Vol. II, p. 384

65. *Amrita Bazar Patrika,* May 19, 1928.

66. Irish revolutionaries.

67. *Bengalee,* December 25, 1928.

68. *Proceedings of the Indian Congress,* 1928.

69. Sir Subba Rao Iyer denounced his title.

70. Mrs. Shiva Kamu, later sister-in-law of Mr. Arundale left the Medical College.

71. Prakasa, Sri, *Annie Besant,* Bombay, 1954, p. 144.

72. The following table showing the province-wise proportion of electors in the general constituencies to population, for the 1926 electorate, testifies the statement:

Province	Population of the electoral areas in 1921	Electors male and female. Male electors in brackets	Proportion of electors to population	Proportion of male electors to adult male population	Proportion of female electors to female population
Madras	4,23,19,000	116,000 (18,65,000)	3.2%	11.6%	1.0%
Bombay	1,92,92,000	39,000 (7,59,000)	3.9%	13.4%	.8%
Bengal	4,62,14,000	38,000 (11,73,000)	2.5%	9.7%	.3%
United Provinces	4,53,76,000	51,000 (15,89,000)	3.5%	12.4%	.4%
Punjab	2,06,75,000	21,000 (6,97,000)	3.4%	11.9%	.5%
Bihar & Orissa	3,38,20,000	None (3,73,000)	1.1%	4.6%	
Assam	67,35,000	About 3,000 (25,000)	3.7%	14.2%	.2%
Central Provinces including Berar	1,27,80,000	None (1,69,000)	1.3%	5.2%	-

73. Her account appears in the next chapter.
74. She was born in 1886 in Pudukottah State (now merged with the Madras Province).
75. Details given in the next chapter.
76. Writing to the Governor, Madras, on May 8, 1930, she said: "I am obliged to take this step as a mark of respect for the great soul Mahatma Gandhi who has been arrested and imprisoned by the Government. I feel it my bounden duty to express to Your Excellency on this occasion that life has been a source of inspiration to me in all my activities. (*My Experience as a Legislature* by Reddi, Dr. S. Muthulakshmi, Appendix B).
77. A place near Surat in Bombay Province.

78. Maniben Patel was the daughter of late Sardar Vallabhbhai Patel known as the Iron Man. She was born in 1904 at Gana near Bombay and received her early education at Queen Mary's High School and St. Joseph's Convent at Bombay. She later studied at Gujarat Vidyapith, Ahmedabad.

79. Desai, M., *The Story of Bardoli*, p. 154.

8

THE CIVIL DISOBEDIENCE MOVEMENT: 1930-1935

The failure of the Government to take up the Nehru Report and take note of the demand of the people within the stipulated period forced the Indian National Congress to proceed with its plans of launching Satyagraha as had been decided at its session in December 1928, at Calcutta.

Therefore, the Indian National Congress which met in December 1929, at Lahore declared on the midnight of December 31, 1929, the goal of the Congress to have complete independence instead of Dominion Status.[1] Thus the new year was ushered in with new hopes, a changed creed and the prospect of an active fight ahead.

The Congress members of the legislature were instructed to boycott elections and 26 January 1930, was declared as Independence Day which was to be celebrated throughout the country every year. Gandhiji was empowered to initiate the Civil Disobedience Movement in any manner he considered best.

Gandhiji selected the breaking of Salt Laws as the centre of gravity. He felt that since salt was a thing of common use, salt tax was unjust for the poor in the land.

Salt Satyagraha

Gandhiji started his historic march to Dandi on the sea coast near Jalalpur on 12 March 1930, and formally inaugurated the Campaign.[2] For breaking the Salt Law he was arrested on the 6th of April.

Mahatma Gandhi's arrest was the long awaited signal and the campaign started with countrywide hartals. It specially electrified the patriotic zeal in women which not only gave a twofold strength and support to the cause but also invited attention and appreciation from the outside world.

At first, women had not been allowed to participate as Gandhiji had thought they would complicate matters. But the women of the land, coveting a place of equality with men, could not sit back at the call of the nation. They protested that in these critical days there should not be any watertight compartments of services. Women demanded that "no conference, no congress or commission dealing with the welfare of India should be held without the presence on them of their kind. Similarly, they must ask that no marches, no imprisonment, no demonstrations organised for the welfare of India should prohibit women from a share in them." Later they were permitted to take part in all phases of the campaign.[3]

They (the women) started their march on the road to liberty by breaking salt laws, forest laws, taking out "Prabhat Pheries', processions, picketing schools, colleges, legislative councils and clubs. The Government met the just demand with lathi charge, shooting, arrests, Section 144, Press Ordinance, Unlawful Instigation Ordinance and Intimidation Ordinance.

Women had determined to participate in the movement in the face of various punishments inflicted by the government. The Provincial Secretary of the Bengal Congress Committee reported that sex was no protection. Two women had been caned on their bare backs.[4] In another incident at Allahabad the police did the most hideous thing by lathi charging a procession led by Smt. Swaroop Rani Nehru, wife of Shri Motilal Nehru who also received a lathi blow as a result of which she became unconscious.[5] In Delhi ten women were injured including the mother-in-law of Pandit Jawaharlal Nehru as a consequence of lathi charge; while in Madhya Pradesh three women were killed as a result of firing in connection with the defying of Forest laws.

These atrocities did not discourage the women, but activated their desire to suffer more, to sacrifice more and to achieve more.

As a protest against the high-handed measure of the government the women in high places resigned their posts. To name a few, Muthulakshmi Ammal resigned her seat in the Legislative Council and her office as Deputy President of the Council. Mrs. Hansa Mehta and Kamalbai Lakshman Rao resigned their offices as Honorary Magistrates. Miss Dickson, the first woman member of the Central Legislative Assembly not only resigned her seat but also refused the Kaiser-i-Hind Medal.[6] Besides, a large number of women took active part in the Civil Disobedience Movement. First and foremost among them was Sarojini Naidu.

Sarojini Naidu

Sarojini Naidu, known as the poetess, politician and peace-maker, was born in Hyderabad on February 13, 1879. Her father Dr. Aghonath Chattopadhya, a Bengali gentleman, was the founder of the Nizam College and till his death, laboured hard in the field of education. He was a scientist of repute. After matriculating at Hyderabad, Sarojini was sent to England in 1895, for higher studies on a scholarship awarded by the Nizam. She studied at King's College, London, and then Girton College, Cambridge University. She could not pursue her studies due to ill health and came back to India in 1898. She spent a few months in Switzerland and Italy before returning to India. The rich historic past of Italy seems to have kindled her heart for freedom. She married Dr. Naidu in 1898, breaking that barrier of caste and religion.

Mrs. Naidu appealed in 1909, to the students in the Byramji Jeejabai Institution, Bombay, that "The highest ideal, the climax of modern spirit should be the unification of the races of India, the unity, which of mutual industry of a common education, of disinterested labour, of breaking up ancient barriers, of eliminating ancient hatred and of the recognition of common brotherhood, that bound the Hindus and Mohammedans, the Mohammedans with Parsis and the Parsis with Christians."[7]

In the same year she attended the Social Service Conference and moved a resolution for the protection of the Hindu widows. Later she dwelt upon the education of women. "Until and unless," she said, "they raise the fallen women in this country and make their voice heard, India's salvation was only a distant dream."[8]

Mrs. Naidu appeared for the first time on the political platform as the "ambassador of Hindu Muslim unity" in 1913 when she attended and addressed the Muslim League Session.[9] Three years later, in 1916, Mrs. Naidu spoke from the Congress platform sponsoring the resolution on self-government. Then onwards she took a prominent part in the country's political life. The period that followed was fraught with difficulties and as such of ceaseless activities for the people who were determined to serve the motherland.

Sarojini Naidu, who saw the salvation and joy of life in the service to the country, fought for self-government on the one hand and women's rights on the other.[10]

Mrs. Naidu led the deputation of leading women in social and political field in December 1917. This deputation waited on Montagu with a view to secure voting rights for women.

Next year in September 1918, she attended the special session of the Congress at Bombay and was instrumental in getting the resolution on women's franchise passed, whereby they were not to be disqualified on account of sex.[11]

Mrs. Naidu went to England in 1919 as a member of Home Rule League Deputation to give evidence before the Joint Parliamentary Committee. She took this opportunity to put forward women's case for franchise as well. Mrs. Naidu felt that without effective propaganda the Montagu-Chelmsford Constitution was likely to be marred with sex disqualifications. She, therefore, organised a powerful agitation in England. She also headed a Joint Deputation of all the different Indian political organisations then in England and made a powerful claim of the Indian women for franchise. She demanded that the provinces should be left free to decide whether or not special arrangements were needed where purdah existed.[12]

Early in 1919 when Gandhiji inaugurated the Satyagraha Movement, Sarojini Naidu was one of the first to take the pledge. After this she went to Bombay, Madras and Ahmedabad and worked incessantly to propagate the cause. Sarojini Naidu made special appeals to women of the land against the Rowlatt Act. She also sold prescribed literature and took part in the Satyagraha demonstrations in Bombay.

At a public meeting at Ahmedabad she criticised the Montagu-Chelmsford Reforms. Speaking about the visit of the Secretary of State, Montagu, she said, "His sentimental journey through the length and breadth of the land in the company of Lord Chelmsford and their expression of sympathy bore no fruit, for in one hand they had the sword and a cup of poison in the other and seemed to say: 'here is bread for you but before you reach out for it you must drain this cup of poison to the dregs'." But she asserted: "As long as Indians have rectitude and strength in them, as long as they have any sense of self-respect they will stoutly refuse to empty the cup of poison."[13] She was in England, in 1920, for treatment and continued her work there. She acquainted the public in England with the highhandedness of the Martial Law authorities. Her speech in Kingsway Hall, London, resulted in what is known as Naidu-Montagu controversy.[14]

Unmindful of her shattered health, this courageous soldier went on working for the redress of the Punjab and Khilafat wrongs. She attended the debate on the Punjab issue in the British Parliament and was pained at the indifferent attitude of the participants.[15]

The same year Mrs. Naidu attended the International Conference in Geneva. She was questioned by people as to why she took to politics. Her answer to the question was a symbol of her desire to bring the Hindus and Muslims closer. She said: "I think it is inevitable that one should become interested in politics if one is a true Indian. The importance of Hindu-Mohammedan unity appealed to me. I lived in a Mohammedan city and you see, I had so many Mohammedan friends. Very few Hindus have had such intimate relations with Mohammedans as I, for I have taken part in all their political and educational movements. I have presided over their meetings and spoken at mosques. That is the thing which counts most among men and women, especially men. The first political speech I made was at a meeting of the Moslem League."[16]

For her, unity was an important thing. Whether she spoke to the students, women or the politicians or the people at large, her watchword was unity among the races. Naidu felt that unity would quicken the attainment of freedom.[17]

She had hardly recovered from her heart disease when she came back to India. These were the days of Non-Cooperation Movement which was launched by Gandhiji in 1920. Like a loyal follower she followed Mahatma Gandhi's programme and was once again in the midst of the fight.

There were riots in Bombay followed by the visit of His Royal Highness, the Prince of Wales, in 1921. Mrs. Naidu personally went to the affected areas to disperse the crowds and to make peace.

Then came the Moplah outbreak, referred to earlier. Mrs. Naidu went to Malabar with a view to quieten the atmosphere. She criticised the Martial Law authorities operating in the area. The Government of

Madras threatened to prosecute her if she did not apologise for the statements and criticism made by her. However, Sarojini was unaffected by these threats. She invited the Government's attention to many more statements made in this regard by other people which corroborated hers. So she challenged the Government to withdraw the remarks or make good the threats.[18] Sarojini gave back the Kaiser-i-Hind Medal to the Government. Gandhiji was arrested in 1922 and his parting message to her was: "I trust the unity of India in your hands."[19]

Heavy work again had its effect on her health and Sarojini had to leave for Ceylon in 1922. But she could not keep herself away from political activities for long. Even there she delivered a number of lectures pleading India's cause and on her way back to India she stopped at many places to propagate the cause and to shake the country from its slumber.

Mrs. Naidu stood for unadulterated Gandhian non-cooperation and opposed the suggestion of the Council entry. She attended the All India Congress Session at Calcutta in November 1922 and opposed in vehement terms the resolution favouring the Council entry. The Akali movement[20] also invited her attention and she moved a resolution[21] in the Indian National Congress of 1923-24 condemning the stand taken by the Government. Mrs. Naidu said: "I feel that I am but discharging a very small portion of the debt of inspiration that I owe to the ideals and the achievements of that dauntless little section of Indian humanity who, in their black robes and their black turbans, stand in the vanguard of the army of India's freedom. So great was the inspiration... when I rose from my sickbed almost unable to walk, I, none the less re-entered public life by marching at Amritsar in the 'Unlawful' Akali Dal as a protest against the tyranny of the Government and as a practical token of my resolution not merely to stand by and support but to participate if necessary in the activities of the Akalis."[22]

Early in 1924 Mrs. Naidu went to South Africa to study and improve if possible, the sad condition of Indians in that country. She raised her voice against the Anti-Historic Bill (1924), which was calculated to exterminate the Indian community in South Africa. She also presided over the East African Congress. In her presidential address she urged the audience: "You must with one united voice give an answer to the Government and say though in natural history rivers don't flow backward, we shall make the river of your decision flow backward."[23] She held discussions over the Indian question with the

Government and members of the Parliament of South Africa and thus became well-acquainted with the viewpoint of all concerned and hence was able to present the matter to the Government of India in all its details.

Mrs. Naidu's services were amply rewarded when she was elected President of the Indian National Congress in 1925. Mrs. Naidu was the first Indian woman to be placed in charge of such an exalted office. Her election to the presidentship was an honour to the womanhood and recognition of their rights. She herself made reference to this fact in her presidential address at the 48th session of the Congress at Kanpur in 1925. She said: "I am fully aware that you have bestowed upon me the richest gift in your possession... but rather ingenerous tribute to Indian womanhood and as token of your loyal recognition of its legitimate place in the secular and spiritual councils of the Nation."[24]

Sarojini Naidu outlined a scheme creating different departments relating to divergent needs of the people like a department for the re-organisation of villages, for the industrial workers and for education. She held that the education system of the time was unsuited to the special trend of our racial genius. She felt that military training should form an integral part of education. She was in favour of having a national militia by voluntary conscription of which the nucleus might be the existing volunteer organisations. The question of giving aerial and naval training was also considered.[25]

Sarojini's message of the new year as President of the Congress was: "Mine, as becomes of a woman, is a most modest domestic programme merely to restore to India her true position as the supreme mistress in her own home, the sole guardian of her own vast resources and the sole dispenser of her own hospitality. As a loyal daughter of Bharat Mata, therefore, it will be my lovely though difficult task, through the coming year, to set my house in order, to reconcile the tragic quarrels that threaten the integrity of her old joint family life of diverse communities and creeds and to find an adequate place and purpose and recognition alike for the lowest and highest of her children and foster children, the guests and strangers within her gate."[26]

From 1923 to 1929 she was in America visiting parts of the United States and Canada. She delivered two hundred lectures during her tour and acquainted the people with the conditions in India.[27] Speaking at a banquet given in her honour by the Hindustan Association of America, in New York, on November 10, 1928, Mrs. Naidu said: "It was futile to aspire for the freedom of the world without a free India."[28]

Sarojini's lectures in these countries for the major part were on "Interpretation of Hindu Womanhood," "An ultimate study of Mahatma Gandhi", and "Interpretation of the spiritual life of India."

In April 1929 Mrs. Naidu sailed for England where she had interviews with the members of the Government. The same year, presiding over the First Provincial U.P. Youth Conference, she exhorted young men to understand the meaning of "give me liberty or death"[29] as the only choice before them in the interest of the country.

Sarojini was specially nominated by Gandhiji to initiate raid upon Dharasana[30] Salt Works in May 1930. Before taking charge of the raiding party she declared in a public speech, "The time has come in my opinion when women can no longer seek immunity behind the shelter of their sex, but must share equally with their men comrades all the perils and sacrifices for the liberation of the country."[31]

It was on May 15, 1930, that she raided the Salt Works. Sarojini and her comrades were arrested, but were released the same day. Sarojini led another batch of twenty-five hundred raiders upon the same Salt Works on May 21, 1930. Webb Miller who was an eye-witness to the happenings at Dharasana wrote that Sarojini called the volunteers for prayers before the march. She exhorted them thus: "Gandhi's body is in jail but his soul is with you. India's prestige is in your hands. You must not use any violence under any circumstances. You will be beaten but you must not resist; you must not even raise a hand to ward off blows."[32]

After the prayer the volunteers started marching towards the salt deposits which were surrounded by ditches filled with water. A batch of volunteers reached near the barbed wire stockade which was guarded by the police. This batch was ordered to disperse but the volunteers did not care to obey the command as a result of which the "police rushed upon the advancing marches and rained blows on their heads with their steel shaft lathes."[33] The injured men were removed and then many a batch of volunteers advanced to meet the same fate. Ultimately the volunteers changed their tactics and sat on the ground near the salt pans.

The authorities could not even bear their assembling in this way and orders to disperse them were given again. They (volunteers), as usual, paid no heed to this order. As a consequence the police "commenced savagely kicking the seated men in the abdomen and testicles." The injured men writhed and squealed in agony, which seemed to inflame the fury of the police.... The police then began dragging the sitting men by the arms or feet, sometimes for a hundred yards and throwing them into ditches.[34]

Mrs. Naidu was arrested the same day, i.e., May 21, 1930. In a message to her comrades, she said thus: "Whatever happens, strictly adhere to the law of non-violence. Don't budge an inch from the place you have taken.[35]

Mrs. Naidu was released following the Gandhi-Irwin Pact[36] signed on March 5, 1931. During the year the Second Round Table Conference was convened in London. Mrs. Naidu attended the conference as an official representative of the women of India.

The Gandhi-Irwin Pact was not respected by Lord Irwin's successor, Lord Willingdon, with the result that most of the national leaders were again put in jail.

Gandhiji returned to India on December 28, 1931, after attending the Round Table Conference at London. He was arrested on January 4, 1932, and was confined in the Pune jail.

Mrs. Naidu became the acting President of the Indian National Congress in 1932. The Reception Committee of the Congress was declared unlawful. This did not deter her from her determination to hold the conference and she shifted the venue of its session to Delhi.[37]

On April 20th Mrs. Naidu was served with an order directing her not to act in furtherance of the Civil Disobedience Movement and not to leave the city limits without the permission of the Commissioner.[38] She did not pay attention to this order and left for Bombay by Frontier Mail. The train was stopped at Bandra, ten miles short of Bombay, and she was arrested.[39] She was sentenced to one year's imprisonment.

BOMBAY

Kamala Devi Chattopadhyaya

Smt. Kamala Devi Chattopadhyaya is another woman of this time who did outstanding work for the furtherance of the cause of national freedom.

Kamala Devi was born in Mangalore in 1903 and was married while she was yet in school. Her husband died and Kamala became a child widow. She continued her studies which was contrary to the customs of the time and later joined the Queen Marry's College at Madras. She was remarried to Harindranath Chattopadhyaya, brother of Mrs. Naidu, setting an example to inter-caste, inter-provincial and widow remarriage.

Kamala decided to join active politics in 1922 and joined the Congress the same year. She always remained in the thick of the fight for freedom. This courageous lady was the first woman to contest election for the Legislative Assembly of Madras in 1926.

Kamala Devi was associated with many women's organisations and attended the International Congress of Women's League for peace and freedom which was held on August 23, 1929, in the city of Prague. She acquainted the gathering there with the conditions in India.[40]

Presiding over the Youth Conference at Ahmedabad in 1929, Kamala Devi complained: "We are very fond of holding ourselves as ready for martyrdom but when the time comes for baring our necks we retreat and say wait till the next blow. Each time the coward gets the better of it. Start Civil Disobedience, declare an independent republic, establish a parallel Government, do it at any cost."[41]

During the Civil Disobedience Movement of 1930, Kamala Devi addressed meetings, prepared salt and picketed foreign cloth and liquor shops. In one of the meetings that she addressed at Esplanade Maidan, Bombay, she exhorted the people to follow the lead given by Gandhiji by defying the laws as that would paralyse the Government.[42]

Kamala Devi offered passive resistance and guarded the salt pans when the police raided the Congress House, Bombay. Salt was publicly prepared by her and was sold in the open market. She even chose High Court premises for selling salt. The salt was sold at a high price.

While it was the privilege of Sarojini Naidu to raid the Dharasana Salt Works, it fell to Kamala Devi to plan a raid on the Salt Fields in the precincts of Bombay city.[43] Before she could realise her dream, she was arrested. Her parting message to the people was: "Carry on the fight until British Imperialism becomes only a dark shadow of the past; India's freedom will open the gate for world freedom."[44]

Kamala Devi was taken to Court for trial. Instead of taking notice of her trial the fearless soldier invited the Magistrate to buy salt and started selling it in the Court Room. She also asked the Magistrate to resign the job and join the Satyagraha Army. For this act she was awarded six months imprisonment and a fine of Rs. 150, and three months more under the Salt Act and a fine of Rs. 20, or in default two week's imprisonment. Both the sentences were to run consecutively.[45]

Kamala was released in 1930. This was the time for the preparation of a bigger fight ahead. She, therefore, made a whirlwind tour of the country with a view to opening branches of the Hindustani Seva Dal. This organisation was an autonomous body which for the last seven years had been training workers for the service of the country. In the beginning it had only recognition from the Congress but later it was administered and controlled by the Congress itself.

Kamala Devi was in charge of women's organisation under the Hindustani Seva Dal. She arranged camps for the training of women workers. The training course was separate for the girls. The course of training included literary education, training in domestic hygiene, child rearing, sewing and spinning, in organising meetings and course of study in Indian history and geography. The course was designed to make women fit for all that the country expected them to do.[46]

During the year Kamala Devi addressed the students also. She was the Vice-Chairman of the Bombay Youth League. Kamala Devi presided over the Students' Conference at Lahore in October 1931. She condemned the education system and said, "It is a frame that ill fits us for it is cast in a sinister mould and that we have slipped it round our neck, it is strangulating us in slow, deliberate manner."[47] She exhorted the students to organise study circles, study the political and economic problems and explain them to the masses.

Kamala Devi was arrested in 1932 and was sentenced to one year's imprisonment. She joined the Congress Socialist Party in 1934 and presided over its All India Conference at Meerut the very next year.

There were a large number of other women in Bombay who participated in the great struggle. But special mention must be made of Jaishri Raiji, Hansa Mehta, Perin Captain, Sofia Somjee, Lilavati Munshi, Maniben Patel and Khurshedben, the granddaughter of Dadabhai Naoroji. They worked in various ways—led processions, held meetings, picketed cloth and liquor shops and organised classes for women to prepare them for the national struggle.

Picketing of shops was not easy; but these brave ladies had a lot of patience and determination at their command. They asked the shopkeepers and traders to stop dealing in foreign cloth. Since picketing cloth shops was declared illegal women had to suffer rigorous imprisonment, lathi charge and rude behaviour of the police. In the prison they received harrowing treatment. Maniben Patel, who was arrested in connection with the Satyagraha Movement, was treated as 'C' class prisoner. There were many political prisoners who were kept along with the criminals. Seventy-seven prisoners with four babies including fifteen ordinary criminals were locked up in a single barrack. There were no proper bathrooms. In addition they had to sweep the barracks and verandahs twice a day, clean the vessels and wash latrines.[48] But these difficulties did not shatter their faith. Many more were taking training to enlist themselves for the service of the country. A class to train women to take part in the Satyagraha campaign of Gandhiji for breaking salt laws was started under the supervision of members of the Satyagraha Ashram and Khurshedben. These trainees were taught to sing propaganda songs and to organise village meetings, to show how to preserve peace and order at the meetings, sanitation, first aid to the injured, nursing and spinning.[49]

Rashtriya Stri Sabha, another organisation of women, launched an intensive campaign for the propagation of Swadeshi throughout the city. Members of this organisation paid house to house visits and secured signatures for the pledge of swadeshi.[50]

Gujarat was the citadel of this campaign. The province was well-trained under the direct teaching of Gandhiji. The womenfolk showed marvellous power of organisation and steered the movement successfully. In Gujarat most of the dictators were women. The men were rounded up in the first few days and it was left to women to come out as war dictators one after the other.

The women of Gujarat informed the Governor that they supported Gandhiji's policy and action. They were determined to fight for prohibition and Swadeshi because the two questions affected them personally.[51]

BENGAL

The women of Bengal not only participated in Mahatma Gandhi's Civil Disobedience campaign but also in the revolutionary activities. They were encouraged to adopt the revolutionary creed by Subhas Chandra Bose and a good many young girls came into the fold of the revolutionary party.

An annual report of the Police Administration stated that "Organised attempts, seldom successful, were made to hoist the Congress Flag on Government buildings in the mofussil. An increasing share of the work was taken up by women, both because it was becoming more difficult to find male recruits and because the presence of women-folk was calculated to prove an embarrassment to the police."[52]

This, of course, was a twisted statement. Women did not join the ranks primarily to embarrass the police. The distinction of sex never worried the police authorities much, as the women were often punished the same way as men, i.e., they were dragged, their processions lathi-charged and life sentence passed on some.[53]

In spite of such treatment, women went along their chosen path, and picketed colleges, schools, clubs and courts. Women's organisations, like Ladies Picketing Board, Nari Satyagraha Committee, Nikhil Jatiya Nari Sangh and Mahila Rashtriya Sangha were declared unlawful.[54]

Mahila Rashtriya Sangha

Lotika Ghose was entrusted with the organisation of women. She, with the help of Subhas Chandra Bose, founded the Mahila Rashtriya Sangha and Subhas Bose's mother was the first president. This body had its branches in other districts as well. Women joined the Salt Satyagraha by preparing salt in the seaside districts. Rashtriya Sangha was able to send batches for nearly six months for picketing and courting arrests.[55] The members went in batches picketing schools and colleges and this work was supervised by Lotika Ghose while another member of the Sangha, Arunbala Sen, undertook the work of picketing the foreign cloth shops in the Bara Bazar and several women's organisations visited this place to stop the sale of foreign cloth. The trade in foreign cloth virtually came to an end for the time being.

Nari Satyagraha Committee

Another institution which played a prominent part during this period was Nari Satyagraha Committee. Smt. Urmila Devi, sister of Deshbandhu C.R. Das, was its president and amongst its vice-presidents were important Congress women workers of standing like Mohini Devi, Jyotirmoyi Ganguli, Hemprabha Das Gupta and Ashoklata Das. Samiti Das and Bimal Pratima Devi were the secretaries. They took out processions violating government orders. They were harassed and intercepted by the mounted police, but nothing intimidated them, so they were arrested by police.

The *Amrita Bazar Patrika* of May 25, 1930, reported that for the first time in the annals of Calcutta the game of football had to be abandoned on Saturday owing to lady picketers making their appearance at club tents.

Ladies Picketing Board

In May 1931, a Picketing Board was started by the women of Bengal to boycott and picket in collaboration with Bengal Provincial Congress Committee.[56] The work of this Board was to propagate against the use of foreign goods; to popularise home industries and to help develop cottage industries; specially those of spinning and weaving Khadi; to arrange processions and meetings; emphasise the importance of liberty and equality of nations; the need for removal of untouchability; to enlist members of the Congress, who would follow the directives of the National Congress stipulating that the Bengal Provincial Congress Committee work in close cooperation with the National Congress.

Boycott and Picketing Section

The work of this section was to carry out peaceful picketing in different markets and shops against the sale of foreign goods, especially cloth.

Swadeshi Prachar Section

To popularise and preach for the use of Swadeshi goods, specially Swadeshi cloth and Khadi in private homes; and to recruit women workers to join the Board and enlist as members of the National Congress.

Prabhat-Pheri Section

To carry on Prabhat-Pheries (morning processions) in different parts of the city in accordance with the instructions of the Board and to recruit members for the Picketing Board.

Constructive Workers Section

To demonstrate the use of Charkhas and Taklis and to help spinners to get in touch with weavers for the yarn spun by them. To help manufacture a variety of handmade goods and to get markets for the same; to establish Ashrams where little girls and boys are instructed to spin yarn.

General Section

This section engaged itself in holding meetings and taking out processions.

The aforesaid scheme was very comprehensive and the women of Bengal did a lot of work in various parts of Bengal.[57]

Conferences and meetings of the ladies was an everyday occurrence in Bengal. In a conference at Comilla which was presided over by Urmila Devi the following resolutions were passed:[58]

(i)   The formation of Mahila Samitis.
(ii)   Boycott of foreign goods.
(iii) Establishment of Hindu-Muslim unity.
(iv)   The removal of untouchability and purdah.
(v)   Demands for open trial of detenus in jails.
(vi)   Urging the ladies to support the Congress cause.

The prominent worker at this place (Comilla) was Hemprabha Majumdar, President and first Dictator of the Tippera District Congress Committee. She was later arrested for her anti-government activities like taking out processions. She was sentenced to one year's rigorous imprisonment for leading a procession and six months rigorous imprisonment for distributing unauthorised Congrsess bulletins. The sentences were to run concurrently.[59]

Revolutionary Activities

The cult of violence which, perhaps, never died in Bengal was renewed with the Civil Disobedience Movement. The organisation of the revolutionaries was very active in Dhaka, Comilla and Chittagong and young college girls came into its fold. The famous group of the women revolutionaries consisted of Samiti and Suniti, Bina Das, Kalpana Dutta and Preetilata Waddedar.

The Chittagong Armoury was raided by the revolutionaries on April 13, 1930. This resulted in a clash between the revolutionaries and government officials in the village of Dhalghat near Chittagong. Two of the revolutionaries and Captain Cameron of the Chittagong Armoury were killed. An old Brahmin lady of the village gave shelter to the absconding revolutionaries. She was arrested and tortured in a variety of ways for eliciting facts of the case. Later she was joined in the jail by Kalpana Dutta whom she warned not to be cowed down by police tricks. She said: "They might torture you but even then you must never tell them anything, they might even threaten you with hanging, but you must never give way."[60]

This lady wrote a poem on the atrocities of the police:

"The wicked men come politely

And sit close to you;

They extract words by giving threats

And take away your life at the end."[61]

She was ill-treated in jail. But she did not worry much about the rules and regulations of the jail. Her son died in prison and she could not get permission to see him. She was released at the expiry of her sentence in a desperate condition. Later she joined the Nari Samiti when a branch of it was opened in Dhalghat.[62]

Kalpana Dutta and Preetilata Waddedar were revolutionaries of a high order. Both of them were together at school and since their youth had disliked the British domination. While studying in the senior class in the school they wanted to change the pledge "to be loyal to God and King" into "to be loyal to God and Country."[63] After completing their studies Preetilata joined the Dhaka University and attended Deepwali Sangha, an organisation to train the patriots in lathi and sword play. Kalpana Dutta joined the Calcutta University and became a member of the Ladies Association. They both came in contact with the revolutionaries in 1931-32.[64]

It was on September 24, 1932, that Preetilata Waddedar led a raid on the Pahartali Railway Officers Club. As a result of this raid one European lady was shot. In an attempt to shoot those who had gathered in the club she had to lose her life by taking potassium cyanide.[65] Some revolvers, live cartridges and red leaflets threatening the authorities were found in her pocket.

Preetilata was the first woman who died in action. She was a courageous lady and had a number of interviews with Ramakrishna Biswas, a revolutionary who was hanged. She also faced the machine gun of Captain Cameron who was shot at Dhalghat. She was suspected of anti-government activities but the police could not catch her as she went underground.

Kalpana was another active worker of the revolutionary party. She was seen quite often, dressed in male attire, in the vicinity of Pahartali.

She was suspected of revolutionary activities so a police watch was kept on her. But the authorities could not find anything substantial to put her on trial. When the Pahartali Club was raided the police became convinced that she was a party to the raid. But lack of evidence kept the authorities from taking any action against her. So she was sent for trial under Section 109.[66] She was later released on bail. Kalpana escaped while still on bail before the trial was completed. She was again arrested after three months and tried by a special tribunal in connection with the Chittagong Armoury Supplementary trials.[67] She was sentenced to transportation for life.[68]

Suniti, daughter of Uma Charan Choudhry, and Samiti, daughter of Debendra Lal Ghose, a professor in the Comilla College, shot the Magistrate of Comilla, on December 14, 1931.[69] They were arrested and were awarded a life sentence.[70]

The next action was that of Miss Bina Dass.[71] She was a student of Diocesean College. She moved from her house to the college hostel on the pretext that it would enable her to devote more attention to her studies, but this move was to perfect her plans for the forthcoming University Convocation.[72]

On February 6, 1932, the day Calcutta University had its convocation, Bina was one of the recipients of Bachelor of Arts degree. As the Governor got up to address the convocation she fired five shots in an attempt to kill him.[73] She was caught immediately. Following this action on the part of Bina Das, a number of arrests were made. A search of her belongings at the Diocessan College was made and a number of documents came into the hands of the police. It was discovered that she was a member of the terrorist party. In a written statement of the Court she boldly pointed out:

> I fired at the Governor impelled by my love of the country which is being repressed. I thought that the only way to death was by offering myself at the feet of my country and thus make an end of all my suffering. I invite the attention of all to the situation created by the measures of the Government which faced even a frail woman like me, brought-up in all the best tradition of Indian womanhood. I can assure all that I have no personal feeling of animosity against Sir Stanley Jackson, the man who is just as good as my father and the Hon'ble Lady Jackson who is as good as my mother. But the Governor of Bengal represents the system which has kept enslaved three hundred million of my countrymen and countrywomen.[74]

She was sentenced to nine years' rigorous imprisonment.[75]

Another girl, daughter of late Bankim Chandra Gupta of village Mirzapur, district Mymensingh, was arrested because a suitcase containing seventy-eight packets marked dynamite, three coils of fusewire and a large number of revolutionary books was found in her possession. She was awarded five years' rigorous imprisonment under Section 5 and 5A of the Explosive Substances Act. Her mother was also arrested for harbouring declared political offenders.[76]

There were many more women who took part in the revolutionary activities and served varying terms of imprisonment. To name only a few who went to jail, were Kamla Chatterjee, Bimal Pratibha Devi, Shobharana Dutta, Ujjala Devi, Parul Mukerjee, Jyotikanta Dutta, Banala Das. Santishda Ghose of Barisal was arrested while trying to encash a forged cheque of twenty-seven thousand rupees in Grindlays Bank, Calcutta. The money was needed to carry on revolutionary activities.[77]

PUNJAB

The women of Punjab inaugurated the Civil Disobedience Movement by taking out a procession of five thousand ladies at Lahore in 1930. Processions, meetings, picketing and Prabhat Pheries in defiance of Section 144 became their daily routine. Day after day they held demonstrations before the gates of the Council Chamber. The police and their lathi charge had ceased to scare them. When the Viceroy came to address the Council members they shouted slogans like "Long Live Revolution," "Up! Up! the National Flag", "Long Live Bhagat Singh", "Gandhi Ki Jai".[78] The life and soul of the movement were Mrs. Lado Rani Zutshi, Parvati, daughter of Lala Lajpat Rai, Smt. Kartar Kaur, Atma Devi and many others.

Lado Rani Zutshi was the leading woman of the time. She was married to the late Pandit Ladli Prashad Zutshi, a leading lawyer of Lahore. Her interest in politics began in the Martial Law days in the Punjab in 1919; and ever after, she was an active Congress worker. During this movement she gained importance for her singular activities and was appointed the eighth Dictator of the War Council and steered the movement successfully.[79]

This courageous woman and her daughters and other women offering Satyagraha picked the cloth shops, law courts and the quarters of Members of the Legislative Assembly. She had arranged a uniform of red trousers, green shirts and white Gandhi caps resembling the National Emblem[80] for volunteers.

Addressing a meeting outside Mori Gate, Lahore, she appealed to women to follow the example of those of Bombay: "The arrests of women show the weakness of the Government." She went on to say, "Government imprisons persons for one offence or another because it wishes to prevent those people from carrying on Congress work outside jails,"[81]

In another speech on June 23, 1930, she encouraged the people "to bear the tyranny of machine guns and lathi blows. How much can the government tyrannize us?"[82] she asked. She also distributed sedious matter, the publication of which was punishable under Section 124A or 153A of the Indian Penal Code.[83]

Speaking at the death anniversary of Bal Gangadhar Tilak, she referred to the highhandedness of the government. "These people," she said, "are wild beasts and devoid of humanity. Their civilisation is only temporary. They have come into power only temporarily, and have forgotten what humaneness is. They are now to learn to what extent this tyranny can go."[84]

As a result of these activities she was called upon to show cause why she should not be ordered to execute a bond of ten thousand rupees with sureties of rupees five thousand each for good behaviour for a period of one year.[85] She was sentenced to one year's imprisonment but was released under the Gandhi-Irwin Pact in 1931 before the expiry of the sentence, only to be re-arrested in 1932. This time she was sentenced to eighteen months' imprisonment. She had to be released before the end of her term on account of ill-health.

Lado Rani had instilled patriotic zeal in her daughters also, and they all shared her responsibilities in this struggle. As many as seventeen women were arrested on October 9, 1913, including Prof. Janak Kumari Zutshi and Swadesh Kumari Zutshi[86] for picketing educational institutions. This was the first time such a large number of women were apprehended in the course of a single day. The Lahore Women's College students did not attend the college as a protest."[87]

Later when the Zutshi sisters were put on trial they refused to attend it unless their relatives were allowed to witness the proceedings. The case had to be adjourned. They were fined and to realise the fine the police attached the clothes and beddings belonging to the convicts. These things were however returned later.[88]

Mrs. Manmohini Sehgal (then Manmohini Zutshi), daughter of Lado Rani, also joined hands with the freedom fighters. She started her career in the political field by becoming Chairman of the Reception Committee of the Second All Punjab Students Conference, presided over by Subhas Chandra Bose, in October 1929.[89] She later became President of the Lahore Students Union founded by Bhagat Singh of the Lahore Conspiracy Case, in December 1929.[90] Manmohini was threatened by her college authorities with expulsion if she did not resign from the Students' Union. Later her degree was withheld by the university. It was only with the good offices of Dr. S. Radhakrishnan[91] that she was able to get the degree of Master of Arts.[92]

She was arrested for picketing educational institutions on October 8 and followed her mother to jail. She was sentenced to six months' imprisonment. Manmohini was released from jail only to be arrested again in January 1931 along with her sisters for picketing shops. This time she was sentenced to one year's imprisonment. She was, however, released under Gandhi-Irwin Pact. Manmohini was again arrested in March 1932, for defying a notice served on her by the Punjab Government and was sentenced to a year's rigorous imprisonment.[93] She had to undergo her full period in jail.

Manmohini had become a member of the Provincial Congress Committee in 1933-34 and also was one of the Punjab delegates to the Swaraj Party Conference convened at Ranchi by Shri Bhulabhai Desai and Dr. M.A. Ansari.[94]

Manmohini worked as Headmistress of Bihar Mahila Vidyapith till she was married in 1935. She had to curtail her political activities after her marriage and involved herself in social work. She became the Honorary Secretary of the Simla Branch of the All India Women's Conference and took up work in the villages also. Manmohini became the General Secretary of the National Council of Women (affiliated to the International Council of Women) in 1945.

Manmohini gave evidence before the Cripps Mission in 1946 as representative of the National Council.[95] She continues to be associated with a large number of social work organisations.

Another important woman of this period was Parvati Devi, daughter of Lala Lajpat Rai. She was a steadfast Congress worker. Parvati took part in all the programmes of the Satyagraha Committee. She was arrested under Section 124A Criminal Procedure Code

(Sedition) for her patriotic activities. She was asked to execute a bond for rupees ten thousand with two sureties of rupees five thousand each. During the pendency of the case she was further required to execute another bond of two thousand rupees to ensure her attendance. She preferred to go to jail. She was sentenced to two years rigorous imprisonment, and was fined twenty thousand rupees.[96]

Laxmi Devi also took a leading part in the various activities of the freedom movement. She was the wife of Mr. Trikha, then President of the District Congress Committee, Simla. Speaking at a public meeting on, July 30, 1931, she alleged that "the government had started committing such tyrannies that we can't find any peace."[97] In another speech she observed that the government only listens to the police and gives punishment to innocent people.[98] She condemned the death sentence passed on Ranbir Singh, Durga Das and Chuni Lal, in connection with the conspiracy to shoot the Governor.[99]

Laxmi Devi was convicted for her activities and was asked to pay two thousand rupees or undergo imprisonment for one year. She preferred to go to Jail.[100]

Madras

In Madras Smt. Rukmini Lakshmapati[101] had the honour of being the first lady to be arrested in connection with the Salt Satyagraha. She was the President of the Tamil Nadu Provincial Congress Committee.

The women of Madras played a prominent part in organising youngsters into the "Vanar Sena"[102] or the Monkey Army, as it was called in the memory of the monkeys who according to the Hindu mythology, joined together to assist Rama. The dynamic energy of these youngsters was thus utilised into systematic and disciplined activity.

Durgabai Deshmukh

Another famous woman of this time was Mrs. Durgabai Deshmukh who became the war dictator in the city of Madras and carried on the movement sponsored by the Congress till she was arrested.

Durgabai was born in 1910 in a village near Rajamundry, Andhra Pradesh. She was married at the age of eight into a conservative family. Durgabai became a widow at an early age. "Durgabai was not an ordinary child. She was the daughter of liberty, the nursing of not just her cultured parents but of the peerless, powerful sea, the intrepid winds, the master of her own thoughts. In the midst of limitations she never faltered, freedom and light were stored in her heart, and when the time came these became her inspiration and strength."[103]

Her interest in politics can be traced back to the year 1921 when she was merely a child. It was during this year when the Non-Cooperation Movement was at its height that she, along with her mother, went around the town selling Khaddar.

Durgabai was well versed in Hindi, a knowledge which came in very handy at the time of the Kakinada Session of the Indian National Congress 1923. She had trained nearly six hundred volunteers who were to work for this session in this language. Her interest in politics was further accentuated after meeting Gandhiji at this session. She participated in processions and prepared salt openly during the 1930-31 movement. Later she was nominated as the second War Dictator after Sri Prakasham. She was arrested for her activities on May 25, 1930, at Arcot and was sentenced to nine months imprisonment.[104]

Durgabai joined the Hindustan Seva Dal and was again arrested for her political work. This time she was sentenced to three years imprisonment.[105] While in jail she took up the study of English. After her release she wanted to join the men's college of the Andhra University to study Political Science as a subject. She was refused admission on the plea that there was no hostel arrangement for the girls. As a challenge to the authorities she started a hostel for women. She took up her Master's degree in Political Science and a Bachelor's in Law as well.

The year 1942 saw her as a practising lawyer and she was the first woman to appear and argue in a murder case. In 1946, while a practising lawyer, she became a member of the Constituent Assembly and later a member of the provisional Parliament.

Durgabai was taken as a member of the Planning Commission. She went to China which further widened her horizon. She married C.D. Deshmukh, then Union Minister, in 1953.

Women's cause remained dear to Durgabai Deshmukh. She started the Central Social Welfare Board and was its chairman from 1953 to 1963.[106]

DELHI

It was in this great city that twenty-four girl guides refused to salute the Union Jack as a result of which their names were struck off the rolls.[107]

Mary Campbell, who was a temperance worker in India, writing in the *Manchester Guardian* of June 1931, described the courage of Delhi women in the following words: "I was in Delhi when Mr. Gandhi, on his way back to jail, sent word—'I leave the work of picketing and drink and drug shops to the women of India.' I thought he had made a mistake this time that the Delhi women, so many of whom lived in purdah, could never undertake the task. But to my astonishment, out they came, and they picketed all the shops in Delhi, sixteen or seventeen in number. I watched them day after day. They stood there saying nothing but politely *salaaming* each customer who approached. The same thing happened repeatedly. The man would stop and say: 'I beg your pardon, sister. I forgot myself in coming here' and go away. That went on for some days until the licensees appealed to the Government. The hefty policemen arrived with police vans and warned the women to go away. I thought those delicate sheltered women would give in now; they would never endure being touched by a policemen. But they did, and as fast as one relay was arrested, another took its place. Altogether about sixteen hundred women were imprisoned in Delhi alone. But they had done their work. Though the shops were opened no one went in.... At last the licensees themselves closed them, and so far as I know they are still closed today."[108]

It was again in this historic city that a thousand women went to the court with a view to persuading the lawyers and the authorities to close down the courts. Mrs. Sahni and the mother-in-law of Pandit Jawaharlal Nehru were amongst the injured on that day. Pandit Motilal Nehru who witnessed the scene, wrote that the police officer declared the assembly unlawful. When he was asked for an order to this effect, he had none. There was no magistrate accompanying him. He threatened to open fire, if the crowd did not disperse. In the meantime five armoured cars reached the scene. The ladies refused to leave the place unless the police was withdrawn and they were allowed to return in procession. The police later withdrew to the farthest end of the courtyard and left the road free when the ladies and others marched back to the city.[109]

Satyawati

The great city of Delhi also witnessed a martyr's death. Satyawati, granddaughter of Swami Shradhanand, was another important leader of this movement in Delhi. She was a revolutionary. In defiance of social taboos, at the age of twenty-three she plunged into the Congress movement, heart and soul, in 1930. She held meetings, led processions, picketed foreign cloth shops not only in the market place but also on the river Jamuna where usually the Marwari ladies in their foreign clothes came to bathe.[110] As a result of her efforts some fifty per cent of women took to wearing Khaddar.

Speaking at a public meeting on May 3, 1930, Satyawati exhorted the audience to remain steadfast in their endeavour and boldly face the machine-guns parading the streets. On May 12, 1930, at the mourning procession of Ami Lal, who died of a gun shot, she pointed out "such things do happen in attaining freedom and that flames of such fire would reduce the tyrant to ashes."[111] She was arrested under Section 108 of the Indian Penal Code (to furnish security to cease dissemination) and was asked to furnish security of five hundred rupees or show good behaviour for six months. She refused to furnish the security and was sent to jail.

At her trial in Delhi, Satyawati remarked: "We have abandoned our homes and children to redeem our motherland from foreign bondage, and neither the threat of the dungeons nor of bullets and the merciless beatings can deter us from the duty which we owe to ourselves and the coming generation. I and thousands of my sisters are ready to suffer, but we must win India's freedom."[112] She was sentenced to six months imprisonment. In a parting message to the nation she said: "So long as there was even a single child she would not let the government rest, nor would she rest herself."[113] She was released only to be arrested again in 1932. This time she was sentenced to two years imprisonment. During her incarceration she contacted pleurisy which later developed into tuberculosis. This did not deter her and she continued political work.

Satyawati was again active in 1937 in anti-government activities. Consequently she was arrested. She was assaulted by the police. This question came up before the Assembly resulting in a successful adjournment motion. Satyawati was asked to execute a bond for good behaviour, but on her refusal she was sentenced to one month's imprisonment which was later reduced.[114] The moment Satyawati was out of the lockup she was again active. She attended the Punjab Political Conference held in April 1938. She was ordered to leave Punjab within twenty-four hours, and her entry into the Punjab without permission was prohibited for one year. She defied the order and was arrested.

During the years 1940 and 1941 Satyawati was tried twice for sedition and imprisoned. She had hardly been released when she was arrested again in August 1942, and detained as a security prisoner until her condition became so serious that the doctors gave up all hope of her life. She was released but was directed by the authorities not to enter Delhi. She naturally refused to obey such an order and even Gandhiji supported her in this matter. She defied the order and was arrested. She was later released and the case against her was withdrawn.[115]

Satyawati was admitted to the hospital. Just two days before her death in 1945, Pandit Jawaharlal Nehru went to see her. She said to him: "My only desire is India's freedom."[116]

UTTAR PRADESH

In Allahabad Swaroop Rani, wife of Motilal Nehru, inaugurated the campaign by preparing salt in front of the police station. It was in this place that the police lathi-charged a procession led by her as a result of which Swaroop Rani got a blow on her head and fainted.[117]

The spirit of patriotism was ingrained in the Nehru family. There was a time when all the members of the family found themselves in jail. In fact the jail had become a second home to several of them. Pandit Jawaharlal Nehru, writing about the activities of his wife and sister, makes a mention of the part played by them in this struggle. He writes: "Salt suddenly became a mysterious word, a word of power. Long before the movement began volunteers were being given the necessary training. Krishna[118] and Kamla[119] had joined the ranks of the volunteers. The volunteers, of course, were unarmed, the idea was to make them more efficient in their work and capable of dealing with large crowds. Krishna Nehru along with Shyam Kumari Nehru were arrested for taking out a procession. They were fined fifty rupees or in lieu of it to undergo one month's simple imprisonment. The fine was paid by some unknown person and they were released the next day."[120]

Kamala Nehru went about like a whirlwind, organising women volunteers, peasants and the students. She played a prominent part in organising No-Tax campaign in the province. Presiding over the U.P. Women's Political Conference she made a fervent appeal to women to prepare for the forthcoming struggle and asked them to use Khaddar.[121] Kamala became the dictator of the war council and the acting President of the Congress Working Committee.[122] She was, however, arrested on January 1, 1931. As she was arrested, a pressman asked her for a message. She said: "I am happy beyond measure and proud to follow in the footsteps of my husband. I hope the people will keep the flag flying."[123]

Another woman who was active in this period was Mrs. Mukund Malviya, daughter-in-law of Pandit Madanmohan Malviya. An attempt to hold the District Conference at Allahabad proved a failure. The police guarded all the public places to prevent any meeting. Mrs. Mukund Malviya came forward to defy the authorities and to hold the meeting near the Clock Tower in the city of Allahabad. She was arrested and sentenced to one year's rigorous imprisonment.[124]

Chandravati Lakhanpal[125] played a prominent part in this struggle. Her interest in politics dates back from her student days. She took an active part in the movement of 1930. Chandravati went from village to village organising villagers to make them politically conscious till she was arrested in 1932 and sentenced to one year's imprisonment.[126]

Uma Nehru,[127] who had been interested in the uplift of women for many years, now came forward to take her place in the Satyagraha Army. She became Dictator of the Provincial Congress Committee and as a result suffered imprisonment. Later she went to jail several times.

Margaret Cousins

Any account of this period would remain incomplete without mentioning Margaret Cousins.[128] She played a significant role in the general awakening of the masses more especially the women.

Mrs. Cousins came to India in 1915 and joined Mrs. Annie Besant at Adyar (Madras). Her interest in this country, to begin with, was mainly in the sphere of education. Later she joined the Home Rule Agitation of Annie Besant and contributed to this demand.

Margaret Cousins and her husband were the progenitors of the idea of 'Vote for Women' in 1917. Montagu was expected in India at the close of the year and she wanted to take this opportunity to put this demand before the Secretary of State. Margaret, therefore, set about organising a deputation. Rani Lakshmi Bai Rajwade said: "The official leader of the delegation was, of course, Mrs. Sarojini Naidu. But the unofficial ones were Annie Besant and Margaret Cousins. In fact, if I mistake not, the idea of such a deputation had really originated with

Cousins, herself an ardent suffragist—and always a champion of women's cause anywhere in the world."[129]

It was easier for Margaret Cousins to organise the women for this purpose with the rich experience she had of this work. In fact, the years between 1910 and 1913 were fateful for her. She founded the Irish Women's League and joined the agitation for votes for women under this league and had to suffer imprisonment in connection with this movement.

Margaret was instrumental in starting the Women's India Association and was one of the Joint Secretaries. She edited the monthly journal of the organisation *Stri Dharma* for many years. At one time there were forty branches of the Women's India Association spread over the country. She visited these branches and guided the workers.[130]

From the year 1921, whenever the question of franchise for women was taken up in the Legislature of the various provinces, she always made it a point to be present to organise either a women's deputation or canvass support for such a motion.

Margaret Cousins set up another organisation in 1927 called the All India Women's Conference.[131] In the 1930 Civil Disobedience Movement when women were forbidden to take part in it, she at once wrote to Gandhiji and also wrote in the *Stri Dharma* pointing out that it was an injustice to women. Margaret Cousins left India in 1932 for America where she organised and spoke at several protest meetings held against the imprisonment of Mahatma Gandhi, Kasturba Gandhi and Sarojini Naidu. She came back to India in October 1932. She made a public protest against the prevailing official ordinance. She addressed several meetings as a result of which she was prosecuted on December 10, 1932, and was sentenced to one year's imprisonment.[132]

Margaret Cousins gave an interesting statement at her trial. She said: "The fact that I am in this court today is no accident. It is the result of seventeen years of intimate living and working with my Indian sisters and brothers. In moving freely with them, in attempting to do constructive work I and my husband learned how exploitation and injustice through foreign rule is crushing them down."[133]

In prison Margaret Cousins used to sing with other prisoners Mrs. Besant's song—"God save our motherland" instead of "God save the King."[134]

Influenced by Gandhiji, Margaret Cousins joined in the work being done among the backward classes, visiting scavengers' and smiths' settlements at Kotagiri.[135] She continued her work for the Harijans in Madras till she became sick in 1943.[136]

The part so courageously played by women in the struggle for freedom attracted attention and was appreciated not only within the country but outside as well. Writing in the *Asiatic Review*, Mrs. Gray observed: "If the women are to be judged by deeds rather than by words it is within the Congress that they have shown the greatest courage....They have picketed, walked in processions, gone to prison and thus have proved their courage in many a dangerous riot."[137]

Desh Sevikas or Storm Troops amongst Congress women were in the forefront of the movement. They were first enrolled in 1930 and constituted a band of volunteers prepared to do active work. Some fifty of them went to prison during the first year. Most of these ladies had never left their homes until the call of Gandhiji came to them. "They had first to learn the courage necessary to be seen abroad in the streets. Presently, they learned to walk long distances, to stand in the sun all day, to picket cloth and toddy shops, to hurry to danger points when summoned by the Congress, or the police, to remove stones, pipes and other obstacles placed in the middle of the road to obstruct traffic, even to shed their fear at night and of hooligan crowds."[138]

In addition to these active Desh Sevikas who courted arrests, thousands more joined in processions, flag salutations and hartals, cooked and nursed in the Congress hospitals, and sold Khaddar. Many of these women gave up their life of ease and comfort to suffer imprisonment and picket shops and went from town to town engaged in needful propaganda and unmindful of the heat or cold.[139]

Margaret Cousins writing under the caption 'Towards Progress and Freedom' remarked: "The response to the call of Mahatma Gandhi was magnificent. Within the next three years over five thousand women had served terms of severe imprisonment, they had suffered lathi charges, loss of property, loss of livelihood from ill health, loss of caste, loss of reputation. They willingly faced publicity of the most trying kind in picketing drink shops and foreign cloth shops, in walking in public processions, in proceedings in law courts. They sacrificed all kinds of cherished privileges of caste, ceremonial purity and privacy."[140]

The police had adopted all sorts of ways in dealing with women. The Provincial Congress Committee reported off and on the ill treatment these women received. It was reported from Andhra that "the police seems to be mean enough not to spare women even from their undignified behaviour." The report describes nine cases of ill-treatment.[141] While in Karnataka in Siddarpur Taluka "they were dragged along the road, beaten with lathis and canes and even whipped. Their sarees were pulled and torn and they were abused in the foulest language."[142]

The Kerala authorities had adopted a novel way of punishing the ladies. They were taken by night trains to distant places and left uncared for at midnight at wayside stations. Fifty or sixty-days'-old babies were often separated from their mothers.[143] The darkest part of the repression was the treatment meted out to the female Satyagrahis. "There appears to be a general lack of the sense of respect for women in all provincial governments. Abuses, beatings of women and even raping have been calmly allowed to be practised."[144]

This repression, however, did not worry the women and they remained unyielding and constant to the stand they had taken. Thus, women showed that gaining freedom of the country was not only the responsibility of men and that when entrusted with a responsibility they were able to steer through as successfully as men. This added strength to the movement. During the Civil Disobedience Movement of 1930-31 twenty thousand women were imprisoned. In other words for every six persons who courted arrest, there was one woman."[145]

This period of five years has been taken up for consideration because the movement which started in 1930 continued till April 1934. It was one long continuous struggle except for a brief period when Gandhiji was attending the Second Round Table Conference in London in 1931. During this period the Simon Commission's report was also published; but it did not satisfy the aspirations of the people. Even this report had recognised the strength of the women. It says: "No document discussing India's constitutional system and the directions in which it can be developed and improved could omit the women of India today."[146]

The period also witnessed three Round Table Conferences convened by the British Cabinet to reconcile different shades of opinion in the political field of India with a view to giving a new constitution to this country. Finally, the British Parliament passed the Government of India Act 1935, thereby giving a new Constitution to India.

Notes and References

1. *Congress Bulletin*, January 9, 1930.
2. The programme was embodied in the following seven points:
    (i) All-India Satyagraha at Dharasana Salt Works and technical breaches of salt elsewhere.
    (ii) Appeals to government servants, students and lawyers to make sacrifices.
    (iii) Intensive boycott of foreign cloth.
    (iv) Initiation of campaign for non-payment of land revenues and taxes in certain provinces and areas.
    (v) Breaches of forest laws.
    (vi) Boycott of British goods and British banking, insurance, shipping and other institutions.
    (vii) Boycott of liquor shops.
3. *Stri Dharma*, Vol. 13, December 1929 to October 1930, p. 247.
4. *Congress Bulletin*, May 30, 1930, p. 4.
5. *Amrita Bazar Patrika*, April 10, 1930; Nehru, J., *An Autobiography*, p. 334.
6. *Stri Dharma*, Vol. 13, October to December 1930, pp. 336-384.
7. *Hindoo Patriot*, March 8, 1909.
8. *Indian Ladies Magazine*, Vol. VIII, 1908-1909, p. 262.
9. *Modern Review*, Vol. 39, January-June 1926, p. 104.
10. She seems to have been greatly influenced by Gokhale to take up political work. Naidu describes herself how one evening he spoke to her. He said, "Stand here with me, with the stars and hills for witness, and in their presence consecrate your life and your talent, your song and your speech, your thought and your dream to the motherland. O'poet, see visions from the hill tops and spread abroad the message of hope to the toilers in the valleys." (*Modern Review*, Vol. 39, Jan-June 1926, p. 104).
11. G.A. Natesan & Co., Madras, *Speeches and Writings of Sarojini Naidu*, p. XVII.
12. *Modern Review*, Vol. 27, January-June 1929, p. 45
13. *Amrita Bazar Patrika*, April 4, 1919.
14. For correspondence see Appendix G.
15. In a letter to Gandhiji she wrote: "I am in a very bad health. But the twin question of the Punjab and the Khilafat absorb all my energies and emotions. But it is in vain to expect justice from a race so blind and drunk with the arrogance of power, the bitter prejudice of race and creed and colour, and betraying such an abysmal ignorance of Indian conditions, opinions, sentiments and aspirations. The debate on the Punjab in the House of Commons last week shattered the last remnant of my hope and faith in British justice and goodwill toward the new

vision of India. The discussion in the house was lamentable and indeed tragic. Our friends revealed their ignorance, our enemies their insolence, and the combination is appalling and heart-breaking."

In another letter she wrote: "The specialists think that my heart disease is in an an advanced and dangerous state but I cannot rest till I stir the heart of the world to repentance over the tragedy of martyred India." (G.A. Natesan & Co. Madras, *Speeches and Writings of Sarojini Naidu*, pp. xxi-xxii).

16. *Modern Review*, July to December 1920, Vol. 28, p. 342.

17. Moving a resolution in the 38th session of the Congress she exclaimed: "Here are we with you in that independent commonwealth of common human responsibilities, in which united India dares to be one with you—not isolated, not ringed round, not separated by that refuge of the weak called independence, but without partition, without walls, without barriers but on a common ground of endeavour sharing the common heritage of a common dream realised by a common constitution by the progress of humanity." (*Proceedings of the Indian National Congress*, 38th Session, 1923, p. 134).

18. G.A. Natesan & Co., Madras, *Speeches and Writings of Sarojini Naidu*, p. XIII.

19. *The Indian Review*, Vol. XXIV, January-December 1923, p. 322.

20. Akalis were an enlightened section of the Sikh community who worked to bring reforms in their places of worship. The Sikh places of worship had fallen under the hands of disreputed Mahants (preachers) who refused to abdicate them. The Government sided with the Mahants as a result of which the Akalis started an active movement.

21. The resolution reads: "This Congress declares that the attack made by the Government on the Shiromani Gurdwara Prabandhak Committee and the Akali Dal is a direct challenge to the rights of free Associations of all India, for non-violent activities and being convinced that the blow is aimed at all movements for freedom, resolves to stand by the Sikhs and calls upon Hindus, Musalmans, Christians, Parsees and all people of India to render all possible assistance with men and money." (*Report on the Indian National Congress Session*, 1923-24, p. 174).

22. *Report on the Indian National Congress Session*, 1923-24, p. 174

23. G.A. Natesan & Co., Madras, *Speeches and Writings of Sarojini Naidu*, p. XXIV.

24. *Congress Presidential Address from 1911 to 1934*, Madras, p. 772.

25. *Congress Presidential Address*, op. cit., p. 774.

26. Sitaramayya, Dr. Pattabhi, op. cit., p. 290.

27. *Times of India*, November 29, 1929

28. *Times of India*, January 1, 1930.

29. Mittra, N.N., *Annual Register*, Vol. II, 1929, p. 401.

30. Dharasana Salt Works are about 150 miles north of Bombay.

31. *Times of India*, Bombay, May 8, 1930.
32. Webb Miller, 'I Found No Peace', pp. 190-196; quoted in Jack A. Homer, *The Gandhi Reader*, Bloomington, 1956, p. 249.
33. ibid., p. 252.
34. ibid.
35. *Amrita Bazar Patrika*, May 22, 1930.
36. Gandhi-Irwin Pact whereby the Civil Disobedience Movement was suspended by the Congress and the Government agreed to release the prisoners.
37. *Advance*, April 6, 1932.
38. ibid., April 21, 1932.
39. ibid., April 23, 1932.
40. *Stri Dharma*, Vol. 12, November 1928 to November 1929, p. 565.
41. *Annual Register*, Vol II, 1929, p. 401.
42. *Advance*, May 19, 1930.
43. Kamala Devi described the raid which was planned by her: "A similar raid (referring to Dharasana Salt Works) was planned on the salt fields in the precincts of Bombay city. It fell to me to plan it, but unlike Dharasana, where only a small group was entrusted with the task of the raid, here I visualized a mass raid embracing a large part of the city two million population. I was sure that no force, not even machine-guns, could stop this raid. On the eve of the raid I was arrested but my parting message to my colleagues and the vast populace was to execute this plan. I was represented by my son of seven who proudly carried the banner and engaged in the drama of this first battle." (Publications Division, Delhi, *Women in India*, p. 21).
44. *Stri Dharma*, Vol. 12. Nov. 1928 to Nov. 1929, p. 565.
45. *Amrita Bazar Patrika*, May 17, 1930.
46. *Amrita Bazar Patrika*, November 19, 1931.
47. *Advance*, November 5, 1931.
48. For details of the treatment accorded to women see Appendix H.
49. *Times of India*, March 24, 1930.
50. ibid., May 2, 1930.
51. *Amrita Bazar Patrika*, May 2, 1930.
52. *Annual Report of Police Administration*, Bombay, 1932, p. XI.
53. Smt. Hem Nalini was hit on the head by a lathi while attending a meeting. Samiti and Suniti and Kalyani Das were sentenced to transportation for life.
54. *Amrita Bazar Patrika*, January 5, 1932, p. 5.
55. *Modern Review*, 1930 (Article by J.C. Bagal), Vol. 94, p. 56.
56. *Amrita Bazar Patrika*, May 14, 1931.
57. ibid., May 14, 1931.
58. ibid., April 29, 1931.
59. ibid., April 2, 1931.

60. Dutta, K., *Chittagong Armoury Raiders Reminiscences*, p. 41.
61. ibid.
62. ibid.
63. ibid., p. 51.
64. Kalpana Dutta came in contact with the revolutionaries in 1929 but did not accept their creed till 1931. Preetilata came into the fold to this group in 1932.
65. Dutta, K., *Chittagong Armoury Raiders Reminiscences*, p. 41; *Annual Register*, Vol. II, 1932, p. 10.
66. This Section is applied only in case of those who conceal their identity for immoral purposes.
67. Dutta, K., *Chittagong Armoury Raiders Reminiscences*, p. 41.
68. *Annual Report of the Administration of Bengal*, 1932-33, p. 20.
69. *Amrita Bazar Patrika*, January 20, 1932.
70. *Modern Review*, 1953, Vol. 94, p. 57.
71. She was the daughter of a Government pensioner, the former Headmaster of Sanskrit Collegiate School, Calcutta.
72. *Annual Report of the Police Administration of the Town of Calcutta and Its Suburbs*, 1932, p. 11.
73. *Amrita Bazar Patrika*, February 16, 1932.
74. *Annual Register*, Volume I, Jan-June 1932, p. 11.
75. *Modern Review*, Vol. 51, Jan-June, p. 344.
76. *Annual Report of Police Administration*, op. cit., 1933, p. 16.
77. ibid., pp. 16-20.
    Modern Review, 1953, Vol. 94, p. 57.
78. *Amrita Bazar Patrika*, July 11, 1930.
79. ibid., August 19, 1930.
80. ibid., July 16, 1930.
81. ibid.
82. ibid., September 2, 1930.
83. ibid.
84. ibid.
85. *Annual Register*, Vol. I, Jan-June, 1932, p. 22.
86. Two daughters of Lado Rani Zutshi.
87. *Amrita Bazar Patrika*, October 10, 1930.
88. ibid.
89. Papers obtained from Manmohini Sehgal.
90. *Times of India*, Bombay, February 5, 1930.
91. He was the 2nd President of India.
92. Papers obtained from Manmohini Sehgal.
93. Papers in possession of Manmohini Sehgal.
94. ibid.
95. This Council was started in 1925.
96. *Amrita Bazar Patrika*, October 15, 1930.

97.   ibid.
98.   ibid.
99.   ibid.
100. ibid.
101. Rukmini Lakshmipati was born in 1892. She graduated from Madras University and was associated with all the activities of Women's India Association. She was the Secretary of the All India Women's Conference (local branch). She was elected as Municipal Councillor and also served as a Health Minister of Madras Government for 1946-47.
102. The Vanar Sena was originally started in Bombay by Shri Johri from among the Bombay Youth League leaders, and was later taken up by the All-India Youth League leaders, over the whole country. Active women participants were Kisan Dhumatkar in Bombay. Rameswaramma in Madras, Vidya Killewala and Mrs. Kamala Devi in Bombay, while at the tender age of 12, Indira Gandhi, daughter of Pandit Jawaharlal Nehru organised six thousand children in Allahabad. (Publications Division, New Delhi. *Women in India*, p. 21)
103. *Illustrated Weekly of India*, January 27, 1957, p. 39.
104. *Amrita Bazar Patrika*, May 27, 1930.
105. *Social Welfare*, Delhi, 1959, p. 5.
106. She resigned from the Board in 1963.
107. *Amrita Bazar Patrika*, March 11, 1930.
108. Zacharia, H.C.E., *Renascent India*, pp. 263-264.
109. *Annual Register*, January-June 1930, Vol. I, pp. 150-51.
110. *Amrita Bazar Patrika*, June 4, 1930.
111. ibid., May 29, 1930.
112. Brockway, A.F., *Indian Crisis*, London, p. 163.
113. *Amrita Bazar Patrika*, May 27, 1930.
114. *Congress Bulletin*, May 13, 1937.
115. *Modern Review*, Vol. 78, July to December 1945, p. 260
116. ibid.
117. *Amrita Bazar Patrika*, April 10, 1932.
118. She was the sister of Pandit Jawaharlal Nehru.
119. Wife of Pandit Jawaharlal Nehru.
120. Nehru, Jawaharlal, *An Autobiography*, p. 210
121. *Amrita Bazar Patrika*, November 5, 1931.
122. *Advance*, November 4, 1931.
123. Nehru. J., op. cit., p. 334.
124. *Annual Register*, Vol. I, January to June, 1932, p. 24.
125. She is the daughter of Pandit Jainarain Shukla. She was born in 1904 and received her education at Allahabad and Banaras. She is at present a member of the Council of States.
126. *Women on the March*, December 1957, p. 22.

127. She is the daughter of Pandit Niranjan Nath Huku and was born in Agra in 1884. She was educated in St. Mary's convent at Hubli (Karnataka). She was married to Pandit Shamlal Nehru in 1901. She was a member of the Lok Sabha and was associated with many a woman's organisations and educational institutions.

128. She was born on November 7, 1878 at Boyle (Ireland). She passed her Matric in the Deny Boarding School and specialised in the study of Bachelor of Music Degree of the Royal University at Ireland. She married Dr. Cousins, and joined him in India in 1915.

129. Women's India Association, Madras, *Mrs. Margaret Cousins and Her Work in India*, (A tribute) to Mrs. M.E. Cousins by Rani Lakshmi Bai Rajwade, p. 1.

130. *Modern Review*, Vol. 95, p. 306.

131. ibid.

132. ibid.

133. *Stri Dharma*, Vol. 16, 1932-33, p. 127.

134. *Modern Review*, Vol. 95, p. 306.

135. Ootacamund (Madras).

136. Margaret Cousins died in the year 1954 at Ootacamund.

137. *Asiatic Review*, Vol. XXVIII, 1932, p. 565.

138. ibid.

139. ibid.

140. Chattopadhyaya, K., *The Awakening of Indian Womanhood*, p. 56.

141. *Congress Bulletin*, October 15, 1932, p. 3.

142. ibid., p. 25.

143. ibid., p. 27.

144. *Special Bulletin* issued by the All-India Congress Committee, March 15, 1933, p. 1.

145. Morton, E., *The Women in Gandhi's Life*, p. 182.

146. *Indian Statutory Commission*. Vol. I. p. 49.

9

WOMEN ADMINISTRATORS: 1935-1939

When it comes to the details of administration and the applying of principles to practice, you will constantly find that a woman's brain has a mastery of administrative details which makes her most valuable where organisation is concerned...in all places where the poor are gathered together and where the young have to be thought of. There it has been found that women's genius for detail is invaluable in the question of administration. It is found that she will look into details that never strike the mind of man.

—Annie Basant[1]

It was the inauguration of provincial autonomy under the Act of 1935 that gave Indian women an opportunity to be elected to the State Legislatures and also act as administrators. This Act no doubt was the result of long deliberations over a number of years. It was based on various recommendations of different bodies, such as the three Round Table Conferences, the Joint Select Committee Report, the Lothian Committee Report,[2] etc.

In its first part the Act had envisaged a federal form of Government at the Centre; but this part never came into operation as it was stoutly opposed by almost all the political parties of the country.

The second part relating to provincial autonomy was gone through and under it elections took place for the Legislative Assemblies of the different provinces. As a result of these elections Congress came to have an absolute majority in seven out of eleven provinces and in two it came out as the single majority party. But the Congress agreed to assume responsibility for running the administration in the provinces only after it had successfully secured an assurance from the Governor-General that Governors would not interfere in the day-to-day administration of the ministers and that they would make use of their special powers and discretionary authority only in exceptional cases. The assumption of this responsibility gave Indian women a chance to become administrators.

In the elections of 1937, eight women were elected from the general constituencies and forty-two from the reserved constituencies. Five were also nominated to the Upper House. When the ministries were formed, six women took office, one as minister and the others as deputy speakers and parliamentary secretaries.[3]

No doubt, Anasuyabai Kale (Madhya Pradesh), Sippi Milani (Sind) and Khudsia Rasul (Uttar Pradesh) came to occupy the positions of Deputy Speakers, and Mrs. Hansa Mehta (Bombay) and Begum Shah Nawaz (Punjab) as Parliamentary Secretaries, in the Legislative Assemblies of these provinces, but in the field of actual administration the credit goes to Vijayalakshmi Pandit.

Vijayalakshmi Pandit

Vijayalakshmi Pandit who suffered privations and hardships in the struggle for freedom, was born on August 18, 1900. She is the daughter of Motilal Nehru, a leading lawyer of Allahabad, who became one of the prominent national leaders. Both her father, and mother Swaroop Rani Nehru, were ardent supporters of the national cause. In fact, it would be right to say that the young and old in this family held the cause of the country dear to their heart.

Vijayalakshmi had her education at home. At the age of fifteen, she, for the first time, attended the Congress Session at Bombay in the company of her parents. She witnessed her father presiding over the Congress Session of 1919 at Amritsar.[4]

Vijayalakshmi's political interests were further accentuated when she was married to Ranjit Pandit, Bar-at-Law, on May 9, 1921. He was one of the followers of Gandhiji. She attended the Congress of 1929 at Lahore which was presided over by her brother Pandit Jawaharlal Nehru. She was a witness to the passing of a resolution whereby the goal of the Congress was changed from Dominion Status to complete Independence.

Vijayalakshmi took active part in the Civil Disobedience Movement of 1930 and 1931-32. She delivered lectures, and led processions. A notice was served on her prohibiting her from taking any part in the movement. Unaffected by the threat she continued her activities. She was arrested on January 27, 1932 and was sentenced to one year's imprisonment. She was elected to the Allahabad Municipal Committee in 1935 and was elected the same year as Chairman of the Education Committee.[5] She also served as Vice-President of the Women's League for Peace and Freedom.

Vijayalakshmi Pandit contested elections in 1936 from Kanpur.[6] She was elected and appointed Minister for Local Self-Government in the Uttar Pradesh Cabinet, on July 29, 1937.[7] As a Minister Vijayalakshmi took a keen interest in the health and educational services and tried her best to make these facilities available to the wider public.

These ministries were however shortlived and the ministers had to resign in 1939 as a protest against the Government's war policy.

In 1940, Gandhiji started an individual Satyagraha and allowed only a chosen band of workers to participate in it. Vijayalakshmi was one such privileged person. She was arrested, but was released after four months' imprisonment.[8]

Not long after the Congress launched the Quit-India movement. Vijayalakshmi became active and went about kindling the fire of freedom in the hearts of thousands of people.[9] She was arrested, tried and imprisoned in 1942. She was released in 1943. She went to America and addressed a number of meetings upholding the cause of her country.[10] She condemned fascism and upheld the ideals of democracy. She criticised the British Government for its failure to tackle the outbreak of famine in Bengal. She courageously criticised President Roosevelt for not supporting India in her national struggle. Her speeches were widely reported in England. Amery described her statement that "India was a vast concentration camp" as fantastic. She challenged Amery to disprove it. She also exhorted the English to lay down the "white man's burden which they had borne long enough."[11]

Addressing a meeting of the Council of World Affairs at New York, Vijayalakshmi said that India was a major stumbling block in the path of world peace and asked how the democracies fighting for the preservation of democracy could suppress India's four hundred million people. In a nation-wide broadcast from New York, she asserted that Asia would be the testing ground for all the theories advanced on behalf of the proposed United Nations. She further added that the continuation of colonial empire would be a constant danger to world peace and progress of humanity.[12]

Vijayalakshmi was in America for the San Francisco Conference held in May 1945 to work on the United Nations Charter. The official representatives were Ramaswami Mudaliar and Feroze Khan Noon. She was not invited to attend the conference, but she made herself available to give information to the delegates and the press when the Pacific Colonial Policy came under discussion.[13] In an interview to the United Press of America she assailed the British, Dutch and French insistence on keeping the subjected people of Asia and Africa under the Trusteeship.[14]

Vijayalakshmi appealed to the United States not to allow American traditional position and vast prestige to be tarnished by conceding European imperialistic demands.

The *mangum opus* of the period, May 1945, was the comprehensive memorandum presented by her as the mouthpiece of the American India League to the San Francisco Conference in which she spoke not only for India, but for the six hundred million people of India and South East Asia. She said that India was the test case for the conference; that Fascism and Nazism having been formerly liquidated, only imperialism remained.[15]

On May 18, 1945, Vijayalakshmi sent a cable to British Labour Party Conference in Lancashire. She appealed to the labour leaders to help India to get independence. She said: "The Indian people have already lost confidence in the present British Government and if existing conditions continued they will also lose faith in the British nation. British labour can help to save the situation if true to its own ideal of democracy, it takes steps to end the deadlock by releasing untried political prisoners."[16]

Addressing the California Legislature in 1945 Vijayalakshmi called for the sympathy for India's campaign for independence. She said: "So long as the colonial vested interests remain, there can be no peace, there can be no security. And so long as there is no security or peace, we shall go on destroying all that generations and centuries of human efforts have built up. I believe these ties will work for common good between people of the world who are going to build up the world structure."[17] Vijayalakshmi further asserted: "I would like you in America to understand how vital it is for the future of the world that problems are approached in terms of realism. This independence which is something so dear to you which you have fought to preserve is something those, who have not yet achieved it, value even more dearly than you who now possess it."[18]

Vijayalakshmi was returned unopposed to the Uttar Pradesh Legislative Assembly from the special women's constituency, Kanpur district[19] (North-West). She became a Minister for the Local Self-Government and Health Department in the Uttar Pradesh Cabinet during 1946-47.

Vijayalakshmi Pandit had the distinction of leading her country's delegation to the United Nations Assembly in 1946-1948. She was the first Indian woman to be elected as President of the United Nations Assembly in the year 1953. She had the honour of being the first woman to represent her country in two important world capitals — Moscow and Washington. She was also India's High Commissioner in London, and the Indian Ambassador to Ireland and Spain.

Notes and References

1. Women's India Association, Madras, *Women's Work in Madras, Reminiscences*, p. 2.
2. The Lothian Committee was constituted in 1932 to look into the possibilities of enlarging the scope of franchise.
3. *Roshni* (Journal published by the All India Women's Conference, Delhi), April 1935, p. 10.
4. Sengupta, Padmini, *Pioneer Women of India*, p. 155.
5. ibid.
6. Pandit, Vijayalaksmi, *So I Became a Minister*, Allahabad, 1939, p. 141.
7. Bright J.S., *The Great Nehrus*, p. 269.
8. Sengupta, Padmini, *Pioneer Women of India*, p. 156.
9. Bright, J.S., *The Great Nehrus*, p. 280.
10. Addressing a meeting at New York on 9 January 1945 she said thus: "Whatever differences may exist between the various races of India, they cannot be ironed out so long as the British dominate the country." (*Annual Register*, Vol I, 1945, p. 30).
11. Sitaramayya, Dr. P., *History of the Indian National Congress*, Vol. II, p. 643.
12. *Annual Register*, Vol, I, 1945, p. 47.

13.   She said: "I speak here for my country because its national voice has
      been stilled by British duress. I also speak for those countries which
      are under the heels of alien militarists and cannot speak for
      themselves. I speak in particular for Burma, Malaya, Indo-China and
      Dutch East Indies, all bound to my own country by the closest ties of
      historic and cultural kinship and which cherish aspirations to national
      freedom like our own. Liberation from Japan should mean for them, I
      submit liberation from all alien imperialists, so far as this conference is
      concerned." (*Roshini*, December, 1953, pp. 5-6).
14.   Sitaramayya, Dr. P., *History of the Indian National Congress*, Vol, II,
      p. 643.
15.   Annual Register, Vol. I, 1945, p. 66.
16.   ibid., p. 63.
17.   Khan, Abdul Majid, *The Great Daughter of India,* Lahore, p. 217.
18.   ibid., p. 219.
19.   *The Tribune*, February 8, 1946.

10

THE LAST PHASE: 1940-1947

There was no power in the world that could set any limitation to women's achievements. There was no Salic Law which would hold good in the world when women were determined that they would rise to the full height and stature of their capacity.

—*Sarojini Naidu*[1]

Political Conditions of the Period

The year 1939 witnessed the beginning of the Second World War in Europe. England declared war on the German Reich on September 3, 1939, professedly in defence of democracy and the weak nations. And yet Britain did not want to grant freedom to India which was her dependency. India had no independent foreign policy and had to follow the one laid out by England. Lord Linlithgow, the then Governor-General of India, proclaimed India to be at war with Germany the same day (September, 3 1939). The Congress ministries in office were not consulted and as a mark of protest they resigned.

The Indian National Congress had made it clear in its election manifesto, as far back as 1936, its "opposition to the participation of India in an imperialist war."[2] This stand of the Congress was further emphasised by the Working Committee of the Indian National Congress which met in September 1939. The Working Committee held that the "declared wishes of the Indian people... have been deliberately ignored by the British Government," and while the committee "unhesitatingly condemns the latest aggression of the Nazi Government in Germany against Poland... the issue of war and peace for India must be decided by the Indian people."[3]

The Congress Working Committee also demanded from the Government a clear declaration of its war objectives and a promise of independence for India. India would be ready to render help to the British Government in her perilous hour if these demands were acceded to. However, the demands of the Congress were rejected. The Congress then decided to propagate against and obstruct people from rendering any help in the war effort. To intensify its campaign Mahatma Gandhi launched an individual Satyagraha. It was "to carry on non-violently and openly anti-war propaganda" and "to preach non-cooperation with the Government in their war efforts."[4]

As a result of this campaign, which was opened by Vinoba Bhave on October 17, 1940, thirty thousand men and women courted arrest.[5] The campaign continued till the end of the year when the Government had to release the political prisoners in view of the prevailing situation. The Japanese were at the doorstep of India and the fate of the British was in jeopardy.

Sir Stafford Cripps was sent to India with seemingly new proposals to win over the popular support. But Cripps's proposal was rejected by all the parties. All hopes of a settlement receded to the background and Cripps's Mission, instead of goodwill and a calmer atmosphere, left ill-will and bitterness among the Indian people.

In a mood of desperation, the Congress Working Committee passed a resolution in July 1942, calling upon the British to withdraw from India. The All India Congress Committee which met in Bombay on 7th and 8th August 1942, endorsed this decision. It resolved "to sanction for the vindication of India's inalienable right to freedom and independence, the starting of a mass struggle on the widest possible scale so that the country might utilize all the non-violent strength it had gathered during the last twenty-two years of peaceful struggle."[6]

The people were in a defiant mood and they were encouraged by the British reverses at the Japanese hands. The suffering of the war refugees and the inhuman treatment meted out to them further incensed them. As a matter of fact force and intimidation had been used against those who had shown reluctance in contribution to war funds.

Gandhiji was arrested on August 9, 1942 and he left a brief but significant message to the nation in three words: "Do or Die". This message became a motto for the millions and a source of strength and sacrifice which was increasingly demanded at the altar of freedom.

The moment the news of Gandhiji's arrest was received, there were hartals in Bombay, Ahmedabad and Poona. By August 11, 1942, this infection had spread all over the country. Alongside also people took out processions, held meetings and demonstrations; the universities closed down for want of students. Industrial labour in Ahmedabad, Bombay, Kanpur, Indore, Bangalore and Mysore, struck work.[7]

The movement affected the rural areas as well. In several places people declared themselves free, courts and offices were seized, police stations were occupied. Flags were hoisted on secretariat buildings, courts and other Government offices. The Government machinery was paralysed in several districts, mainly in Bihar, Central Provinces, Andhra, Uttar Pradesh, Gujarat, Karnataka, Assam and parts of Bengal.

The Government reacted with counter-measures. It enacted "the Penalties Enhancement Ordinance, Collective Fine Ordinance, the Special Court Ordinance, the Whipping Ordinance." These ordinances legalised certain forms of plunder, loot, flogging and even killing of political offenders. Searches were made and properties confiscated. Congress offices and its funds became the property of the Government. India had become a "big prison".[8]

Leaders were arrested in the first round-up and in their absence women carried on the movement and bore the brunt of the British wrath.

The women not only took out processions and held demonstrations but also organised camps in which they were given training in civic duties, and first aid, education democracy and the Indian constitution. Training in lathi and drill was also imparted in these camps.[9]

The women organised Political Prisoner's Relief Fund and collected large amounts. Some women went underground and directed the movement from there. In every province there were stories to tell about the heroic part played by women.

Assam

The women of this province took a prominent part in this movement. It was perhaps the sudden unbounded passion for liberty which made them take over the command of the battle for freedom. "The struggle waged by Assam to break down the shackles of slavery", observed Mitra and Chakraborty in *Rebel India,* "is largely a struggle for Assam's womanhood."[10]

It was on September 20, 1942 that Kanak Lata Barua, a girl in her teens, marched towards Gohapon Thana,[11] at the head of five hundred people to occupy the Thana building. She was asked to leave the premises by Rabati Mohan Shome, the Officer In-charge, Police Thana, but she boldly replied: "Unless the Thana Officer and his men wanted to act as the servants of the people they must clear out and allow the people to take possession of the place."[12]

The Daroga threatened her that firing would be ordered if she did not move. She was not discouraged and told him to do his duty and she would do hers. She was fired in the chest which killed her and the flag was taken by her male comrade Mukunda who was also shot dead.[13] Many more were killed, one of the women killed was pregnant and six others were injured.[14]

There was another elderly woman, Bhogaswari Phoo Kanani, who went to see her granddaughter, Ratna Prabha, carrying the national flag proceeding towards the Congress office to attend a social feast. The Congress office was then seized by the Government. The flag was snatched from the unwilling hand of the girl, but the grandmother unable to bear this, got hold of another flag and hit the official with it. The next minute she was shot dead.

The women's organisation sprung up under Smt. Annupriya Barua and Sudhalata Dutta, as a result of excesses committed by the military and police. The women visited the terrorised areas and encouraged and cheered the people. Again it was left to the women to face the military and armed police and to lead processions in places like Gohpur, Barapujjia, Teok and Barhampur.[15]

It was in Assam that "Free India's Fighting Force" was organised. Women also joined this force and they took charge of providing amenities. They organised the Red Cross First Aid parties and distributed warm clothing, bandages and many other things to the workers and countrymen all over Assam. The Government later broke up the organisation but the women carried on their work.[16]

Tezpur is another place in Assam where women from surrounding villages paraded the streets of the town, sang songs, shouted slogans and hoisted the tricolour.

In some places the women were treated inhumanly when they refused to disclose to the police the whereabouts of their relatives who were underground. Mrs. Anna Prava Barua bore police torture for two long years. Failing to arrest her husband the police took charge of all her possessions including the image of the family deity. The police would visit in the night and lift the mosquito net to see if Barua was there. As a result it became impossible for the female members and specially Anna Prava Barua to sleep with ease[17] and privacy.

Ten thousand women of village Bajali came out *en masse* on October 7, 1942, to meet at the Pata Churkuchi Police Station platform. The women sang national songs and hoisted the national flag. The police tried to disperse them, but without success. They also requested the police officials to resign their posts.[18]

On January 26, 1943, one thousand women gathered to celebrate the Independence Day. Since public meetings were banned they called a prayer meeting at Kirtan Ghar. Chandra Prabha Saikiani was dragged out and arrested while delivering a lecture. The 'prasad' was mixed with dust and the police also assaulted some of the women of whom Sita Bhuwaneswari Devi was the worst affected.[19]

BENGAL

The women of Bengal had been participating in the freedom struggle ever since the battle began. The people of Midnapore District played a notable part in the movement of 1942.

The Tamlauk sub-division had organised itself against the Japanese invasion. They raised an army of volunteers which included men and women. Several camps were opened to give training to those who joined the ranks. Local relief committees were formed. A Khadi Centre was also organised where four thousand spinners were working. Most of these were women.[20] A National Government was formed within the limits laid down by the Congress Committee. It was assisted by the various Ministries. The National Government kept on functioning till August 8, 1944. It was dissolved at the instance of Gandhiji.[21] The women of Tamlauk division took out processions and in one of these seven women were arrested and two years' rigorous imprisonment was awarded to each.[22]

One such procession was led by a seventy-three-year old lady, Manangini Hazra. The processionists wanted to occupy the Thana. The police hit her hands but she did not let the flag drop. Instead she exhorted the officials to cease firing and to give up their jobs to join the freedom movement. A bullet was fired at her which killed her.[23]

Seventy-four women of this division were raped by the Government employees. One of them died as a result of the assault. Women with daggers tried to offer resistance collectively which proved effective.[24]

It was reported on November 7, 1942, that forty-three persons were killed and seventy wounded in the Tamlauk sub-division. The houses of people engaged in political activities were set on fire. In some cases the women were not allowed to leave the houses. After setting fire to the houses the police or military remained on guard. The women had to be rescued by the volunteers through back doors or by ladders thrown over the roof.[25]

On January 9, 1943, six hundred soldiers surrounded three villages of Masuria Dalmasuria and Chandipur in Mohishadal Thana. Those soldiers not only plundered the villages but also committed criminal assault on 46 women in a single day.[26]

The women started an organisation called Bhagini Seva Sangha with the object of protecting their chastity and honour. Some of them faced the soldiers and the police with weapons. Two ladies were prosecuted under the Arms Act for drawing out daggers in self-defence.[27]

Kalpana Dutta

Kalpana, who was arrested for her revolutionary activities in 1932 was released in 1937, when the Provincial Autonomy was introduced in the country. Special efforts for her release were made by Rabindranath Tagore, C.F. Andrews and Mahatma Gandhi. In the Midnapore Jail Gandhiji met her. Writing about herself in her book Chittagong Armoury Raiders Reminiscences, she said: "Gandhiji came to meet me in the Presidency Jail. After a little conversation Gandhiji spoke to me 'Nazimuddin[28] is extremely angry with you and says none of the Chittagong Armoury Raid cases would be released, but yet I am trying for you."[29] She was released in 1939. She busied herself in studies and also engaged in communist propaganda. She worked in labour areas and Dhobi Para. Kalpana worked in the Kisan Sabha Office and later joined the Tramway Workers' Union Office as a whole time worker.[30]

Kalpana joined a post-graduate course. By this time the Second World War broke out, the authorities ordered her to leave Calcutta within twenty-four hours and interned her in her house in Chittagong.

Her activities at this time were to carry on the secret work of the party and see to its efficient running. It included the despatching of all Provincial Committee and Central Committee circulars, books and papers to different areas, fixing up shelters and dumps in the town, organising distribution of leaflets etc. In 1941 the restrictions on her activity were relaxed.[31]

UTTAR PRADESH

Following repressive measures adopted by the Government, the Congress office was seized by the police. On August 10, 1942, a group of girl students raided the office and took possession of it.[32]

Batches of girl students toured the districts and rendered whatever relief and succour they could to the people. Women of respectable Hindu families were asked to leave their houses at the point of bayonets including the mothers of the newly born babies. They were asked to part with their ornaments. In some cases the ornaments were removed from their bodies forcibly. In Samanwal village of District Ghazipur an Ahir woman was shot down when she was running away from the soldiers.[33]

It was reported from Banaras that the ladies who had suffered at the hands of police related lamentable stories. In some cases the women were dragged by their long hairs; they were asked to perform sit-ups; no food was given to them. In one case a child was roasted alive before his mother's eyes. Some women were tortured to disclose the whereabouts of their husbands.[34] Nine students were externed from Banaras Hindu University for actively participating in the movement.[35]

PUNJAB

Punjab energetically responded to the call of Mahatma Gandhi—students, both boys and girls, unhesitatingly came forward in the field. It was in the city of Lahore that on November 10, 1942, one hundred and four students were arrested. This number included twenty-two girls. The girls were courageous, they distributed the badges. The girls even did not pay any heed to the presence of the police and did not get into the police van till they were told by their principal to do so. At the police station they were asked several questions:

Q. What is your name?
A. Bagi No. 1, 2, 3, ...22.
Q. What is your father's name?
A. Gandhiji.

Q. What is your mother's name?

A. Bharat Mata.[36]

In Amritsar the girl students were given a highly objectionable treatment.[37]

Rajkumari Amrit Kaur

During the movement Rajkumari Amrit Kaur played a leading role in organising processions and protest meetings. Rajkumari came from the royal family of Kapurthala State. She was the daughter of Sir Harnam Singh and was born in 1886 in Lucknow, Uttar Pradesh. Her mother was one of the pioneer social workers and the daughter not only learnt to fight for social freedom but also for the political freedom of the country.

Amrit Kaur had most of her education in England and was a keen sportswoman. On her return to India she set about organising sports and games in the Punjab.

Gokhale was a great friend of Amrit Kaur's father. She said: "The flames of my passionate desire to see India free from foreign domination were fanned by him."[38]

Rajkumari Amrit Kaur first came in contact with Mahatma Gandhi in the stirring days of Martial Law in 1919. She later became his secretary, a place she occupied for sixteen years.[39]

Amrit Kaur was instrumental in bringing about the birth of the All India Women's Conference in 1926 and she was its secretary for many years. In the year 1932 she gave evidence before the Lothian Committee on Indian franchise and later, as a member of a delegation of Women's Organisation, she testified before the Joint Select Committee of Parliament on Indian Constitutional Reforms.[40]

Rajkumari took an active part in the Salt Satyagraha and was arrested in Bombay. Later, when the Communal Award[41] was announced, she condemned it and moved the following resolution at a conference of the All India Women's Conference held on December 23, 1932:

This conference stands united (i) in its protest against the Communal Award as touching the womanhood of India, and (ii) in its demand for a system of joint electorates.[42]

The Rajkumari went to Bannu in the North-West Frontier Province to advocate the case of the Congress. She was convicted on July 16,

1937, by the Assistant Commissioner, Bannu, on a charge of sedition and was sentenced to imprisonment till the rising of the Court and to pay fifty rupees fine.[43]

Amrit Kaur was most active during the Quit India movement in 1942. She led processions day after day. One procession was subjected to ruthless lathi charge in Simla. From August 9 to 16 the processions led by her were subjected to lathi charge fifteen times.[44]

The Government could not let her be free and finally she was arrested at Kalka. She was taken by car to Ambala Jail and was allowed to take with her a bedding roll, a bag containing her spinning wheel, her Bible and Gita, which she insisted on taking, and her brass vessel for drinking water. Her suitcase containing clothes was not allowed with her and she had to manage for more than one month with one change of clothes. The filth in the jail was indescribable. Pigeons and rats were her constant companions. There was a foul smelling latrine in the living room which she refused to use on hygienic grounds. She had to bathe in the open.

The food was very bad. She was unable to eat it. Within a week she was put on the hospital list. In eight weeks she lost one stone weight and had to be sent back to Simla. Here she remained interned for twenty months. She lost her brother while in jail. Her letter to her sister-in-law was not even allowed to be sent.[45]

After India attained independence, she was Cabinet Minister in the Government of India.

Amar Kaur

Amar Kaur, wife of Mohan Lal, an advocate of Gurdaspur who renounced his practice in response to Gandhiji's call in 1921, entered public life at the same time.

Next year, Amar Kaur shifted to Lyallpur with her husband and started her real political work. She went about in the district advocating the cause of the Congress, and, according to Dobson, the then Deputy Commissioner, she "had set the agitation fire ablaze in the whole district."[46]

The next movement came in 1930 and this brave lady started her work in Jalandhar district and was ultimately arrested at Banga[47] on charge of sedition.

In the year 1932 Amar Kaur attended the Political Conference at Lyallpur where a number of arrests were made but somehow or the other she escaped arrest.

Amar Kaur and Adarsh Kumari, daughters of Lala Pindi Das, a veteran Congress worker, and many others found a novel way of disturbing the authorities. On their way from Lyallpur to Lahore on August 23, 1932, they pulled the chain in the running train at Badami Bagh Railway Station, a couple of miles from Lahore. After stopping the train they shouted slogans like "Inquilab Zindabad", "Videshi Mal Boycott" and "Gandhi ki Jai". They exhorted other passengers to join them in their endeavour to free the country.[48]

Amar Kaur and others were tried[49] and sentenced to five months' imprisonment and a fine of forty rupees each. Amar Kaur was awarded one month's extra imprisonment for stopping the train.[50]

The Lahore Bar filed a revision and the High Court ordered that they could be released on furnishing a security of five hundred rupees each pending the decision of the case. Amar Kaur and Adarsh refused to come out on bail and decried the action taken by the High Court Bar.

Amar Kaur did not restrict her activities to Punjab only. She visited North-West Frontier Province. She was arrested and convicted at Bannu for her political activities.

Following the policy of individual Satyagraha launched by Gandhiji in 1940, Amar Kaur offered Satyagraha at Kasur in Lahore District. She was released from jail only to be rearrested in September 1942. During this period she organised women's training camps in Lahore and Amritsar for which she was arrested. The treatment meted out to the political prisoners was humiliating. So she, along with Satyawati, decided to organise demonstrations in jail. They were able to hoist a national flag on the jail gate on October 9, 1942. This enraged the jail authorities and these two ladies were transferred to Ambala District Jail.[51]

Amar Kaur's husband was not allowed to see her. While in Ambala Jail she became ill. Her husband again approached the authorities to see her but permission was refused.[52]

She was released in April 1944 in shattered health, after one year and four months in jail.

Pushpa Gujral

Pushpa Gujral[53] is yet another woman of Punjab who took a prominent part in the movement of 1942.

Her interest in political work began in 1919, but she became active only during the movement of 1930. At this time she was elected President of the City District Congress Committee. She collected funds for the families of political prisoners.[54]

Pushpa Gujral went to jail for first the time in 1940 for offering Satyagraha and was sentenced to six months' imprisonment.

The year 1942 witnessed the passing of the famous Quit India resolution and the family was active again. Pushpa was arrested along with the whole family. She was sentenced to six months imprisonment.[55]

Pushpa Gujral became the Convener, Punjab Pradesh Congress Committee (women) and was also associated with many other social work agencies. She was member of the Punjab State Social Welfare Advisory Board. This soldier of freedom struggle is no more with us.

NORTH-WEST FRONTIER PROVINCES

The freedom movement had taken such a strong hold amongst the women that even purdah-stricken Bannu was no exception. They took out processions and marched proudly, raising slogans against the alien usurper. The procession was taken out as a mark of protest against the arrests of Hindu-Muslim merchants for giving food and shelter to the Khudai Khidmatgars.[56] It was the first demonstration arranged by the women in the history of the province and as a result it had far reaching effect on the people.[57]

SIND

The women of this area took out processions. The police of Karachi adopted new methods to harass them. The women were abused and taken away to far off places and released in the middle of the night. The City Magistrate, Rup Chand, while conducting the case of a girl, slapped her on the face because she refused to apologise. Two girl volunteers entered the City Magistrate's Court and ordered him in writing to vacate the post as he had been found incompetent. Copies of this order were distributed in the court. Both of them were arrested, tried and convicted to long terms of imprisonment.[58]

MADHYA PRADESH

In every province novel methods were being tried to do away with the foreign yoke. In this province women approached officials and members of the bar on Raksha Bandan Day and requested the former to resign and the latter to refrain from attending the courts.

In this province women of the village Chimur[59] had to suffer a great deal at the hands of the police and military. On August 19, 1942, a special train with 200 European soldiers and fifty Indian constables reached Wardha. The sepoys and soldiers plundered the property of the inhabitants. Women were raped. In many cases they were able to save themselves by putting a united front. There are reports of cases where women in advanced stages of pregnancy or in confinement or in menses, and girls of tender age were raped by them.[60]

Enquiries were made into the happenings at Chimur by a committee composed of officials and non-officials. It was revealed that thirteen women were actually raped and some of them were raped by more than one European. Four girls were also molested. One of them was molested by one European soldier and later by one Indian soldier. They took her ring and ten rupees from her mother.[61] The wife of the sarpanch (chairman of village panchayat) who was pregnant was also raped.[62]

Anasuyabai Kale

Anasuyabai Kale's interest in public work began in 1920 when she organised Bhagini Mandal, a women's organisation. Later she was an active member of the All-India Women's Conference.

Anasuyabai Kale became a member of the Central Provinces Legislature in 1928 and was its Deputy Speaker—an office from which she resigned as a protest against Gandhiji's arrest in 1930 in connection with the Salt Satyagraha.[63]

Anasuyabai took active part in the Civil Disobedience movement of 1930. She was imprisoned for her political activities.

When the popular ministries were installed in 1937 Anasuyabai became the Duputy Speaker of the Madhya Pradesh Legislature. She had to resign from this office again in pursuance of the Congress policy regarding the Second World War.

The Quit-India movement saw her in the field of active politics. It was due to her efforts that the lives of twenty-five young men,[64] who were associated with the Ashti Chimur chapter of the annals of the freedom struggle of 1942, were saved.[65]

After India gained independence Anasuyabai became a member of the Central Legislature.[66]

BOMBAY

Bombay was the first province which was affected by the political upsurge and it was in the vanguard of the fight for freedom.

Sarojini Naidu

Mrs. Naidu of the fame of Dharasana Salt raid was again active during this period.

In the course of these few years Sarojini Naidu strove hard to bring the two communities closer. She addressed meetings and spoke from various platforms. Addressing a political conference at Vellore (Madras) she said: "The Hindus and Muslims are the two eyes of the nation and if both eyes were to be focused together on the Swaraj image under the leadership of Mahatma Gandhi, freedom would be theirs ere long."[67]

Sarojini was arrested on December 3, 1940, for taking part in the individual Satyagraha inaugurated by Vinoba Bhave. She fell ill and had to be released on December 11, 1940.

As soon as Sarojini's health permitted she started her political work. She was again arrested immediately after the passing of the Quit-India resolution on August 9, 1942. Sarojini came out of the Aga Khan Palace in shattered health and remained inactive for ten months after her release in March 1943.

Sarojini appeared in public again on January 7, 1944, and addressed a meeting at Bombay. Later in the month, on January 26, 1944, she came to Delhi on her way to Lahore. As soon as she reached Lahore railway station, a notice was served on her by the Punjab Government prohibiting her from making any public speech or taking part in a procession, or writing to the newspapers. She returned the notice with the remarks that she was already under the instruction of her doctor, whom she was obeying and was not addressing any public meetings of joining any procession. Therefore so far as she was concerned the order was non-existent.[68]

Immediately after India attained independence, Sarojini had the privilege of being the first woman Governor of Uttar Pradesh in 1947, one of the largest States of India. She occupied this place up to March 1949 when death took away this nightingale, ambassador of Hindu-Muslim unity and the champion of women's rights.

Kamala Devi Chottopadhyaya

Kamala Devi, who had participated in the Salt Satyagraha actively, now took her place in the movement again. In fact, this soldier of Satyagraha army was never tired and continued her work throughout the period. She was arrested for her political work a number of times between 1939 and 1944. She visited the United States with a view to acquainting the people of that country about the true conditions in India.

After India attained independence, Kamala Devi's interest was diverted from politics to cooperative movement. She sponsored the Indian Cooperative Union. She set up the Theatre Centre of India, a federation of theatre organisations all over the country. She was awarded Padma Bhushan in 1955.

Kamala Devi is, at present, chairman of the All-India Handicrafts Board. Her contribution in reviving the traditional cottage industries of the country has been great.[69] She died two years ago.

Miraben (Madeleine Slade)

Madeleine Slade did not actively participate in the political struggle, but supported the cause of the freedom of India.

She was the daughter of Sir Edmund Slade and was born in 1892. She belonged to an aristocratic family of Great Britain. Madeleine Slade had a good education, but she changed her interests very often. In the year 1923 she moved to Paris and "was living a life of thoughtless luxury in those days, idling away the time between London, Paris and Berne. Her parents were well-to-do and she had nothing to worry except the pursuit of pleasure and the ways to appreciate and enjoy the life that was bestowed on her by her parents."[70]

During this period she read a book written by Romain Rolland, a French philosopher, on Gandhiji. The book greatly influenced Madeleine Slade. She has herself described how the change came about: "Then something happened one night. I had never thought of religion before but it came all of a sudden. I read this book and I decided then and there that if possible I must give life to Gandhi and to India.

Accordingly she wrote to Gandhiji requesting him if she could join the Ashram in India and serve for the rest of her life."[71]

Slade took one year to get prepared to come to her new master. She sent for Khadi so that she could get the necessary garments made before she came to India. She also spent her days and nights reading the Hindu scriptures. After she was fully prepared she came to her new home. Her parents tried to dissuade her but to no avail. She came to India in 1925. Here she was given a new name, Miraben.

Miraben went to England in 1931 with Gandhiji when he went to attend the Second Round Table Conference. During this period she sent news releases concerning Gandhiji's campaign to the press in England, America, France, Germany and Switzerland. The Government sent her a warning that unless she stopped sending news to foreign countries she would be arrested. She did not stop her work.

As soon as Miraben came back from England she started on a Khadi selling tour throughout the country. When she returned, Mira was ordered by the Government of Bombay not to enter the city. She defied the order and was arrested. She was charged under Section 21 of Emergency Ordinance and sentenced to three months' imprisonment.[72]

Miraben went to England again in 1934 to educate the people of England in Gandhiji's philosophy. She was again arrested during the Quit-India movement of 1942 along with Gandhiji and was confined to the Aga Khan Palace for twenty-one months.

In 1946, Miraben was appointed Special Advisor to the Government of Uttar Pradesh for "Grow More Food" campaign. From 1947 to 1960 she was Advisor for Development. She was running an Ashram at Rishikesh in the Himalayas. She died some time back.[73]

Khurshed Behn

Khurshed Behn, a famous organiser of the Volunteer Army in 1930, went to the North-West Frontier Province in 1940 to spread the gospel of non-violence amongst the people there. She went from village to village, meeting the Pathans, Pirs, Maliks and Khans and spoke to them of the cruelty of kidnapping people. She met the members of the Hindu community also, instilling in them the spirit of courage and bravery. At the close of the year she wanted to go to Walo Tangi, a trial territory, and sought the Government's permission to cross the border. When the Government did not respond she informed the Government of her intention of crossing the border. In an attempt to cross the border she was arrested on December 4, 1940, and was tried. She was sentenced to pay a fine of one thousand rupees or in dafault thereof to undergo three months' imprisonment. However, she preferred to be imprisoned rather than pay the fine.[74] After the expiry of her sentence she was externed from the Frontier Province and was interned in Bombay.

Khurshed challenged the validity of such an order in a letter dated March 31, 1941. But the Government did not pay any attention to her protest. She was later allowed to move within the Bombay Presidency. This relaxation could not satisfy her as she wanted to move out of Bombay. Khurshed was willing to accommodate the Government as regards its policy of externing her from North-West Frontier Province, but she could not possibly be externed from other parts of the country. Khurshed Behn finally decided to defy the Government orders and accordingly informed the authorities on July 31, 1941, of her intention of leaving for Wardha on August 1, 1941.[75] She, however, could not reach Wardha.[76] Khurshed was arrested on the day of her departure and was sent to Central Jail, Yerwada, (Pune).

Khurshed also took part in the Quit-India Movement. She made a careful study of the atrocities committed by the police.

Bombay was greatly effected by the 1942 movement. In addition to the usual processions, Womens' Day was celebrated. Three processions were taken out in Ahmedabad. A procession was lathi-charged and seventy-six women were arrested.[77]

On a similar occasion in the month of October, processions of women from ten different parts of the city started. The police attacked one such procession and seized the national flag. As a result the women squatted on the road and refused to move unless the tricolour was restored to them. The police answered with ruthless teargas attack. Some women fainted while others got hurt. One Satyawati Mehta was seriously injured on her head with the bursting of a gas cylinder and had to be removed to hospital. About eighty men were injured but volunteers were prohibited from giving water to the wounded.[78]

The women of Bombay took out processions on the 9th of every month, the 9th August being the day of Gandhiji's arrest. The police had made arrangements to meet them. Exactly at the appointed hour, Jayshriben came out. No sooner did she come out than she was arrested along with other ladies. As they were being arrested a procession of

Desh Sevikas appeared on the scene. They were arrested and their arrest served as a signal for spontaneous processions. The procession was lathi-charged. A girl of fourteen years tried to hoist the flag but was beaten by the police. Another girl, named Manfule, was also beaten for a similar attempt. The police opened fire on these women processionists five times and total arrests numbered two hundred and fifty.

Usha Mehta

Bombay kept up the struggle through the radio. Usha Mehta [79] was one of the prominent workers of the Congress Radio Conspiracy Case. She had a leaning towards the Congress Socialist Party. She had earlier attended the Congress session but this time when the famous Quit-India resolution was passed she was present and was a witness to this important decision. It was her great desire to do something to make this resolution a success. Picketing of foreign cloth shops and liquor shops was distasteful to her. She wanted to do something different.

Usha Mehta's dream was realised when some friends decided to run a secret transmitting station. "It appealed to me immensely and I jumped at the idea and plunged into the movement in spite of staunch opposition from my father who being a government servant did not approve of my idea and who wanted me to finish my education."[80] Nothing deterred this brave girl, not even the danger it presented to her father who was a Judge at the time.

The prominent leaders were in jail by August 9, 1942 and it was from this day that preparations for setting up a radio in the name of "Voice of Freedom" speaking from somewhere in India, were taken in hand.[81] A transmitter was necessary for successfully carrying on the movement. It was felt that the press would be censored and as such the required propaganda could easily be done through the radio for the cause. It was Babubhai and Usha who first started working for the radio. Money had to be obtained. A woman relative of Usha offered her jewellery. Usha was hesitant to accept this offer. Ultimately Babubhai Khakar got the required amount and a transmitter was set up with it.[82]

Another group led by Vithalbhai K. Jhavari, now one of the editors of the birthday volume on Gandhiji, was also trying to set up another transmitter. Besides these two, there were several other groups. Dr. Rammanohar Lohia, a famous socialist leader, was in the know of these groups and tried to coordinate the work. The most active group was Babubhai's in which Usha worked.

The Congress Radio had its own transmitter, transmitting station, recording station, its own call sign and last but not least a distinct wavelength. It started broadcasting on August 14, 1942. "This is the Congress Radio calling on 42.84 metres from somewhere in India."[83]

It was not easy to fool the police, so the workers of the Congress Radio had to change their abode very often. Usha described how they camouflaged their moves. "Fortunately for us, one uncle from upcountry or our sister or some other relative would come to our rescue. Uncle wanted a flat for one month. One of his nephews would go and hire it, take all the luggage there and would anxiously wait for him. But by the time uncle was expected another flat would have to be hired for some other fictitious purpose. Every time the process was to go from the broadcasting station to the railway station and from there again to the new transmiting station. This had to be done every fortnight or so. Once Babubhai and I found a very good place; quite safe according to us. We were extremely happy at the idea that we would be able to carry on at least for a month or two. We went to the owner to pay the rent. A queer apparatus was lying there. We said 'Sethji, what is this supposed to be?'[84] 'A detecting machine to catch the illegal radios,' came the reply. 'Detecting machine', I exclaimed in my mind, but I took care to see that the face did not betray the expressions. Babubhai cleverly joined him in abusing all those who did such illegal acts and we were off. We thanked our stars for having been cautioned in time. The first words of Babubhai were 'Behn, we are saved from the tiger's jaws.'[85]

"Babubhai had warned me not to be in white Khadi sari that day but I had insisted on it. Since that day, however, I changed my dress slightly so as to be less conspicuous."[86]

Usha Mehta was mainly assigned the task of broadcasting news and giving talks in Hindustani. It was this broadcasting station which first gave the news of Chittagong bomb raid, Jamshedpur strike and the news about atrocities in Ashti Chimur. In the speeches, attempts were made to clarify and explain the Congress stand, both from the national and international points of view. Broadcasting on world peace it said: "The Congress sends its message of goodwill and peace to all the people of the world who are suffering, to countries still resisting and to countries batrayed by their own governments. India is at present suffering...."[87]

Explaining the Quit-India Movement the comments were: "So far we were conducting a movement, but now we are conducting a revolution. In a revolution, there is victory or defeat. This revolution is not of one party or community, but of the whole of India, we hope you will not rest content till the British Empire is burnt to ashes."[88] The speeches were mostly delivered by Dr. Lohia.

However, this Radio could not function for a long time. The Government came to know of it and raided the place on November 12, at night. The Superintendent of Police and his military technicians and a troop of fifty odd policemen came to take possession of the belongings of this broadcasting station. The entry of the Deputy Commissioner did not worry the brave soldiers and they did not even care to move from their seats. Babubhai and Usha Mehta along with many others were arrested in this Radio Conspiracy case. The police tried its best to get the details from Usha Mehta but she refused to answer any question relating to this subject. During the interrogation period she was also kept in the lock-up. Describing life in the police custody she says: "The lock-up period is perhaps the most trying time in the life of a prisoner. During the day you have to face the policemen and at night your only possible activity could be either to kill the bugs or to kill time. Again it is humanly impossible to sleep in a cell full of filth, dirt and nauseating smell."[89]

"In spite of six months continuous interrogation, the police could not get any information from her and finally charged her with agreeing in conspiring among and between ourselves and others, to do or cause to be done illegal acts like possessing, establishing, maintaining and working illegal wireless telegraph without lawful...authority or excuse prejudicial acts and spreading prejudicial reports."[90]

The case was Emperor versus Babubhai Khakar, Vithalbhai Jhaveri, Usha Mehta, Chandrakant Jhaveri, Nanak Motwant. "Throughout the trial," says Usha Mehta, "we enjoyed so much that I am tempted to say that it was a golden period of my jail life. All along, we used to chew chocolates or peppermints unperturbed by the efforts of the Prosecutor who was hard at proving the case against us. The revelations of the approvers likewise failed to disturb our equanimity."[91]

The case was decided and Usha Mehta was sentenced to four years' imprisonment.[92] She remained in the jail till April 1946.

After her release in 1946 she took to teaching and later obtained her doctorate degree on a thesis on the "Social and Political Thought of Mahatma Gandhi."

Kasturba Gandhi

Bombay witnessed a martyr's death. Kasturba Gandhi, who had shared the responsibilities of the freedom struggle with Gandhiji, died as a prisoner on February 24, 1944. She could not even get the required medical help. It was after a great deal of correspondence by Gandhiji that physicians of her choice were allowed to attend her.

Hansa Mehta

Hansa Mehta plunged into the freedom struggle early in life. Greatly inspired by the leaders of the day she travelled all over India, meeting women to create awareness among them. This, however, was disliked by the British Government. The Abhudaya, dated August 30, 1930, reported on a trick played by the railway authorities to send engines to drown the voices of the people shouting 'Inquilab Zindabad' on the arrival of Kamala Nehru and Hansa Mehta at Delhi Railway Station. The engines were made to hoot non-stop.

An eminent educationist and a dedicated social worker, she believed that unless there was improvement in the quality of life of women, social reform was not possible. Her tremendous contribution in the field of education won her many distinctions. She was the first woman Vice-Chancellor in India (Baroda University) and was actively associated with the All India Women's Conference since its inception. *The Times of India*, in its issue of August 15, 1947, described the uprecedented scenes of enthusiasm on the ushering of the freedom of India at the hour of midnight. In the Constituent Assembly, "Pandit Nehru made a speech which was at once notable and a masterpiece of literature." After the oath of dedication, the report says, "Smt. Hansa Mehta presented a national flag to the Constituent Assembly on behalf of the women of India."

Mridula Sarabhai

Mridula Sarabhai was a renowned political and social worker. She was the daughter of Sarla and Ambalal Sarabhai, the fabulously rich industrialists and philanthropists of Ahmedabad. She became a prominent worker in the cause of freedom, in 1927. Like other people of her time, she was deeply moved by Gandhiji's message and participated in the Salt Satyagraha (1930), the Rajkot Satyagraha (1938), and was in and out of prison several times. She worked actively during the INA Trials in 1946. She played a commendable role in the restoration of abducted women during the communal riots, which shook the country in the wake of the partition of India in 1947.

MYSORE

Consequent upon the arrest of Gandhiji the Congress leaders of Isur and neighbouring villages formed Panchayats and called upon officials to resign. The Patil[93] of Isur refused to resign. A party of children took over the papers and other things and thus relieved him of his duty forcibly. As a result the village was raided by the Inspector of Police. The children summoned the police officials and asked them to wear Gandhi caps and remove their hats. The Sub-Inspector however ordered a lathi-charge on children. A girl, the daughter of Shanker, removed his hat and replaced it with a Khadi cap. The Sub-Inspector shot at the girl who was wounded. This enraged the villagers, and they attacked the police party and killed the Sub-Inspector and Amildar. A trial followed. Fourteen persons were sentenced to be hanged and twenty-three, including three women, sentenced to transportation for life. The High Court confirmed the death sentence of five and the transportation sentence on three women."[94]

KARNATAKA

The students took active part in the movement. The share of the girl students in these activities was by no means small. The government dealt lathi blows and indiscriminate beatings on these law-defying students. Thirty-two girls were severely beaten at Kumtha Adoni[95] (Karnataka).

Balamakki Bamakka, the old mother of two influential merchants, led a procession with a flag and Gandhiji's photo. She appealed to the Sub-Inspector of police who stopped the procession to resign and lead the movement against the government. She was arrested.

At Dharwar, on October 23, 1942, two lady students, Hemlata Shenolikar and Gulvadi, entered the District Courts and hoisted the tricolour on the Judge's seat. Gulvadi addressed the members of the Bar present in the court and summoned the Judge and asked him to resign and dissolve his court within eight days, otherwise he would be tried as a traitor. The police came on the scene. Gulvadi escaped. However, Shenolikar was sentenced to pay a fine of fifty rupees or to suffer imprisonment for one month. She refused to pay the fine and preferred to go to jail.[96]

Gulvadi again came to Dharwar Bar and addressed it again, exhorting them to support the cause of independence. She was arrested and was sentenced to pay a fine of one hundred and fifty rupees or to undergo three months' imprisonment.[97]

Sucheta Kriplani

Sucheta Kriplani's[98] interest in politics dates back from the days she was a lecturer in Banares University in 1934. Her marriage to Acharya J.B. Kriplani, then General Secretary of the All India Congress, further accentuated her interest. She left her job in the Banares University and plunged into political activities. Individual Satyagraha was launched by the Congress in 1940 and she was one of the chosen ones who was permitted to take part in this Satyagraha and was arrested.[99]

By the time she came out of jail, another movement was under way. Most of the leaders were in the prison. She did not think it proper to surrender to the police and went underground. She had to face many hardships to carry on her activities, but escaped arrest by the police.[100]

During this period a women's department of the Indian National Congress was started in 1943 with Sucheta Kriplani as Secretary-In charge. She issued circulars to the Pradesh Congress Committees to organise women's department effectively. It was felt that women must be provided with correct information to save them from getting panicky over trifles. With this aim in view it was decided to hold meetings at regular intervals in mohallas so that the uneducated, ignorant women were kept informeed regarding war and the Congress activities. The information could be given through hand bills and bulletins.[101]

Another work undertaken by this Department was to organise a Volunteer Corps. The volunteers were taught simple drill, first-aid and the art of self-protection in an emergency. The Corps were also required to help the refugees when they came to the town or left it.[102]

In the towns a Central Committee with branches in each mohalla was formed. The Committee through its branches had to (a) convey to each home the day-to-day instructions of the local Congress Committee, (b) collect information regarding the difficulties of the mohalla and convey them to the Congress Committee, (c) arrange to teach spinning to the mohalla women, (d) arrange lectures on useful general information, (e) organise a short course of physical culture with special emphasis on how to evade personal assaults, (f) find out cases of assaults and oppression on women, explain to victims that such incidents were not to be kept secret under false ideas of modesty and honour, give publicity to such incidents and render help in bringing criminals to books, be they civil or military, and (g) keep in touch with men's Volunteer Corps to be able to ask for assistance in any emergency.[103]

The Mohalla Committee had to make arrangements to teach carding, spinning etc. It had to supply charkhas and cotton, take the spun yarn and arrange for the weaving of cloth.[104]

In addition to this work, the Women's Department was to undertake to (i) study the difficulties of women and their causes and cures, (ii) try to increase the membership of women and devise ways and means of securing their active cooperation in various Congress activities, (iii) coordinate the activities of women Congress workers, (iv) suggest ways and means of increasing the capacity of women workers so as to take up more responsibility when called upon to do so, (v) suggest ways and means to Congress women representatives for their effective working in local government bodies, assemblies and institutions for constructive work like Khadi, village industries, labour, kisans, and (vi) to keep in touch with women's activities in India.[105]

Sucheta Kriplani was however arrested in 1944. After her release in 1945 she engaged herself mostly in the social and relief activities. She went to East Bengal during the communal riots in 1946 to rescue the women and children from the hands of Muslims. When Mahatma Gandhi went to East Bengal and undertook to work for rehabilitation of the refugees, Sucheta joined him in the work.

During the year 1947, when the partition of India took place, riots broke out in Punjab. Sucheta Kriplani rushed to the affected areas and organised relief operations. She was taken as a member of the Congress Working Committee in 1947 in recognition of her work.

Sucheta Kriplani was a member of the Uttar Pradesh Legislative Assembly and later became a member of the Lok Sabha. She had been the Chief Minister of Uttar Pradesh.

Aruna Asaf Ali

Aruna[106] has been an ardent soldier of the army of freedom fighters. She became prominent during the days of Salt Satyagraha. She went about addressing meetings, preparing salt and she also led processions. The

Chief Commissioner of Delhi was greatly alarmed by her activities. As a consequence he prosecuted her not for sedition "but for being a vagrant having no ostensible means of livelihood."[107] She was asked to furnish security for good behaviour, which she refused. Aruna was arrested and was sentenced to one year's imprisonment. A few months later most of the political prisoners were released under the Gandhi-Irwin Truce. The government, however, did not think it advisable to release Aruna who was in Lahore jail. Her women co-prisoners refused to leave on the ground that unless Aruna was released they would not move. Gandhiji had to intervene and the prisoners left Aruna in jail.[108] Later in response to a strong public agitation, Aruna was released after a few days.

Aruna was again arrested in 1932. In addition to imprisonment, she was fined two hundred rupees. Failing to get the fine so imposed, the police adopted a novel way of taxing her patience. They seized several of her most expensive sarees.[109]

This time Aruna was lodged in the Delhi District jail. The political prisoners were being treated callously as a consequence of which Aruna took the lead and went on a hunger strike. The authorities conceded to the demand of the political prisoners, but Aruna had to suffer heavily. She was transferred to Ambala jail and was kept there in solitary confinement.[110]

After Aruna's release from jail, she kept away from active politics and for the next ten years she watched the developments in India with interest and formed her own ideas about the programme and methods of achieving freedom. Aruna accompanied her husband to Bombay for the All India Congress Committee meeting in August 1942. She was a witness to the famous 'Quit-India' resolution of August 8, 1942.

Soon after the arrest of the members of the Congress Working Committee and other leaders on August 9, 1942, Aruna presided over the national flag hoisting ceremony at Gowalia Tank Maidan, Bombay, the site of the All India Congress Committee meeting. A vast crowd had gathered to witness the function. The police tried to disrupt the function and lathi-charged the crowd. Teargas and bullets were also used. "The sight of so much innocent blood and suffering lit the fire in her. It was Aruna's baptism in the politics of revolution."[111]

Aruna was one of the most important figures of the movement of 1942. For all this period of four years she evaded arrest and was successful. She carried on her activities underground. It was on September 26, 1942, that the property of Mrs. Asaf Ali and Jugal Kishore Khanna was forfeited by the Delhi Administration after the expiry of one month's notice during which they were ordered to surrender themselves.[112] Aruna's property, that is her house, was auctioned for twenty thousand rupees and her car for three thousand and five hundred.

The attitude of the government did not deter Aruna. She published bulletins, participated in the independence movement, went from place to place for her work. She even met Mahatma Gandhi during this period but the police was not able to get her. She was a prominent leader of the underground movement.

Aruna edited *Inquilab*, a monthly journal of the Indian National Congress, Eastern Zone, along with Rammanohar Lohia.

In the March 1944 issue of *Inquilab*, Aruna called upon the fighters for freedom "to choose his field of work and if the aim is common do not allow any academic and therefore futile arguments on questions like violence and non-violence to divert your attention from the stern realities of today.... This revolution is the most opportune moment for taking stock and making preparation for our next effort. I want every student and youth to think and feel as soldiers of the revolution that is to come."[113]

Aruna was able to earn the admiration of many a government servant for her courage and resourcefulness. Pyarelal writes: "An Englishman who was also a government servant meeting her accidently at the house of a friend, after hearing from her the story of her adventures, instead of informing the police complimented her for her courage saying, he himself would have done the same thing in similar circumstances."[114]

A prize of five thousand rupees was announced by the authorities for her capture.

Aruna became ill. Hearing of her failing health Gandhiji wrote to her: "I have been filled with admiration for your courage and heroism. I have sent you a message that you must not die underground. You are reduced to a skeleton. Do come out and surrender yourself and win the prize offered for your arrest. Reserve the prize money for Harijan cause."[115] Aruna, however, could not reconcile herself to surrender and kept on working in spite of her bad health. She came out in the open when warrants against her were cancelled on January 26, 1946.[116]

Aruna explained in a public meeting at Calcutta that she remained underground primarily for the reason that she had to go to several places in order to preserve and promote the spirit of national organisation that was being attacked by the Government.

In February 1946, Aruna suggested the creation of a new Azad Hind Army in India under the banner of Congress to organise revolutionary movement for the overthrow of British rule in India. She said, "We have no place for mere intellectuals, we want practical people who can carry the message of independence throughout the whole length and breadth of the country."[117]

Yusuf Mehrally, while writing about her in the *Tribune,* observed, "The heroine of 1857 was the Rani of Jhansi, that of the 1942 revolution is undoubtedly Aruna Asaf Ali."[118]

Aruna Asaf Ali became the Mayor of Delhi Corporation in 1958, a place she occupied with distinction.

Women in the Indian National Army

It was about the first decade of the century that the revolutionary and terrorist activities were at their peak in India. Some of the revolutionaries escaped to other countries such as Japan, China, Siam and Malaya to avoid repression at the hands of the British Government and with the object of perfecting their plans for liberating their country. The most important person was Rash Behari Bose who sought asylum in Japan after throwing a bomb on Lord Hardinge in 1911.

The number of revolutionaries increased with the passage of time, and the local population of South-East Asia which consisted of three million people strengthened the revolutionary movement with men and money.

There were several organisations established by the Indians in this area. The Ghadar party was active in Shanghai. In Bangkok, Thai Bharat Cultural Lodge[119] was the centre of revolutionary activities. The important revolutionaries were S. Amar Singh, Pritam Singh and Chanda Singh.

Japan declared war on Britain and America in December 1941. It was on December 15, 1941, that Captain Mohan Singh of the Indian

Army, now known as General Mohan Singh,[120] with fifty-four companions, met Pritam Singh near Jitra Cantonment. Mohan Singh and his companions promised to sacrifice their lives for the freedom of India.[121] This was the beginning of the Indian National Army.

The Indian Independence League was formed on January 16, 1942, at Kuala Lumpur. Later branches were founded in Thailand and other places. By now the number of Indian prisoners at Kuala Lumpur was five thousand. Captain Mohan Singh addressed them and exhorted them to join the Indian National Army to fight the British in Malaya and elsewhere.[122]

Ever since the formation of the Indian Independence League the Indian women in East Asia helped to further the cause of India's Independence League. Indian women assisted in the preparation and collection of bandages, first field dressing, collection of funds and articles required by the troops and inspiring young men and women to do their duty in the critical hour.[123]

In March, 1943, the Women's Section of the Indian Independence League was inaugurated. Mrs. M.K. Chidambaram was elected Chairman and Miss Saraswaty as Secretary of the Women's Section of Indian Independence League, Singapore. Dr. Lakshmi Swaminathan was appointed Secretary at the Headquarters. These ladies toured the various parts of Malaya, Thailand and Burma to open branches and to enlist volunteers.[124] Ultimately all branches of the Indian Independence League started the Women's Section. The work of the women for the major part was of collecting funds and providing amenities to the soldiers. But with the arrival of Subhas Chandra Bose there came a revolutionary spirit in the organisation.

It was on July 9, 1943, that Subhas Chandra Bose addressed a meeting and asked for men and women volunteers. He felt that women must be ready to share the burden of freedom's battle. "This caught the imagination of the Indian womenfolk" and a beginning to start a Women's Regiment was made, which later popularly came to be known as the "Ranee Jhansi Regiment".[125]

A women's camp was started on October 23, 1943, in Singapore which was followed by many more in Malaya and Burma. They were given training in nursing, social service and general welfare work. The military part of the training consisted of (1) drill, (2) weapon training, (3) tactics, (4) map reading, and (5) general subjects. They were trained to use rifles, bayonets, sub-machine guns, machine guns, revolvers, grenades, swords and daggers.[126]

The women wore the soldiers' uniforms and had to observe strict military discipline. They were taken out on route marches and had to cover between 6 and 40 miles at times. Their day began with the singing of the National Anthem and common prayer for the liberation of Hindustan. They would, day after day, re-affirm their pledge too—"I shall fulfil our objective in the face of all difficulties, I shall sacrifice myself, my body, soul and properties, all for the fulfilment of my pledge. I promise I shall not do any such thing which may besmear the name of Hindustan and Netajee. I shall obey all the orders of superiors with heart and soul. I shall keep in good condition all the weapons Netaji has given."[127]

The women of Ranee Jhansi Regiment were keen to go on active service. So they sent a representation to Subhas Chandra Bose, the Supreme Commander of the Indian National Army, "It is you, who taught us that there is no distinction between men and women. It is you who gave us training, fit for menfolk, have inspired us with courage and moral stamina required for actual warfare. We have received complete training. In these circumstances why should we not be sent to the battlefront without delay?"[128] This was singed with the blood drawn from the fingers of the signatories.[129]

The first batch was sent to Maymo (Burma) in the beginning of 1945. The members of the Jhansi Regiment could not take part in actual fighting as the Indian National Army was retreating at that time. Before Netaji left for Malaya he issued orders that the regiment be disbanded and members sent to their homes.[130]

Dr. Lakshmi Swaminathan (Mrs. Sehgal)

Lakshmi Swaminathan[131] was an important woman of the Indian National Army. She was in Singapore at the time when the call of the Netaji came. She responded to this call with wholehearted enthusiasm. She was the Commander of the Ranee Jhansi Regiment and also the Minister of Social Welfare and Medicine in the Azad Hind Cabinet.

As the Commander of the Ranee Jhansi Regiment, Lakshmi was designated as Lt. Colonel. When the Indian National Army collapsed she did not surrender to the British. She was captured and later placed under arrest. Her Regiment was disbanded in 1945 and most of the girls were sent away to Singapore from Rangoon. Laksmi Swaminathan was sent to Rangoon Jail. There was a great deal of agitation for her release and the government had to yield and released her on the condition that she would not make any public speech.[132]

Lakshmi, however, defied the order and spoke on the anniversary day, October 21, 1945, of the Azad Hind Fauj and said the object for which the Azad Hind Fauj was formed had still to be achieved. She also organised a protest meeting against the Indian National Army trials at Delhi. Her activities did not please the authorities and she was served with a notice and asked to go to Kalawe.[133] On November 14 a second notice was served on her and the next morning she was flown to Meikilita from where she was taken to Kalawe in a military car.

Lakshmi was released the next year. She came to India and married Captain Sehgal of the Indian National Army.

Towards the Goal

Throughout the war period most of the Indians, wherever they were, continued their efforts to free themselves. The leaders of the major political parties were in jail for two years between 1942 and 1944. The Government was still reluctant to open negotiations with Indian leaders on the constitutional set-up. The Labour Party of England became critical of the policy of the British Government regarding India and condemned it for its failure to arrive at some workable solution. In December 1944 the Labour Party passed a resolution wherein it urged the government for the resumption of negotiations with Indian leaders with a view to securing a place for India as a self-governing member of the British Commonwealth.[134]

The next year was significant for it witnessed a new British offer[135] which was announced by Lord Wavell, the then Viceroy, general elections in Great Britain (July 1945) with Labour Party in power, and the ending of the Second World War.

During this period Indians became more important than ever before. The war had caused a lot of dislocation in the daily life of the people. The food was not only expensive but scarce as well. In some places there was famine. The war also gave an opportunity to Indian soldiers to handle new machinery and armament. The trial of the men of the Indian National Army further fanned the fire of nationalism. There were widespread demonstrations and clashes with the government against the trials.

Early next year came the uprising of the sailors of the Indian Navy at Bombay which slowly spread to other seaports. This uprising claimed the lives of several people.

By now Clement Attlee had replaced Winston Churchill, the war-time Minister. Attlee made an announcement in February that a Cabinet Mission would leave for India to assist the Indian leaders to draw up a new constitution. The Cabinet Mission[136] arrived in India on March 24, 1946, and held discussions with the various political parties and with the Indian Government. The Indian leaders could not come to a common understanding. As a consequence the Cabinet Mission had to give their own formula for solving the constitutional deadlock.

The Cabinet Mission offer was accepted by the Muslim League in its entirety by resolution on May 6, 1946. The Congress, however, only approved the portion relating to the constitution making on June 26, 1946. The government, therefore, had to announce that the interim government could not be formed on account of the difficulties arising out of the stand taken by political parties.

The decision of the government annoyed Jinnah and the Muslim League passed its famous Direct Action Resolution in which both the Congress and British Government were condemned for the breach of faith. Serious riots between Hindus and Muslims broke out in many parts of the country.

It was on August 12 that Lord Wavell invited Pandit Nehru, the President of the Indian Congress, to form the National interim government. Elections to the Constituent Assembly were also held and it met for the first time in New Delhi on December 9, 1946. It had fifteen women members. The Muslim League refused to participate. The Constituent Assembly however went on with its work.

Attlee made the following announcement on February 20: "His Majesty's government wish to make it clear that it is their definite intention to take necessary steps to effect the transference of power to responsible Indian hands by a date not later than June 1948."[137]

Lord Wavell was replaced by Lord Mountbatten on March 24, 1947, as Viceroy. The situation at this time was very tense as a strong agitation for partition was set in motion by the Muslim League. It became evident that the unity of India could not be maintained and Jinnah and the Muslim League would have nothing less than Pakistan.

The Mountbatten plan which amongst other things provided for the partition of India was accepted by the Muslim League on June 9, 1947 and by the All India Congress Committee on June, 15, 1947. The Indian Independence Act was passed by the British Parliament on July 18, 1947. This Act marked the end of the British rule in India.

Notes and References

1. Women's Indian Association, Madras, *Women's Work in Madras—Reminiscences*, p. 7.
2. Nehru, Jawaharlal, *The Unity of India, Collected Writing—1937-40*, London, 1941, p. 401.
3. Nehru, Jawaharlal, *Toward Freedom*, New York, 1941, p. 432.
4. Diwakar, R.R., *Satyagraha in Action*, Calcutta, p. 96.
5. ibid., p. 98.
6. ibid., pp. 99-100.
7. *August Struggle Report*, Part II-Prepared under the aegis of All India Satyagraha Council, U.P. Branch (unpublished), All India Congress Committee Office, Delhi, p. 5.
8. Sahai, Gobind, *42, Rebellion*, Delhi, 1947, p. 9.
9. *Hindustan Standard*, 27 July, 1942.
10. Mitra, Bejin and Chakraborty, P. (Edited), *Rebel India*, Calcutta, 1946, p. 3.
11. ibid., p. 4.
12. A place in Darrang District.
13. The Congress report says that one after another four stepped into her place and defied the bullets by laying down their lives, (*August Struggle Report* prepared under the aegis of All India Satyagraha Council, U.P., p. 157).
14. Mitra, Bejin and Chakraborty, P., *Rebel India*, 1946, p. 4.
15. ibid., Calcutta, 1946, p. 5.
16. ibid.
17. *August Struggle Report* prepared under the aegis of All India Satyagraha Council, U.P. Branch (unpublished), A.I.C.C. Office, New Delhi, p. 5.
18. *August Struggle Report* (Assam) (unpublished), A.I.C.C. Office, Delhi, p. 62.
19. ibid.
20. Mitra, Bejin and Chakraborty, P., *The Rebel India*, Calcutta, 1946, p. 22.
21. ibid., p. 22.
22. ibid., p. 25
23. ibid., p. 25
24. Mitra, Bejin, op. cit., p. 22.

25. *August Struggle Report* prepared under the aegis of All India Satyagraha Council, U.P. Branch (unpublished), A.I.C.C. Library, New Delhi, p. 120.
26. Mitra, Bejin, op. cit., p. 28.
27. *August Struggle Report,* op. cit., p. 120.
28. Nizamuddin was Home Minister of Bengal.
29. Dutta, K., op. cit., p. 25.
30. ibid.
31. ibid.
32. *August Struggle,* op. cit., p. 78.
33. ibid., p. 88
34. *The Report of the Banaras August 1942 Disturbances—Enquiry Committee* (unpublished), A.I.C.C. Library, New Delhi, p.3.
35. ibid.
36. *August Struggle Report,* op. cit., p. 173.
37. *Punjab Congress Committee Report on Disobedience in Lahore,* August 9, 1942, p. 4.
38. Morton, E., *Women Behind Gandhiji,* London, 1954, p. 139.
39. *Illustrated Weekly of India,* January 1957
40. *Women's Work in Madras—Reminiscences,* Women's Indian Association, Madras.
41. Award given by Ramsay Macdonald when Premier in 1932, regarding the political rights of major and minor communities in India.
42. *Annual Register,* Vol. II, July to December 1933, p. 357.
43. *Congress Bulletin,* September 4, 1937.
44. Punjab Congress Committee—*Report on Disturbances in Punjab,* p. 8.
45. Sitaramayya, Dr. P., op. cit., Vol. II, pp. 761-62.
46. "Brief Account of the National Activities of Bibi Amar Kaur Ahluwalia"—a hand bill.
47. Banga is in tehsil Nawanshahr, District Jalandhar.
48. *The Tribune,* Lahore, August 26, 1932.
49. The others with her were Smt. Yashodan Kumari and Krishna Kumari, daughter of Gobind Ram Khanna, Adarsh Kumari, daughter of Lala Pindi Das.
50. *The Tribune,* Lahore, September 1932.
51. "Brief Account of the National Activities of Bibi Amar Kaur Ahluwalia"—a hand bill.
52. Letter No. 5950-JL-42/54484, dated October 8, 1942; Letter No. 8245-JL-42/73492, dated December 31, 1942 (in the possession of Amar Kaur).
53. She was born in 1900 in Sanglai (Jhelum) now in Pakistan. She was educated at the village school and was married at the age of sixteen to A.N.Gujral, Advocate of Jhelum.

54. All India Congress Committee—*Women on the March*, April 1958, p.7.

55. ibid.

56. Followers of Khan Abdul Ghaffar Khan, a leader of the national movement in the North West Frontier Province.

57. ibid.

58. *August Struggle Report*, Part II, op. cit., p. 145.

59. Chimur is a village with a population of about six thousand people in Chanda District.

60. *India Ravaged*—Being an account of atrocities committed under British aegis, over the whole sub-continent of India in the latter part of 1942, Chimur-Bhansali, Professor, p. 2 (A.I.C.C. Library, New Delhi).

61. *India Ravaged*, Bhansali, Professor, p. 13.

62. ibid.

63. *Times of India*, October 8, 1930.

64. These men were to be hanged for taking part in the 1942 movement. They were responsible for the killing of some people in the two villages of Ashti and Chimur.

65. *Mahila Pragati Ke Path Par*, September, 1957, p. 13 (Hindi); *Women on the March*, September 1958, p. 4.

66. She died in 1958

67. *Annual Register*, Vol. I, 1940, p. 79.

68. Sitaramayya, Dr. P., *History of the Indian National Congress*, Vol. II, pp. 577-578.

69. *Illustrated Weekly of India*, January 20, 1957.

70. *Amrita Bazar Patrika*, February 25, 1930.

71. ibid., p. 4.

72. *Advance*, February 19, 1932.

73. *Women on the March*, July 1957, p. 11.

74. *Congress Bulletin*, January 8, 1942, p. 42.

75. ibid., 1942 p. 44.

76. A district of Madhya Pradesh.

77. *August Struggle Report*, Part II, op. cit., p. 59.

78. ibid., p. 62.

79. She was born on March 24, 1920, at Satara, district Surat (Gujarat). She took her Bachelor of Arts degree in 1939 by standing first in the University from Wilson College, Bombay. She worked as a fellow in the College. Usha interested herself in law and passed the L.L.B. Examination in 1941. She had intended to do her Master of Arts degree, but joined the Quit India movement and her attention was now diverted from studies to politics.

80. From papers in possession of Usha Mehta.

81. The Congress Radio Calling. Accused No. 3 in the Congress Radio Conspiracy Case (Papers in Possession of Usha Mehta), p. 1

82. ibid.
83. ibid., p. 2.
84. The Congress Radio Calling, op. cit., pp. 2-3. Mitra, Bejin and Chakraborty, P., (Ed), *The Rebel India*, p. 154.
85. ibid.
86. ibid.
87. Radio Calling. op. cit., p.4.
88. ibid., p.6.
89. Radio Calling, No. II (Papers in possession of Miss Usha Mehta).
90. ibid.
91. ibid.
92. Sahai, Govind, *42 Rebellion*, Delhi, 1947, p. 86.
93. A petty official in charge of collecting the land revenue in a village.
94. *August Struggle Report*, Part II, op. cit., p. 184.
95. *Report of the Pradesh Congress Committee on the happenings in Karnatak*, August 9, 1942 to September 20, 1942, p.3.
96. Karnatak Pradesh Congress Committee Report on the happenings in Karnatak, October 11, 1942 to October 31, 1942.
97. Karnatak Provincial Congress Committee, *Brief Report on Happenings in Karnatak*, November 1, 1942, to November 15, 1942.
98. Sucheta Kriplani came from a well known Bengali family settled in Punjab. She was educated at Lahore and Delhi. She took her Master of Arts degree from Delhi and became a Professor in Banaras University.
99. All India Congress Committee, *Women on the March*, August 1957, p. 13.
100. ibid.
101. *Annual Register*, January to June, Vol. I, 1942, p. 301.
102. ibid.
103. ibid.
104. ibid.
105. ibid.
106. Aruna comes from a respectable Gangoli family of Bengal. She had her early education in Sacred Heart of Jesus at Lahore and then in a Protestant School at Nainital. After completing her education she took up work in the Gokhale Memorial School for girls at Calcutta. She met Asaf Ali, a promising lawyer and a Persian scholar, at Allahabad and they became attached to each other. There was a lot of opposition, for they both belonged to different communities, Asaf Ali was a Muslim and Aruna, a Hindu. She was almost 23 years younger to him. But Aruna clung to her decision and despite opposition married Asaf Ali in 1924.
107. *The Tribune*, February 1946.
108. ibid.
109. ibid.

110. ibid.
111. ibid.
112. *Advance.* September 29, 1942.
113. *Inquilab,* monthly journal of the Indian National Congress, Eastern Zone. Edited, Rammanohar Lohia and Aruna Asaf Ali, March 1944, A.I.C.C. Library, New Delhi.
114. Lal, Pyare, *Mahatma Gandhi, The Last Phase,* p. 37.
115. ibid.
116. ibid., p. 43.
117. *The Tribune,* February 18, 1946.
118. ibid.
119. This Lodge was opened by Swami Satyanand Puri, a great Indian scholar and philosopher and a disciple of Rabindranath Tagore.
120. General Mohan Singh originally comes from Ugoke in District Sialkot, West Pakistan. He was with the 1/14th Panjab Regiment in Burmah fighting against the Japanese.
121. Giani, K.S., *Indian Independence Movement in East Asia,* Lahore, 1947.
122. ibid., p. 64.
123. ibid., p, 80.
124. ibid.
125. *The Tribune,* March 7, 1946.
126. Benarjee, Bejoy, *Indian War of Independence,* p.82; *The Tribune,* March 7, 1946.
127. ibid., pp. 85-86.
128. ibid., p. 116; Mehta (Mrs.) Gurcharan, *Azad Hind Fauj,* Amritsar, p. 173
129. ibid.
130. *Roshni,* Journal published by the All India Women's Conference. Delhi, May 1947 , p. 41.
131. She was a civilian doctor in Singapore and is the daughter of Ammu Swaminathan of Madras who took prominent part in the various movements launched by the Congress. She passed her M.B.B.S. from Medical College, in 1937. Apart from being a Commander of the Rani Jhansi Regiment, she had a portfolio in the Azad Hind Cabinet being in charge of Social Welfare and Medical Work.
132. Benarjee, Bejoy, *Indian War of Independence,* p. 116.
133. ibid.
134. Wallbank, T. Walter, *A Short History of India and Pakistan,* p. 213.
135. In this offer it was made clear that the responsibility of making a new constitution rested with the Indians. Lord Wavell offered to make important changes in his Executive Council. For this purpose he convened a meeting to which twenty-two representatives of various political parties were invited. Differences among the major political

parties took place over the representation of Muslim League nominees and Lord Wavell had to announce the breakdown of the talks.

136. The Cabinet Mission consisted of Lord Pethick-Lawrence, Sir Strafford Cripps and A.V. Alexander.

137. Banerjee A.C., *The Making of Indian Constitution*, Calcutta, 1948, p. 402.

11

INDEPENDENCE AND AFTER

After attaining independence in 1947, India had an onerous task of social reconstruction, economic development and political awakening to be able to ensure justice and equality to all its citizens. The framers of the Constitution of India, which amongst others, had prominent women like Sarojini Naidu, Hansa Mehta, Durgabai, Renuka Ray and Malti Chowdhry as its members, were aware of the social disabilities and inequalities that existed, gave constitution to the country which conferred equal rights to all its citizens and that all of them are equal before the law. It is in this context that legal, political and socio-economic status of women has to be examined.

Legal status (Article 14 of the Constitution) provides that the state shall not deny any person equality before law or equal protection of the law in the territory of India. Article 15 further elaborates and fortifies the right to equality by laying down that the state shall not discriminate against any citizen on grounds only of religion, race, caste, sex, place of birth or any of them. It goes further and provides that nothing in this article prevents the state from making any special provision for women and children. The Constitution also provides vide Article 16 equality of opportunities for all citizens in matters of employment or appointment to any office under the state.

Besides these provisions, Article 42 lays down that the state shall make provision for securing just and humane conditions of work and for maternity relief. A uniform civil code is envisaged throughout the territory of India in Article 44 of the Constitution.

Women have the right to acquire education to equip themselves for any work they chose to do. Article 29 (2) of the Constitution says "no citizen shall be denied admission to any educational institution maintained by the state or receiving aid out of state funds on grounds only of religion, sex, race, caste, language or any of them."

In spite of the liberal provisions made to ensure equality to all citizens and thereby women as well, the women continue to suffer from oppression in the male dominated society.

In the pre-independence era, the woman had no property rights, she was not legally authorised to adopt a child, she could not validly give away her daughter in marriage, a mother could also not appoint a guardian for her children by will. These and many other disabilities undermined the status of women. Efforts to reduce and remove the disabilities were made by enacting four Acts of Parliament, The Hindu Marriage Act 1955 makes monogamy the rule for both men and women. Divorce is permissible under certain conditions and petition for divorce can be made by the husband or wife. The Hindu Succession Act 1956 empowered the Hindu women to inherit property. The basis of heirship specified in the Schedule to this Act is blood relationship and the daughters, widow and mother of the deceased male inherit equally with the son. The Hindu Adoption and Maintenance Act enables the woman to adopt a child if she be a widow or divorced or if her husband had become ascetic or apostate or has been declared of unsound mind by competent court. In case the husband wants to adopt a child, consent of the wife is necessary. Under the Hindu Minority Guardianship Act 1956, a wife is entitled to maintenance under certain conditions and circumstances. She may live separately from her husband without forfeiting her right to maintenance. Children both legitimate and illegitimate are entitled to be maintained by parents. This right can be enforced against those who inherit the estate of the deceased.

In addition to these four Acts, a number of other laws have been passed to eliminate undesirable practices and protect, promote and safeguard the interest of women. Some of these are Dowry Act, Suppression of Prostitution and Immoral Traffic Act 1958, Plantation Labour Act 1951, Mines Act 1952 and Factories Act 1958. These laws were a progressive measure but these for the major part decorated the statute books, for women were not able to take benefit of the provisions made therein. In many cases illiteracy, lack of information and awareness on their part, expensive and long drawn out legal procedures discouraged them from tacking recourse to law courts. The enforcement machinery also was not adequate to ensure implementation of these laws.

Women not withstanding these handicaps continued to work for a better deal. In the seventies a fresh look began to be taken on the problems, particularly after a committee set up by the government presented the report of the Committee on Status of Women in India "Towards Equality" (1974). Now onwards the debate on law and women was a departure from the past in the sense that emphasis shifted from removing discrimination against women to focusing on the gender bias in the law and inviting attention to the violence and oppression against women within the home. This attitude and a new concept resulted in several important amendments to the existing laws and initiation of new bills.

The year 1976 witnessed passing of Bill for Equal Remuneration to men and women for the same type of work. Another progressive step was taken by amending the Factories Act which made it obligatory on the employer to provide creches for the children of working mothers in the factories. At about the same time Maternity Benefit was extended to those women who hitherto were not covered under the Act of 1958.

The laws relating to dowry, rape and violence against women were amended to make them more stringent to ensure that the culprit is punished. For instance, in case of violence against women, the Criminal Law Amendment Act 1983 recognised for the first time domestic violence inflicted by the husband or any of his relations and such a violence became an offence under the Act. The law was also amended and it provided that if a married woman committed suicide within seven years of her marriage, the presumption in law would be that her husband or his relations abetted the suicide (Section 113/4 of the Indian Evidence Act of 1872).

Similarly the changes that were effected in the Act 1983 with regard to rape were in the interest of women. The Act enjoined that the victim should be protected from the glare of publicity during investigation and trial. There was also a change in the definition of raps and the element of consent was removed. The onus of proving one's innocence was shifted to the accused. Prevention of Sati Act was passed in 1987 which was preceded by amendment to the Dowry Act of 1961 in 1984 and again in 1986. The amendments were made basically to plug the loopholes. The offence has been made cognisable and non-bailable. It also provided for Dowry Prohibition Officers at State level.

The other progressive legislations/amendments related to abortion, marriage, divorce, right to children and right to property, maintenance, family courts for speedy settlements of disputes besides many more bills introduced to ensure a strong legal framework towards attaining equality and improving the lot of women.

The legal framework, even though a step forward and an enabling factor in the development of women, the plethora of Acts could not achieve the desired results. For in the case of social legislation it is also imperative to have a change in the outlook, in the perception of women's role and support services. All these have been very slow to come by. Consequently even after more than a century of social reforms, the change though discernible is far from being indicative of parity between men and women.

The overview of the situation is generally distressing. Rape, dowry deaths, female foeticide, i.e., misuse of sex determination test of the child in the womb and the termination of pregnancy in the event of a female foetus are rampant. It was reported in *The Times of India* dated 12th April, 1991 that between 1978 and 1983, 78,000 female foetuses were aborted after sex determination. This figure is on the conservative side for it is doubtful that each and every case got reported. The Maharashtra Government in response to the women's groups enacted the Maharashtra Regulation of use of pre-natal Diagnostic Technique Act in April 1988. The misuse of test continues. This really is an indication of the horrible behaviour pattern. These may be termed as psychosicknesses, or uncivilised behaviour; but the fact remains that gruesome and a healthy society needs to get rid of them. There is need for a central legislation to check this crime and once the law is there to implement it with the sincerity it deserves. The need is all the more urgent in view of the provisional figure of sex ratio 929 females for 1000 males made available by the census department in connection with the 1991 census. These figures remind us of the prevailing imbalances in the society.

The sad augury of the whole situation is that the crime rates in cases of rape, dowry and violence against women are on the rise. In Delhi alone 132 dowry deaths were reported between January 1989 and February 1990 while in the year 1987, rape cases registered in the Union Territory of Delhi were 103, the number increased to 161 in the year 1989 and 26 gang rape cases.

The conditions in the country elsewhere were no better. In 1985 the data collected by the Police Research Development Bureau for 22 states showed 1689 cases of rape, 13,952 cases of molestation, 7,652 of kidnapping of women and 802 cases pertaining to dowry registered under different sections of the Penal Code. These figures do not represent the totality of the situation in the sense that a lot many cases remain unrepresented.

It has been felt widely by the social activists and the women's organisations that increase in crime is mainly because there is hardly any deterrent and the culprit generally gets away with anything. For instance in all the cases of dowry deaths in Delhi over the last four years there has been only one conviction and out of 6,500 cases registered with the police on crime against women, there were only 1,500 arrests and all of them were released on bail. Not only this, the Police Research Bureau recorded three per cent conviction during the last ten years.

It appears that women had to ask for, agitate, demand and advocate legal remedies to reduce and or eliminate the disabilities inflicted on them. Having obtained this enabling factor, the women have now to struggle for the implementation of laws in right earnest. It has also to be understood that there is still a need for "stringent laws, sensitive judiciary, effective enforcement machinery and vigilant women's groups to deal with such atrocious crimes against women". More than anything else there is a need for total revolution in the attitude, their perspective, their thinking that always blame the women for the crime of which she is the victim and not the perpetrator.[1]

The implementation apart, there are still lacunas in some of the laws partaining to women which need to be amended to ensure equality.

Besides the social legislation 'planned change' played an important role in creating awareness amongst women.

Planned Change

No society is static and as such no two generations are alike. Social change is a continuous process, admittedly it is far slower than what is possible in technological development and scientific discoveries. Social change in some traditional societies is so insignificant that it is not discernible and it gives credence to the fact that society is static. Consequently it becomes important to induce change to awaken it from the long slumber to which it is accustomed. Over 5,00,000 villages of India where almost 80 per cent of our population lives were no better on the eve of independence. The leadership and the planners of the country felt that all around planned change particularly in the economic sector was essential. This challenge was met by formulating the First Five Year Plan.

The First Five Year Plan amongst various provisions for development of agriculture and industries provided for social education at the Block level with three women functionaries (one at supervisory level and two at the village level) to create awareness and improve their lot and to help them to manage their household better, the objective being to acquaint the women with development needs so as to ensure that they appreciated the means and methods that were to be used to increase agriculture production.

The planners, however, soon realised that in the whole process of development participation of the women would be essential and their welfare and development had to be alongside the development in other areas. Two years after the First Five Year Plan became operative, special provisions were made within the plan to create an autonomous body to cater to the welfare of women, children and the handicapped. Thus the Central Social Welfare Board at the National level and State Social Welfare Advisory Boards at the State level were established.

The establishment of the Boards and Project implementing committees at the project level gave an opportunity to women to associate themselves with the planning of programmes and implementing them at the grassroots. Thousands of women came forward to offer their services as volunteers and many of them served on the Boards and helped in formulating policies. Many more women volunteers served in the project areas. In many cases these were uneducated women who were perhaps aware of the problems and were keen to participate to help make a better world for themselves and for womankind in general. It was as if to say that with one stroke the women came around to participate in work outside the home under the dynamic leadership of Mrs Durgabai Deshmukh. Mrs Durgabai Deshmukh was the first Chairman of the Board and remained so for many years. She had the privilege of initiating new programmes and formulating policies and above all maintaining the voluntary character of the Board. The leadership provided by her in those early days laid the foundation of sound services. The Board was full of life and always on the forward march, the enthusiasm and dynamism of the days of Durgabai became unknown once she left the Board.

The Welfare Extension Projects, one of the major programmes of the CSWB (Central Social Welfare Board) had for its component maternity and child welfare services aimed at improving the health, status of the mother and the child, adult education, imparting improved skills for the management of the home, environment sanitation and craft classes with the objective of training women in crafts to enable them to supplement the income of the family if they so wished. Balwadians for children under six years were an important component of the project as well. These project centres became women's centres where they could learn new things, meet and discuss and also have some entertainment. The welfare extension projects were not many but wherever they were started, there was a positive impact of the services. In fact it could safely be mentioned that the Welfare Extension Projects were the first to have services for women's welfare in the rural areas.

The subsequent Five Year Plan widened the scope of services for women even though for the major part, the approach remained welfare. In the Second Plan, apart from maintaining the welfare services already started, the need for implementing the principal of equal pay for equal work was asserted and provisions for training for women to compete for higher jobs was recommended. Thus it would be seen that change in the perception of women's issues and recognition of the social disabilities surfaced.

The Third Five Year Plan went a step further and focused attention on the education of women, promotion of health services with emphasis on maternal and child health, health education, nutrition and family planning. Under social welfare the largest share was allocated for expanding services in rural areas, the unique feature being the condensed courses for education of women which enabled them to pass middle/matric examination in within two years, depending upon their earlier schooling.

In the next plan, education of women received further impetus. In the field of social welfare, the emphasis shifted from women and children to family welfare. Family welfare centres (Griha Kalyan Kendras) were started in many places, even though the target group remained unchanged. Larger funds were provided for the family planning programme with a view to reduce the birth rate to 40 to 50 per thousand live births. High priority was accorded to immunisation of pre-school children, expectant mothers and to supplementary feeding of both these groups besides the nursing mothers.

The period under the Fifth Five Year Plan coincided with the International Year of the Women. The plan as such did not perhaps have anything innovative, taking clues from the earlier plans it gave weightage to the training aspect, protection of women in need, functional literacy to equip women to perform the functions of a housewife (including, nutrition, health care, home economy etc.).

These years however were important in the sense that a Report of the Committee on the status of women in India was presented. This committee, after making a comprehensive study of the questions relating to the rights and status of women in the context of changing socio-economic conditions and issues relating to the advancement of women, pointed out that dynamics of social change and development had adversely affected a large section of women and had created new imbalances and disparities such as declining sex ratio, lower expectancy of life, higher infant and maternal mortality, declining work participation, illiteracy and rising migration.

These revelations in a way was a sad reflection on our development working lasting over two decades. Something had to be done to rectify the situation. The CSWI (Committee on Status of Women in India) Report was placed before the Indian Parliament and it was debated with a lot of interest taken by the members, particularly the women members. Consequently women emerged as critical inputs for national development rather than as targets for welfare policies. Their participation was realised to be of crucial importance in the whole gamut of development work. It also came to light that the process of economic transformation adversely affected the women. Women's economic independence was a distant dream. It was strongly felt that the equality envisaged in the Constitution would be of little value unless the right to economic independence inherent in it becomes a reality.

The recommendations of the CSWI Report coupled with the climate created by the International Women's Year, hastened the passage for formulation of the National Plan of Action for women. The National Plan of Action identified the areas of health, family planning, nutrition, education, employment legislation and social welfare for implementing action programmes for women. The plan also called for planned implementation to improve the lot of women.

During these years, many women's organisations became more active, and women activists highlighted the disabilities with which the women continued to suffer. Not only this, a number of meetings, seminars, workshops etc were organised, in addition to the publication of books, articles in newspapers and research findings which were made public.

The Sixth Plan was a landmark in the struggle for equality. It made far reaching changes in favour of women. For the first time one whole chapter was devoted in the Sixth Plan to development of women and also a shift in approach from welfare to development was clearly perceived. The basic unit however remained the family rather than the women for development programming.

The Plan also provided for joint pattas (titles) to men and women. This was one way to have access to resources which perhaps would contribute to their development.

As a follow-up of the National Plan of Action, a Women's Welfare and Development Bureau was established, this in fact was the forerunner of the Women and Child Development Department organised under the Ministry of Human Resource Development in 1985.

The Department is a Modal point within the government and it has amongst others, the responsibility of co-ordinating, monitoring and initiating policies and programmes.

The Seventh Plan further "operationalised the concern for equity and empowerment articulated by the International Decade for Women". The emphasis has been on building confidence, disseminating information, creating awareness about their rights and privileges. Training for economic pursuits and opening new avenues for employment of women were some of the other areas of concern.

These provisions apart, the women began to have access to the inputs and productive resources, a process which was initiated in the Sixth Plan in the form of Joint Pattas. Another salient feature of the Seventh Plan was the recognition of the work of women at home, like collection of fuel, fodder, water etc. In addition supportive services for women and children became a part of the package.

Today besides the Human Resource Ministry which has a Department of Women and Child Development, a number of other Ministries such as Rural Development, Labour, Education, Health etc. have women's cells. There are also nearly 27 schemes which cater to the needs of women. The University Grants Commission has been instrumental in setting up a Department of Development Studies in a number of Universities in the country.

All these efforts have certainly created an environment for working more vigorously towards parity between men and women. This parity is not easy to achieve, at the same time there is an increasing awareness, women now have tried to assert to some extent, and there has been a visible change in their social status. In this direction the role played by the Non-Governmental Organisations (NGO), especially the women's groups, is no mean achievement. Women's groups have sprung up all over the country. Considering the problems and the population, these groups meet only the fringe of the need. Nevertheless it is a good beginning.

The key to the development is education. Renewed efforts have to be made for girls to get time and opportunities for schooling.

Education

Education is one of the main factors which can help women to attain higher status, economic independence, understanding about their social and legal rights etc. It also plays a significant role in changing the social order and bringing about attitudinal changes.

The Constitution of the country provides for equality of opportunities to all citizens, irrespective of race, sex, caste and communities and directs the state to "endeavour to provide within a period of ten years from the commencement of this Constitution for free and compulsory education for all children until they complete the age of 14 years."

The first census that was enumerated after the independence in 1951 revealed that there were 5.4 per cent girls at the primary level and 0.5 per cent girls at the middle level in schools. It therefore was a herculean task to increase literacy rates amongst women.

The First Five Year Plan underlined the need to have special measures for women's education. "Women must", the plan emphasised, "have the same opportunity as men for taking all kinds of work and this presupposes that they get equal facilities so that their entry into profession and public services is in no way prejudiced." The plan also envisaged vocationalised training at the secondary and university level to enable women to take up vocations if necessary.

Similarly the Five Year Plans that followed have stressed the importance of education. The Report of the National Committee on Women's Education (1959) made an impact on the formulation of the Third Five Year Plan. As a sequel to the Report condensed courses for adult women, Balsavike training and child care programmes besides extending facilities of free textbooks and scholarships were provided. In spite of the concern expressed in the succeeding Five Year Plans there was not an impressive improvement in the enrolment of girls. One of the factors attributed to this situation was the shortage of women teachers. This bottleneck was removed by extending scholarship to local girls to take up to teaching career.

Education was still far behind the overall male literacy rates. The Indian Education Commission (1966) in its report regretted the failure to achieve the target set for it in this field. Realising the resource constraints it recommended the phasing of the programme by (a) providing five years of effective education to all children by 1975-76 and seven years of such education by 1985-86, (b) making partime education for about one year compulsory for all children in the age group of 11-14 who have not completed the lower primary stage and are not attending schools and (c) efforts to liquidate adult illiteracy.[1]

In the year 1971 male literacy rate was 39.5 per cent as against female literacy rate of 18.7 per cent, while in 1981 the rates for male literacy were 46.9 per cent, and for females 24.8 per cent. The situation in rural areas was still worse with 40.8 per cent and 18 per cent for males and females respectively. Female literacy in rural areas varied between 8.99 per cent and 10.17 per cent in states such as Bihar, Uttar Pradesh and Madhya Pradesh and was as low as 5.4 per cent in some parts of Rajasthan.

At the primary level girls enrolment has increased at the rate of 5.5 per cent while the comparable rate in case of boys has been 3.9 per cent per annum. The disparity remains because of the initial setback in the girls education. The rate of growth in girls enrolment at the middle level has been much faster at 8.6 per cent but the fact remains that only 30.6 per cent of girls in the relevant age group are in the middle schools.

The Fifth Five Year Plan pointed out that despite substantial increase in the educational facilities, the targets laid down for both elementary and secondary education registered a shortfall in enrolment, while in higher education these were exceeded. "But shortfalls have been particularly large in case of elementary education, more so in the case of girls." Enrolment in primary education as percentage of the population in the corresponding age group is as follows:

Year	Primary Stage Classes I-IV			Middle Stage Classes V-VIII		
	Boys	Girls	Total	Boys	Girls	Total
1950-51	55.0	20.1	37.8	20.8	4.6	13.00
1960-61	74.0	35.0	54.8	35.5	12.5	24.3
1970-71	109.8	68.6	89.7	66.7	33.0	50.7

The low literacy rate amongst girls is mainly due to poverty and the attitude of the parents to educate boys in preference to girls. It is still accepted in some sections of the society that education is really not necessary for girls for her future role as wife and mother.

The Sixth Five Year Plan was a landmark in the history of education for women. Education for them became a major programme under the special chapter assigned to "Women and Development". The programme was directed towards higher enrolment, strengthening of science teaching in schools, increased entry of women in professional colleges like engineering, electronics etc.

The education of girls, with all the encouragement given and the provision made was far from its goal of universal elementary education as is apparent from the statement:

Enrolment Ratio—Elementary Classes 1984-1985

Year	Class I-V		Class VI-VIII		Class I-VIII	
	Total	Girls	Total	Girls	Total	Girls
1950-51	42.6	24.61	12.9	4.5	32.4	17.4
	(191.55)	(53.86)	(31.20)	(5.30)	(227.75)	(59.15)
1955-56	52.9	32.4	16.5	6.6	42.5	22.5
	(251.67)	(76.39)	(42.93)	(8.67)	(294.60)	(85.06)
1960-61	62.4	41.4	22.5	11.3	48.7	30.9
	(349.94)	(114.01)	(67.04)	(16.30)	(416.98)	(130.31)
1968-69	78.1	59.6	33.5	19.4	82.5	46.5
	(543.68)	(202.11)	(125.36)	(35.47)	(669.04)	(274.58)
1973-74	77.0	59.9	32.8	21.0	61.6	46.5
	(612.55)	(231.09)	(139.50)	(42.97)	(752.05)	(274.06)
1979-80	83.6	65.9	40.2	27.7	67.2	52.0
	(709.43)	(271.81)	(194.83)	(65.28)	(904.26)	(337.09)
1984-85	94.1	76.7	50.6	36.3	78.3	61.9
	(839.32)	(331.93)	(161.53)	(90.68)	(1100.84)	(422.61)

It would thus be seen from the statement that by the end of the Sixth Plan, the education of women still remained a matter of concern. The Seventh Five Year Plan included among its major thrust areas, the future "development of women". "The basic approach being to enable women to acquire confidence in themselves...and develop a sense of responsibility towards the overall betterment of society and their individual personalities."

The Seventh Plan also proposed a number of socio-economic programmes together with provision for financial outlay to ensure implementation. Dr. Manmohan Singh, former Deputy Chairman of the Planning Commission, stated in an interview to *The Economic Times:* "There is growing awareness that in a situation where poverty is pervasive, our perception of needs and priorities must not be merely male perception."

The goal of the Seventh Plan was to achieve universalisation of elementary education. Emphasis however was placed on vocational training, personnel policies, mass education etc. The Plan pointed out that "the educational programme will have to be restructured to remove the stereotyped image of women.... For creating the right type of awareness, important instruments that may be used are radio, television, educational institutions, mahila mandals and voluntary agencies. New areas for providing suitable employment to women have to be identified."

The Seventh Plan period is over. There has been an improvement in the rate of literacy among women, the goal for universalisation of women's education is still not in sight, the school dropout rates are high. The picture is not all that bleak. There is a ray of hope. The 1991 census reveal that even though the disparity between the female and male literacy continues, the gaps between the two are increasingly being bridged. However the regional differences remain. Kerala continues to be ahead of other states with 90.59 per cent 'effective literacy' with Rajasthan the second lowest from the bottom. The four states of Bihar, Madhya Pradesh, Rajasthan and Uttar Pradesh constitute 39.70 per cent of India's population with 30.64 per cent of her population literate. Gender differences in these states seems to be more pronounced. The basic redeeming feature in the overall situation even in these states is the reduction of disparities. There has to be a faster growth in women's education to be able to close this gap.

Another positive factor in the overall assessment of the education of girls is that it is now being generally realised that education for girls is essential even though a hostile attitude towards higher education for girls continues. The acceptance of girls' education is comparatively better in urban areas than in rural areas. The reasons for the slow progress are many. The girl, by the time she is eight or nine and in some cases even earlier, starts helping in the household work like washing, cleaning, collection of firewood, fetching water etc. She also looks after the siblings, especially when the mother is out.

A large number of girls also work and contribute to the income of the family by their own labour. Once a girl has had the taste of freedom and cash money, it is difficult for her to go back to school. Another factor which weighs heavily, is the lack of adequate number of schools exclusively for girls. Indifferent attitude of parents to the education of girls also plays an important role in keeping girls away from schools.

The government, women activists and the voluntary agencies are alive to the problems and. Concerted efforts, social awareness, adequate incentives and need-based educational facilities are likely to improve the situation. It is the imparting of education and training in improved skills besides the vocational training that can raise the status of women for it would be a step towards economic independence.

Economic Independence

Women have always participated in the economic activity of the society ever since man put his foot on this land. It is however a different matter that her work has been hidden behind a thick veil in the man-oriented society.

The women have been engaged in household crafts, in the agriculture sector, in the domestic front, in finding fuel and water for the family and fodder for the animals. There are certain agriculture related jobs which are done by women like transplanting, cutting and harvesting etc. Even in the household industry, whether it is the handloom or the potters wheel, she is there to do the job of preparing the material, colouring it and in the case of pottery of baking it. This is all in addition to the six or seven hours job that she does in the house, cooking, washing cleaning, bearing children etc. Since she does not get any cash money or wages, she is enlisted as dependent. She performs the essential jobs, it may also be that without her contribution the household expenditure is difficult to meet, yet she is neither considered economically productive nor the bread winner.

However, with the advocacy being done for the cause of women, there is greater realisation at least on the women's part, though not widely, of economic independence. Economic independence is imperative to ensure equality among women and men. Pandit Jawaharlal Nehru rightly said, "The habit of looking upon marriage as a profession almost and as the sole economic refuge for women will have to go before women can have any freedom. Freedom depends on economic conditions even more than political ones and if a woman is not economically free and self-earning, she will have to depend on her husband or on someone else and dependents are never free. The association of man and woman should be of perfect freedom and perfect comradeship with no dependence of one or the other."

The data on employment situation leading to economic independence and overall contribution of women to the economic development and economic health of the family is neither accurate nor adequate, since there are variations in the figures available and this variation is born out of the definition adopted by each of the organisations/departments like the census of India National Sample Survey, the Labour Bureau etc. In fact, the employment of women is generally underestimated. The concept of employment revolves around the cash wage earners, her work in the farm and in the house having been taken for granted. According to the 1985 report of the UNICEF about 45 per cent of the total number of working women were unpaid helpers on family farms or non-farm enterprises.

Statistics reveal that there has been seven per cent decrease in women's employment in the two decades beginning from 1961. The census of 1961 showed that female work participation was 28 per cent. In the subsequent census in 1971, it came down to 14.2 per cent and by 1981 it again increased to 20.85 per cent which was lower than that of the 1961 figures. The main reason for variation in the figures seems to be because the workers were defined very narrowly in the 1971 census. This was somewhat corrected at the time of 1981 census and the scope of the definition was widened. The census of 1981 introduced a category of marginal workers which covered a large number of women.

There were 44.97 million, or 13.99 per cent were women main workers out of the total population of 321.93 million females (1981). In case of rural areas the percentage of main workers was 16 while in case of urban areas the percentage was 7.28. Further, of the 44.97 million main workers in the country (excluding Assam,) the majority, that is,

20.77 million or 46.18 per cent were agriculture labour, 14.93 million or 33.20 per cent were cultivators, 20.6 million or 4.59 per cent worked in household industry and 7.21 million or 16.03 per cent were engaged in other activities.

Among the female dominated industries in 1981, bidi making had the highest proportion as there were 1,549 females per 1,000 male bidi workers. The ratio of male-female workers was considerably low as far as women were concerned in industries like manufacture of transport equipment and parts, manufacture of electrical machinery, apparatus and appliances etc.

Women, besides being entrepreneurs, are also joining enterprises being run by others for wages. This phenomenon is visible in rural as well as in urban areas. However, in rural areas the number of self-employed women has declined from 356 thousand in 1971 to 325 thousand in 1981. In urban areas the picture is different. There has been a fairly good increase of 33.07 per cent.

The employment of women has also not kept pace with the growth in population. In the last few decades of planning, the female population has increased by 55 per cent while the female work force has increased only by 15 per cent. This decline may be because there continues to be a decline in the female population as compared to the male population. The literacy rates among women are low, there are also fewer women at the decision-making level. Despite these handicaps, there is qualitative improvement in the sense that there is diversity of occupation and women are now found as doctors, nurses, teachers, administrators, bankers, entrepreneurs, in fact there is hardly a profession where women are not now working. The number of women in such cases is limited.

Women have accepted responsibilities outside the home. They have done equally well if not better than their counterparts, the men. It has however been a difficult task to leave the home and find jobs outside. It has also been not easy for them to move up the ladder.

These apart, consideration of home and children weigh heavily with her. Her work, howsoever important, is taken as of secondary importance. Her first duty even today is considered to be the home and the children. In fact in her case, more often than not, it is the family decision where the employment of women is concerned—whether she should work or not, where she should work, what kind of jobs she should have are all matters where her decision is not final.

Another discouraging factor is that women do not get equal pay for equal work in spite of the legal provisions that exist. It has been the practice that in the agriculture sector women are paid only 40 to 60 per cent of the male wages. With the passage of time the women's earnings are showing a downward trend. Between 1964-65 and 1974-75 the disparity between the earnings of men and women in the farm sector had increased by 50 per cent. The women in the self-employed, home-based industry are facing a crises, for rapid industrialisation is dislocating them. In most of the cases they are being forced to work on fixed rates just as for traders, middlemen and small industrialists.

In the recent plans, particularly in the Sixth and Seventh Plan, the emphasis has been to vocationalise education. Regional Vocational Centres, one each at Bangalore, Bombay and Trivandrum, besides the National Institute at Delhi, have been opened. In addition a number of training institutions have been started all over the country for women.

The economic activity of the women continues to receive attention but economic independence of women still needs acceptance. Some of the constraints that have to be looked into are:

(i)   Lack of enforcement of social and labour legislation.
(ii)   Inadequate access to employment benefits like minimum hours of work, minimum wages, maternal health care, day care for their children etc.
(iii)   New and diverse avenues of employment.
(iv)   Insufficient managements for skill training, management training etc.
(v)   Awareness programme also needs to be strengthened to bring about social change.

The voluntary agencies can help in ensuring better status to the women workers and increase their bargaining power, at least for equal wages, by developing unionisation amongst women. SEVA, a voluntary organisation, has done pioneering work in this direction.

These voluntary agencies can also develop an awareness programme directed towards the facilities available under the law, the employment opportunities, attitudinal changes and acceptance of the new role of women outside the home. The Labour Ministry and the Social Welfare Department have a significant role to play in this field. Economic independence, besides building confidence in women, will also help them to take an active part in the political life of the country.

Political and Administrative Role

Women had participated very actively in the political life of the country, particularly after Gandhiji took the leadership of the freedom struggle in his hands. They took part in the several phases of the struggle. Women also fought and won elections after the Congress decided to form the government under the Government of India Act, 1935. Immediately following the declaration of independence, a number of women alongside the men were elected to frame the Constitution for free India.

There were women who excelled in the international field. Mrs. Vijayalakshmi Pandit became the first woman President of the UN Assembly, a rare honour for the women of the world. Similarly Raj Kumari Amrit Kaur became the Vice President of the League of Red Cross, Hansa Mehta and Lakshmi Menon held offices in the Human Rights Commission and the UN Commission on the Status of Women. At home Mrs. Sarojini Naidu became the first Governor of Uttar Pradesh. Later her daughter Padmaja Naidu was the Governor of West Bengal. Women also fought elections and were elected to both the Central Parliament and the State Assemblies. A few of them became Cabinet Ministers, Ministers of State etc. Mrs Sucheta Kriplani had the distinction of becoming the Chief Minister of Uttar Pradesh and Shashikala Kakedkar was the Chief Minister of Goa. Mrs Satpati Nandini became Chief Minister of Orissa.

Mrs. Indira Gandhi had the signal honour of becoming the first woman Prime Minister of India, a position she occupied for about nineteen years except for a brief period when the Janata Party came to power in 1977.

Born on 19 November 1917, in a very comfortable home, Anand Bhavan, Allahabad, Indira Priyadarshini Nehru was the daughter of Pandit Jawaharlal Nehru, the first Prime Minister of Independent India and a prominent leader of the independence struggle. Indira's political association began when she was four years of age. She witnessed the trial of her grandfather, Pandit Motilal Nehru, sitting on his lap. Later as a young girl she organised the Vanar Sena (Monkey Army). The members of the Vanar Sena, the little children, were to serve water to the marching Satyagrahis. They also helped in distributing literature and carrying messages.

It was during the Quit India movement that Indira Gandhi became actively involved in the freedom struggle. She defied the law by taking out processions. The police lathi charged, the undaunted young Indira continued to hold the flag despite the lathi blows. Indira rose in the Congress (Indian National Congress) ranks and became its President. She became Prime Minister in the year 1966 after the death of Lal Bahadur Shastri, the then Prime Minister. Her years of Prime Ministership have been very eventful. She helped Bangladesh achieve victory in its independence war. She gave new direction to the policies and programmes and was internationally respected as a politician of high calibre. After serving the country for over three terms, she met with a tragic death in the year 1984.

These women were the rare ones, perhaps they were the children of the circumstances; once the opportunity came their way, they exploited it fully and made a name for themselves. This however does not mean that the status of millions of women was in any way related to them and even remotely equivalent to them. To assess the status of women with these examples is not only incorrect but is another injustice to women.

It may be of interest to examine the political status of women on the basis of elections that have taken place so far. In the first elections held in 1951-52, 27 women were elected to the Parliament, at the state level only 16 states out of the 25 states (category A, B & C) had women MLA's (Member Legislative Assembly) with the State of Bihar electing a maximum of 13 women members followed by Uttar Pradesh and Madhya Pradesh with seven each. The position in the next elections did not improve. In fact there were 25 women members of Parliament in 1957 against 27 in 1951. In the State Assemblies 196 women were elected by 13 states. Bihar again took the lead by electing 33 members. This seasaw battle continues even today. There has not been a substantial increase in the number of women that have become members of parliament. The position as it stands today after more than three decades is that in 1984 elections, 46 seats out of the house of 537 seats were occupied by women, an improvement over the past years. The Rajya Sahba had 28 women in the house of 245 members. There has been greater representation of women in the Rajya Sabha by nomination. In the recent elections (in 1989 there were only 24 women in the Lok Sabha and 24 in the Rajya Sabha), the position is not even comparable with the first elections in 1951.

As far as the political offices for women are concerned, these have been slow to come. Today there is no woman amongst the Cabinet Ministers, the strength of women State Ministers is negligible. Women are yet far away from participating in the decision-making level.

The participation of women members, both in the state legislatives and the central parliament, has been significant. They have not only debated and piloted the bills relevant to women's development, dowry, child care, health education etc, but have taken a keen interest in the debates in specialised subjects.

Women, however, have not been able to make pressure groups, this may be because of the insignificant number that are returned to the parliament, lack of awareness, the voting pattern, which is for the major part based on caste and socio-economic status of the candidate, rather than on political ideology, lack of decision-making power. And as such participation of women at the district, state and national level is not commensurate with their numbers. It is also not easy for women to take part in the political life in view of the stringent social practices besides the socio-economic constraints.

Participation of women in the Panchayati Raj Institution has been minimal. There has hardly been any involvement of women in the Panchayati Raj Institutions. Their participation was sought to be ensured by nomination of one or two women members wherever they could not be elected. There has been in the recent years inclination for providing 30 per cent representation to women. Andhra Pradesh and Karnataka already have 30 and 25 per cent seats respectively for women.

Political parties have really not taken the interest that was needed to organise the women power. The Congress Party which has a large number of women members has had only one woman President of the Congress in Mrs. Indira Gandhi after independence. The Bharatiya Janata Party (BJP) has one woman Vice President, Mrs Vijayraje Scindia. In spite of the fact that each of the political parties now project its programme for women and expresses concern for them, in actual practice very few women candidates are fielded in the elections.

Non-Governmental Sectors

Women's contribution in the non-governmental sector also has been praiseworthy. Besides advocating the cause of women and seeking improvement in their status, they have initiated programmes of

protection and development. Some of these organisations are All India
Women's Conference, Bharatiya Grameen Mahila Sangh, Mahila
Mandals all over the country, organisations for Rural Development and
those engaged in providing employment like SEWA of Gujarat and
many others like Saheli of Delhi seeking to render assistance.

The women's cause apart, there have been a number of
organisations started by women for the welfare of weaker sections of the
society. Some of these are the Indian Council for Child Welfare, the
Family Planning Association etc. In recent years women have also
taken part very actively in the Blood Donation programme, particularly
in motivating the public. All this is being done as a labour of love and
for no personal gains.

The Indian Council for child welfare has had prominent women
like Mrs. Indira Gandhi, Hansa Mehta, Pushpa Mehta, Phul Renu Guha,
Rajan Nehru, Mrs. Tara Ali Baig and many others as its President.

Mrs. Tara Ali Baig worked for the 'child' for over forty years. Born
in Mussorie in 1916, granddaughter of Sir K.G. Gupta and wife of the
late Mirza Rashid Ali Baig of Diplomatic Services, was an outstanding
worker. She was responsible for initiating and submitting an eight-point
National Policy to the government which ultimately paved the way for
the government to pass the 1974 Policy for children. Mrs Baig was the
General Secretary of the Council and later became its President. During
her tenure new directions were given to the child welfare work, and it
was taken out from its narrow concept to a broader perspective. In fact,
it would not be wrong to say that she was the founder of the S.O.S.
Children's villages in India. Mrs. Baig worked for a change in the
institutional system of children's orphanages and allied institutions.

Mrs. Baig was recognised as an expert on 'child'. She became the
President of the International Union for Child Welfare, a world apex
body federating 90 countries with child care projects. Mrs Baig also had
the distinction of presiding over the World Congress on the 'child' held
in Sweden in the year 1969.

Besides being a social worker of standing Mrs. Baig was a prolific
public speaker and a writer. She was invited to write the official
biography of Smt. Sarojini Naidu. She authored two books on women
and many articles on varied subjects.

Another prominent leader in the cause of women has been Dr. Phul
Renu Guha, known as a social worker and an educationist. Born on 12

August, 1911 in Calcutta, she had her education in India and UK. In her earlier days she participated in the freedom struggle. She was elected to the Rajya Sabha in 1968 and became the Union Minister of State. Dr. Guha was also Chairman of the Committee set up to study the status of women. She has been actively associated with a large number of women's organisations, like All Indian Women's Conference, Women's Co-ordinating Council, Women's International League for Peace and Freedom. Her work in Calcutta, both in political and social welfare, is well known. Her work continues. Even at the age of 80, she is active, attends meetings and does her best to solve the problems of women.

While Dr. Phul Renu Guha carries on her work in Calcutta quietly, Mrs. Sarojini Vardappan is a name synonymous with social work and women's development in Tamil Nadu. Born in September 1921, in Madras, Mrs Vardappan's association with women's work is of over 40 years. She has been the President of the All India Women's Conference, Chairman of the Central Social Welfare Board, Chairman of the Red Cross Branch of Tamil Nadu and many other organisations. Her mission has been to raise the status of women and sponsor programmes for the needy.

Mrs. Vidyaben Shah, born on November 7, 1922, has been a social worker in the field of child welfare. In fact she started her public career by participating in the Quit India Movement. Once she was out, there was no going back, consequently she has been associated with a variety of organisations engaged in child welfare, women and family welfare and other social and relief work.

As for the child welfare work, it all began in Saurashtra, with the child welfare council and later in setting up and developing the famous Bal Bhavan at Rajkot. She is today the President of the Indian Council for Child Welfare, a position she has occupied for two terms. During her tenure she has tried to develop child welfare councils in areas where these were non existent.

Besides these traditional fields, the women have also come into health-related fields and have found new areas of development. One such area is the Voluntary Blood Donation Programme. The need of this programme is urgent, particularly in view of the threat posed by AIDS all over the world. Mrs Kanta Saroop Krishen born in West Punjab, now a part of Pakistan, started her social work activities in the pre-partition days. She has been associated with the Red Cross and its Hospital

Welfare Section, Women's Defence Council, Bharat Scouts and Guides, and Child Welfare Council. These early years in the voluntary arena helped her in developing the Blood Donation Programme. She can rightly be called the founder of this programme in North India and for developing the voluntary concept all over the country. She feels and rightly so that blood donated by the free will of the donor for a cause is better than the commercial blood. She has made all out efforts to start voluntary blood donation societies in many parts of the country. Her life's mission has been to spread the concept of voluntary donation and eliminate commercialisation of blood.

Mrs. Saroop Krishen can be a proud mother of the movement and can say with pride that there is no commercialisation of blood in Chandigarh. After her initial success in Chandigarh she moved out to larger areas and along with others founded the Indian Society of Blood Transfusion &Immunohaematology. In 1972 she became its Founder-Secretary General, a position she occupies till today. The ISBTI has had its birth pangs but with undaunted courage, Mrs. Saroop Krishen has steered through difficult times.

Her appeal, her visits, her contacts are not only limited to one area or one section of the society. It may be the school students, the college students, universities, offices, housewives, Mrs. Saroop Krishen has a programme for them. She has time for everybody. For her a blood donor is a VIP.

There are many more women, who need to be included but then many more volumes would be needed. This brief description of women is an indication of their achievement and not a detailed account. This work would be incomplete without making a mention of women in the Family Planning Association, particularly the late Lady Rama Rao, the founder of the Association and the current President of the Association, Mrs. A. Wadia.

An area where women have to exert fully are the trade unions. They could have acted as pressure groups. Women workers have co-operated in the activities and programmes of the trade unions. They have participated in the strikes as well. Unfortunately their number is small and as such their issues have not been taken up seriously. Despite the expression of concern at different forums, the trade unions have yet to pay adequate attention to women's problems. They are issues like equal pay for equal work, maternity benefits and child care facilities, etc. In fact, no trade union has gone on strike on these important issues.

It may be mentioned that women have supported action and in some cases have initiated action where they felt grossly wronged. Some of the important events relate to the Chipko Movement, the politics of liquor licensing, government water supply in Himachal Pradesh, struggle for canal water and public lands by poor women in drought-prone Marathwada and struggle for self-respect, employment and justice among Tamil Nadu landless labourers.

More such efforts are needed to restore a place of equality to women on par with men.

After more than 40 years of independence, a change in the position, though not dramatic, is discernible. This may be because of the social legislation, the progress made in education, health or economic field or as a result of technological developments, or perhaps as a process of evolution. There are, though in small numbers, women in almost all spheres of the national life. They are doctors, engineers, pilots journalists, teachers, administrators, diplomats, head of states etc. In spite of these achievements, the fact remains that women's condition even today is a grim reality. According to the 1981 census there were 933 women for 1,000 men, against nearly 47 per cent literate men only 25 per cent literate women. Dowry deaths, child marriages, perpetuation of widowhood, preference for son in every sphere of life continues to have social sanctions.

As for the child marriages, according to the 1981 census, out of 321.36 million females, 147.14 million or 45.79 per cent were married; of these 2.63 million or 1.79 per cent were aged 10-14 years. In the rural areas out of the 115.00 million married females 2.42 million or 2.11 per cent were aged 10-14 years and in the urban areas out of the 32.14 million, 0.68 per cent were aged 10-14 years.

"The level of current fertility among these girls can be judged from the fact that 20,014 births were reported to these girls. It is quite shocking during the last one year proceeding the 1981 census enumeration were not restricted to first order births but almost 10 per cent of them were of second order. Giving birth to a second child before the age of 14 years is really a reflection on the prevailing social system which needs drastic change."

The situation in the economic front or for her economic independence is no better. The women's work in the house which includes collection of firewood, bringing water from long distance, helping in the family business or in the agricultural fields because it is not remunerative and she is also not paid for, is not considered as work. The census does not take note of it nor is it recognised. It is estimated that of the average hours of unpaid work done by women outside their homes, ranges from 6.1 to 7.5 per day with some women working for 10 hours and more. This apart, 89.51 (1981 census) per cent of the women workers are engaged in the unorganised sector. Of these 82.3 per cent are in agriculture and allied occupations. In the organised sector women form 13.3 per cent of all employees. In the public sector, they account for 11 per cent of the total employment and in the private sector, for 17.8 per cent.

In the senior management jobs, women hold 994 posts against 15,993 men in similar positions in the All India Services Constituting 5.8 per cent, There are only 21 women officers in the Indian Police Service as against 2,418 men (0.9%). In the Indian Administrative Services, there are 339 women against 4,209 men (7.5%).

Besides the concern expressed in other fields, the economic independence is greatly being advocated for women. This in a way seems to be the right course. But has it helped? The answer is a big question mark. The woman is now burdened with two jobs, work within the house and a job outside. Does it really leave free time for her to enjoy the fruits of her economic independence? Not only that, she in many cases is perhaps the custodian of her salary till she arrives home, when it becomes a part of the total income of the family, the salary having been passed on to the mother-in-law or the husband.

The economic independence, therefore, is not the total solution; equal emphasis has also to be on the total development of the woman, aware of her rights and responsibilities, recognition of her role and work in the home, awareness amongst the people that women are as good citizens as others in this country. If necessary social system has to change where women do not have to ask for concessions, it is their right and they must have it.

The conditions in the political arena are no better. Each of the political parties contribute to the principle of women's participation. But do we see the reflection of their wishes in Parliament? The percentage of women members of parliament have been reducing instead of increasing. 27 women were elected to the Lok Sabha in the first election while 19 were elected/nominated to the Rajya Sabha. Today after 44 years of independence, there are only 24 women members in Lok Sabha and 24 in the Rajya Sabha.

The women have to travel a long way before they can be equated with men. Having agreed that they have to go a long way to ensure a place that rightly belongs to the women as citizens of the country, a concrete action is called for. How do we reach the women in the remote and backward areas? How do we create awareness amongst men and women of the roles and responsibilities of each of the citizens of this country? How do we bring about acceptance of changed role in the traditional society and how do we ensure that the girl child in the family is equally important if not more, as the creator, as the producer and as the maker? The future lies in her hands. This is not an easy task. It does need both men and women to contribute to this cause. In the past, it has not been only the women who have been in the vanguard of the social reform movement, men have also played leading and important roles. It is, therefore necessary to avoid isolation and have men and women participate in this great task. Let there be a movement, a movement of the type led by Gandhiji for the freedom of the country, in which he invited and encouraged women to participate. Let the men feel the same concern over the condition of almost 50 per cent of the population which, if not totally inhuman, is degrading.

Cited Works

Census of India, 1961, 1971, 1981.

Govt of India, New Delhi, Towards Equality—Report on the Status of Women in India, New Delhi, 1974.

The Tribune, September 23, 1990.

The Times of India, April, 1991.

The Hindustan Times, May 3, 1991.

Indian Management, Special Issue, April, 1988.

Five Year Plan Documents.

Dayal, Rekha (Ed.), *Resource Book on Women and Development*, New Delhi, 1987.

Desai, Dr. Neera, *A Decade of Women's Movement in India*, Bombay, 1988.

Desai, Dr. Neera, *Women in Modern India Bombay*, 1957.

Hansa Mehta, *Indian Women*, Delhi, 1981.

Mankekar, Kamala, *Women in India*, New Delhi, National Institute of Public Co-operation & Child Development, New Delhi. *Report of the National Workshop on Enforcement Machinery and Women*, Feb 19-20, 1988.

Tara Ali Baig, (ed) *Women of India*, New Delhi, 1957.

Verma, S.C., *Women's Vital Role in Rural Development*, New Delhi.

The Tribune, 23 Sept, 1990.

The Indian Education Commission Report 1966, Para 53.

Govt of India, Deptt of Social Welfare, *Towards Equality—Report of the Committee on the Status of Women in India*, p. 237.

APPENDICES

APPENDIX A

Details of the Custom of Widow Burning or Sati

There were a number of ways of performing the rites of sati.

A woman who intended to become a Sati was first given a bath and then she put on all the insignia of a married woman. The Sati took along with her 'kum kum' (a red powder used by women on the forehead), a comb, a mirror and betel leaves. She was then taken to the cremation ground to the accompaniment of music, and women following her singing hymns in the glory of the unfortunate widow. The Brahmin who accompanied her exhorted the Sati to show courage and resoluteness.

In Gujarat and in northern districts of Uttar Pradesh, a small hut, about 12 feet square, was built of reeds and faggots in which small pots of oil and other fuel were kept to make it burn quickly.

The woman was made to sit in half reclining position in the middle of the hut. She rested her back against a post to which she was tied from her waist downwards. In this position she held the dead body of her husband on her knees, chewing betel. After remaining in this position for half an hour she called the Brahmin to set fire.[1]

In some places, especially in the Deccan and western India, the funeral pyre was piled in a deep pit, thus leaving little chance for escape.

Yet there was another method practised in Bengal. A Sati was often bound to the corpse with cords or both the bodies were fastened down with long bamboo poles curving over them like a coverlet or weighed down with logs. After she was laid across, her relatives and friends gave her messages in the form of letters, clothes, or flowers to be delivered to their dear ones who were dead.

In some cases the woman willingly followed her husband to the funeral pyre. Bernier was an eye-witness to one such case. He states: "It is impossible to describe the brutish boldness or the ferocious gaiety depicted on the woman's countenance; her step was undaunted, her conversation was free from all perturbation, her easy air was free from all dejection, her lofty courage was void of all embarrassment. She took a torch and with her own hand lighted the fire. It appeared to be a dream but it was a stern reality."[2]

The custom of Sati had become a symbol of prestige and all respectable women were honour-bound to sacrifice themselves on the funeral pyre of their husbands. Besides, the stigma attached to widowhood and cruel treatment meted out to the widows who did not commit sati was such that women chose to burn themselves, an easier evil than widowhood.

Rajput ladies burned themselves more willingly than those of other castes. It was particularly practised on the junction of rivers and was common in Punjab, Rajasthan, the Ganges Valley, South India, Bengal and Bihar, etc.

It was practised for a number of reasons. The families boasted of their Satis and the rival families tried to surpass each other. In some cases the aged husband did not desire that his young wife as a lonely woman should survive him. It was more in the interest of the departed soul. The son was relieved from the expenses of maintaining a mother. The relatives were happy to get rid of the widows as in the absence of a direct issue the property would be theirs.

Albuquerque, the Portuguese Governor in India in 1510, prohibited sati within the Portuguese territory of Goa. The third Sikh Guru Amar Das (1552-1574) condemned it. Akbar also was against this custom and saved the daughter-in-law of the Raja of Jodhpur from being burnt against her will. Jahangir also prohibited it. The Marathas did not favour the burning of widows. Queen Ahalya Bai Holkar, a famous Maratha ruler of Indore, discouraged it.[3] Sati was also suppressed by the Dutch in Chinsura and by the French in Chandranagar and by the Danes at Sirampur (Bengal).

The Regulation Act of 1813 imposed restriction on the burning of widows. This Act was later amended in 1817. However, the government interference did have its effect in Bombay and Madras and the average number did not exceed fifty annually between 1815 and 1820. But the Bengal Presidency was not affected much. The numbers officially reported were:

1815...378
1816...442
1817...707
1819...839

It was in the year 1818 that Raja Rammohun Roy felt the necessity of eradicating this evil. He propagated against this practice and tried to end this custom by dissuasion. However, he was against the abolition of sati by a Government measure. But Lord William Bentinck took a decisive step after consulting his principal officers and got the Regulation XVII of December 1829 passed. The practice of sati or of burning or burying alive widows became illegal and punishable by criminal courts.

However, this regulation did not reach the whole country. It reached only 37 million people directly and to 19 million people in the Indian States out of the total population of 77 million people. So Sati was prohibited in British India. But it continued to be practised in northern India, western India, Sind, Assam and Orissa.

Slowly, the Act of 1829 was extended to other areas and it lasted till 1860 when another Act[4] was passed whereby any assistance given in the performance of Sati was made punishable as an abetment of suicide.

APPENDIX B

Martin's letter to Damodar Rao indicating that the Rani had no share in the occurrence at Jhansi

"Your poor mother was very unjustly and cruelly dealt with, and no one knows her true case as I do. The poor thing took no part in the massacre of the European residents of Jhansi in June 1857. On the contrary she supplied them with food for two days after they had gone into the Fort—got a 100 matchlock men from Kurrua, and sent them to assist us, but after being kept a day in the Fort, they were sent away in the evening. She then advised Major Skeine and Captain Gordon to fly at once to Dattia and place themselves under the Raja's protection, but this even they would not do; and finally they were massacred by our own troops, the police, Jail and Cas; Este."

APPENDIX C

Translation of a Khureeta of the Rani of Jhansi to the address of the Commissioner and Agent Lt. Governor, Saugor Division, (the date is not given but it is supposed that it was written on June 12, 1857) giving details of the uprising in Jhansi and her inability to maintain law and order.

Foreign Political Consultation No. 354. July 31, 1857

Letter No 1

After compliments. States that the Government forces stationed at Jhansi, through their faithlessness, cruelty and violence, killed all the European Civil and Military officers, the clerks and all their families and the Rani not being able to assist them for want of guns, and soldiers as she had only 100 or 50 people engaged in guarding her house she could render them no aid, which she very much regrets. That the mutineers afterwards behaved with much violence against her and servants, and extorted a great deal of money from her, and said that as the Rani was entitled to succeed to the Reasut, she should undertake the management since the sepoys were proceeding to Delhi to the King.

That her dependence was entirely on the British authorities who met with such a misfortune, the sepoys knowing her to be quite helpless sent her messages through the Tehseeldar of Jhansi, the revenue and judicial Seristadars of the deputy commissioner's and superintendent's courts to the effect that if she, at all, hesitated to comply with their requests they would blow up her palace with guns. Taking into consideration her position she was obliged to consent to all the requests made and put up with a great deal of annoyance, and had to pay large sums in property, as well as in cash to save her life and honour.

Knowing that no British Officers had been spared in the whole district, she was in consideration of the welfare and protection of the people, and district, induced to address Perwannahs to all the Government subordinate agency in the shape of police etc., to remain at their posts and perform their duties as usual; she is in continual dread of her own life and that of the inhabitants.

It was proper that the report of all this should have been made immediately, but the disaffected allowed her no opportunity for so doing. As they have this day proceeded towards Delhi, she loses no time in writing.

Letter No. 2

Translation of a Khureeta from the Rani of Jhansi to the address of the Commissioner and Agent Lt. Governor, Saugor Division, dated June 14, 1857, giving further details of the uprising.

After compliments. States that on the 12th June, she addressed the Commissioner on the subject of the awful events which have transpired in Jhansi and sent the Khut by Gungadhur Daugee and the Bhowanee Hurkara. That she still continues to regret the fate of the Europeans of Jhansi and is convinced that great cruelties could not have been enacted in any other place... a detailed narrative of them is annexed to the Khureeta.

The further news since is that in all the Elaqas subordinate to Jhansi the chiefs have taken possession of the Gurhees, while others are plundering the country. That it is quite beyond her power to make any arrangements for the safety of the district as the measure would require funds, which she does not possess nor will the mahajans in times like these will lend her money. Up to the present time after selling her own personal property and suffering much inconvenience she has managed to save the town from being plundered and has kept up the form of the late Government she has entertained many people for the protection of the town and Mofussil outposts, but without a competent Government Force and funds she sees the impossibility of holding on any further, she has therefore written out some remarks on the state of the district which is also sent herewith and trusts she may early be favoured with orders which she will see carried out.

Enclosure to Letter No. 2

Translation of Narrative of Events which transpired in Jhansi on the 5th of June 1857.

About 1 p.m. all of a sudden about 50 or 60 Sepoys rose and took possession of the Magazine and Government Treasure and commenced firing their muskets towards Captain Skeine's Bungalow. On finding this to be the case, Captain Skeine, his wife and children, in company with Captain Gordon proceeded to the town and made arrangements for guarding it and then proceeded to the Fort. A short time after this other gentlemen also went to the Fort which they guarded with small force and the Rani sent a few of her own guards to the Fort for their aid.

On the 6th June everything remained as on the previous day up to noon, viz., only such of the sepoys as had become disaffected remained so, the rest and Sawars continuing quiet, after 12 o'clock all became disaffected and joined together and killed all their Officers, and burnt their Bungalows as well as all the public offices with their records which were all destroyed and plundered. Then they proceeded to the Jail and released all the prisoners. The Jail Darogah joined the Mutineers and they then proceeded towards the Town and surrounded the Fort, but since the Gentlemen had closed the gates of the Fort and were firing with great bravery from the Fort walls, the Mutineers could not manage to open the Gates.

On the 7th June the mutineers commenced firing guns against the Fort walls and this very much frightened the Town's people, specially when 4 or 5 balls came and fell in the Town but everything remained quiet.

On the 8th June, the Mutineers planned an assault on the Fort and compelled 150 men of the Rani's to join them who then all continued the attack till 3 o'clock p.m.; during all this time the Gentlemen who were so few, continued with their usual vigour to defend the Fort and managed to kill and wound many of the Mutineers with their guns. After this Captain Gordon received a musket shot which killed him. Then Captain Skeine, with his wife and children and other gentlemen came down from the Fort and intended to escape out of the Town, but the cruel Mutineers did not allow them to effect their purpose. After murdering them all in such a cruel manner that the Almighty is sure to punish them for it, they plundered some people in the Town and otherwise did as they pleased. The Rani with the utmost difficulty managed to save her life, but her money and property were plundered. She was not able to report this before to the Commissioner or Agent since the disaffected had stopped all Dawk communication and had guarded all the roads round Jhansi which prevented every one from going out.

On the night of 11th June, they left the place and it is hoped will go to hell for their deeds.

Translation of a Khureeta from the Rani of Jhansi to the Agent Governor-General for Central India dated 14th Jamudee-colewul A.H. 1274 corresponding to 1st January 1858, giving details of the occurrences in Jhansi.

Foreign Political Consultation No. 226, December 30, 1859

(Supplementary)

After compliments. To narrate all the strange and unexpected occurrences that took place during your absence from India is a painful task. I cannot describe the troubles and hardships I have suffered during this period. Your return to India gives me a new life. I take this opportunity to give you a brief statement of my history. At the time when the British forces mutinied at this place and plundered me of my property, and when the chiefs of Dattia and Oorchcha commenced their career of coercion and rapine, I lost no time in writing to the British Officers as per margin, and gave them detailed information as to the state of the country, some of the bearers of these letters are missing, others being plundered before reaching their destination came back to Jhansi, those that were sent to Agra returning stated that they succeeded in sending the letters within the Fort of Agra through a Bhistee, that their life being not safe they did not wait for reply. Major Ellis informed me that my letters were referred to the Officer that was acting for Captain Skeine.[5]

I got a letter from the Commissioner through the Chief of Goorsaray dated 23rd June, stating that I should take charge of the District. Another communication from the same officer dated 10th July, in reply to my three letters was also received; it referred me to his former communications in which a proclamation putting me in charge of the District was said to have been enclosed. On the 29th July, I wrote back in reply stating that I had not received the proclamation.

2.   Taking advantage of the disturbed state of the country, the Chiefs of Dattia and Oorchcha first took possession of the district of Jhansi Illaqa that lay on the border of their respective states, both to the East and West.

3.   On the 3rd September, (both these Chiefs acting in concert) the forces of Oorchcha composed of the Thakoors and relations of the State, and amounting to 40,000 men with 28 guns invaded Jhansi itself and made other Chiefs support them. Although the two letters received by

me from the Commissioner were sent to Nuthey Khan for his perusal, yet he took no notice of them. On this, I again wrote to the Commissioner who told me in reply that British Forces were assembling at Jabalpur. That he will come to Jhansi and examine the conduct of all either high or low and deal with them accordingly. In the meantime I tried my best by selling my property, taking money on interest—collected a party of men and took steps to protect the city, and to meet the invading force. The enemy by firing guns, matchlocks and rockets (Ban) did much mischief and killed thousands of precious souls, my resources failing, I wrote on 20th September and 19th October for reinforcements. After two months the besieging force retired to a village Koma situated about 3 miles from Oorchcha, all the districts that were formerly occupied by the Chief of Oorchcha are still in his possession. In the same manner the Rani of Dattia still holds all the districts that fell into her hands. The authorities at Oorchcha and Dattia do not give up these places, the troops sent to re-occupy them meet with opposition.

As was the case in former days the Pawars and Mawasas are excited to ruin by rapine and plunder the remaining districts. Under the circumstances I can never expect to get rid of these enemies and to clear myself of the heavy debts without the assistance of the British Government.

The Commissioner seems not prepared to move for my help as he states in his letter dated 9th November, that the services of the British troops for the present are required at his quarter. As these short-sighted individuals seem unmindful of the British supremacy and do their best to ruin myself and the whole country, I beg you will give me your support in the best way you can, and thus save myself and the people who are reduced to the last extremity and are not able to copy with the enemy.

APPENDIX D

(Part I)

Proclamation for Jhansi sent by the Commissioner, Saugor Division, authorising Rani Jhansi to take over the administration of Jhansi till British Government is re-established.

Foreign Political Consultation No. 354, July 31, 1857

Be it known to all people belonging to, or residing in the Government

District of Jhansi, that owing to the bad conduct of the soldiers some valuable lives have been lost, and property destroyed but the strong and powerful British Government is sending thousands of European soldiers to places which have been disturbed and early arrangements will be made to restore order in Jhansi.

Until officers and troops reach Jhansi, the Rani will rule in the name of the British Government, and according to the customs of the British Government, I hereby call on all great and small, to obey the Rani, and to pay the Government Revenue to her, for which they will receive credit.

The British Army has retaken the city of Delhi and has killed thousands of the rebels, and will hang or shoot all the rebels wherever they may be found.

(Part II)

A letter from the Secretary of the Government of India to Commissioner, Saugor and Nerbudha, giving conditional approval to the steps taken by the latter.

Foreign Political Consultation No. 355

No. 3032 of 1857

From

    G.F. Edmondstone Esquire, Secretary to the Government of India

To

    Major W.C. Erksine, Commissioner, Saugor and Nerbudha Territories.

For. Deptt.

D/Fort William the 23rd July, 1857

Sir,

    In reply to your letter dated the 2nd instant No. A forwarding translations of two letters from the Rani of Jhansi, I am directed to acquaint you that the Governor-General in Council approves and sanctions the rewards amounting to Rs. 500, which you have authorised to be paid to the most deserving of those who captured or shot the convicts who attempted to escape from the Nagode Jail.

    In respect to the Rani I am to state that though His Lordship in

Council does not blame you for accepting in the circumstances in which you were placed her account of her own proceedings, and sentiments, and entrusting to her the management of the Jhansi territory on behalf of the British Government, yet this circumstance will not protect her if her account should turn out to be false. From the account supplied to Government by Major Ellis it appears that the Rani did lend assistance to the mutineers and rebels, and that she gave guns and men.

I have the honour to be etc.

S/d-G.F. Edmondstone

Secretary to the Government of India.

Fort William

The 23rd July, 1857.

APPENDIX E

A letter from Lakshmi Bai (Rani Jhansi) to Nana Seheb wherein she requested for help.

Foreign Political Consultation No. 617-54 K.W. (Supplement) Dated December 30, 1859

Lakshmi Bai to Peshwa   14 February 1858

Shri,

Lakshmi Bai presents compliments and begs to write from Jhansi that by the grace of the Sarkar news of this quarter is all right up to Falgun 8th. We are not being favoured by your comrades. The master will be kind enough to look after us by letters. Malhar Anand Rao has written to say that the Sarkar has arrived at Jalon which makes me happy. I am anxious to see the feet of the Sarkar (to meet you) and would consider it as a fortunate day when I do so. My request has already been conveyed to you by the said person. Something must be done to cherish the state and afford it protection. There is pressure on Moti Saugor. If the enemy is not held up it would be a serious problem. There was fighting at Rahatgarh and Garalhota. The posts have been evacuated and the Tambra (British forces) has arrived. It is now heading towards Jhansi. Unless aid from Sarkar is forthcoming it is difficult to stop it. It is the duty of the servant to write often leaving to the master to provide for the emergency....

The masters are my ultimate shield. May this be known. This is my request. The last words He' Vidnvapana are in the handwriting of the Rani.

APPENDIX F

Translation of a letter in cypher presumed to be written by Rani Jindan to the address of Churt Singh of Amritsar from Hashee Mir of Nepal (without date. Nepal post mark of October 16, 1858) asking Maharaja Kashmir to proceed to Lahore with a view to attack the British and also informing him of the plans of Maharaja of Nepal, other rebel leaders and Chiefs.

Foreign Political Secret Proceeding No. 1045 of December 30, 1859

Letter No. 1

"Seeta Mata (Maharanee) writes of Rundheer Singh."

After compliments. Ram Singh has written me your message, the receipt of it has given me great pleasure. I was about to send Sirdar Jeeta (Maharanee's Mookhtar) but now my mind has been set at rest. I sent for Jung Bahadur to my house and told him the state of your affairs. He was quite pleased to hear it, and is now entirely satisfied. He has two things to say to you. One is that he sends you his salams, the other is in regard to your request that Seeta Mata should be sent to you along with five or seven thousand men or that Jung Bahadur should come towards Simla. Now Simla is one thousand kos from this place, a great distance difficult of accomplishment. His wish is that you should proceed to Lahore and thence write to him, when he would immediately march with troops and join you accompanied by "Seeta Mata".

With reference to your request for information of the date which he (Jung Bahadur) had fixed on for marching the fact is that he has determined on doing so either in Mughr or Poos/November or December but it is advisable that you should quickly reach Lahore. You may rely on his good faith, he will not fail to join you. Consider his troops to be on their way down.

Koor Singh of Jugdeespoor has 18,000 men and let no ships pass between Patna and Benaras. Umr Singh in the Chunar District has 16,000 men. The Begum is at Bulloca Ghat with 40,000 Horse and Foot. Banee Madho Singh has 20,000 men with him at Sooltanpore. Devi Singh and Mehudie Hoosain are also there with a gathering of 30,000 men. The Nana Sahib with 30,000 more is at Chutter Kote and there are 10 or 20 other chiefs of this kind besides.

Translation of a letter in cypher from Nepal (name of writer nowhere shown) to Churt Singh of Amritsar.

Foreign Political Secret Proceeding No. 1047
Dated December 30, 1859

Letter No. 2

Let Dheer Singh accept my kind regards and be assured of my welfare. The letter dictated by you has arrived. As regards Churt Singh's request that letter should not be addressed to him, there is no danger in doing so. Jung Bahadur consents to everything. By the 10th or 15th of Poos (December) he will go down. Tell this to the Raja. At this season there should be no delay. Further Jung Bahadur says that for certain he will descend in Poos (December) but he will not give battle. On the day that he (the Raja alias Rundheer Singh) strikes, on the day will he (Jung Bahadur) do likewise. Five of the brothers will descend by three different routes. One by Darjialing, himself by Chitalangi and the others by Patna. There will be no deviations from this plan, we hear a great many things, some true and some false, we do not therefore write them.

Here ends the cypher.

Translation of Goormukhi writing on the same paper with the foregoing:

There is but one God and He is to be approached through His appointed ministers.

Written by Myapoorie Jee (Maharanee) to Churt Singh, may blessings attend him. This amulet which I have written do you give to my disciple Dharam Dass with my blessings. My disciple who went to Dwarka has started on his return, and is expected to arrive during Mughr (this month commences in the middle of November) but the future is known only to the teachers (gooroo). He (the disciple) is greedy to excess, and may get entangled somewhere, if this should prove the case, I will write again. The disciple with whom I stay has received this information letter.

Kartick Buddee Ushtamee

Dated 29 October 1858

Translation of a Goormukhi letter from Nepal written by Myapoorie of Churt Singh.

Foreign Political Secret Proceeding No. 1047,
Dated December 30, 1859

Letter No. 3

Give my blessings to my disciple Rampoorie and tell him that my disciple who went to Dwarka 3 to 4 years ago is now on his return. This information has come in a letter to one of my disciples. He will arrive in Mughr (November). I also intend going on pilgrimage. All other pilgrimages have been performed, that of "Umrnath" (this is a shrine in the Kashmir Mountain) remains to be done. The disciple who is with me, is a child and says he cannot accompany me further than Kashee/ Benaras. Let Dherjpoore know this and tell him to come ahead and take me on. Tell him moreover that if he waits on his teacher, he will reap a blessing. Let me know all about Hurdass Singh.

The supports of the earth are steadfast to their engagement to uphold her.

The sea too adheres to her treaty not to molest the earth.

The lightning also maintains its alliance with the clouds.

The example of all compacts is that between the Almighty and Bhil Raja.

Other compacts are as nothing—that alone is the compact, which cannot change.

Translation of a letter⁶ from Nepal from Kashi Ram to Churt Singh of Amritsar in cypher.

Foreign Political Supplement Proceeding No. 1051
Dated December 30, 1859

Letter No. 4

After respects and good wishes. You repeatedly write that you have sent letters and not received replies. The reason of reply not being sent is this that Megh Singh has come to me and I have heard everything from him, viz., that Samer Gir⁷ has done nothing according to my wish, but only gave time-serving replies and said he would do this and that, and held out false hopes. Those who have to act send a trusty messenger to negotiate. I have twice sent each a man but he has sent none in return. I have lived on in hope. Now Jung Bahadur according to his word has come down, his letters have reached me. What am I to say?

You state that Samer Gir says, come by Simla and Sabathao but am I so degraded to listen to this? That road is difficult. He (Jung Bahadur) has marched according to promise. I shall not go on writing and will only now say Ram-Ram.

The letter goes in Gurmukhi, 'Oh Churt Singh iron[8] in this quarter is quoted high. Give this letter to my disciple Ram Giry'[9].

Translation of a Cypher. From Goormukh Singh Subedar to Churt Singh.

Foreign Political Supplement Proceeding No. 1052, Dated December 30, 1859

Letter No.5

Oh Brother, you go to Jammu and tell Sewapooree (i.e., the Maharaja) that Jung Bahadur had arranged everything according to promise; now you should make arrangements on your side. Jung Bahadur complaints to me (i.e., to the Maharanee Jindan) that my minister (i.e., the Maharaja) does nothing and that he will have to assist him; the Maharaja is getting to Lahore. Give compliments to Rattan Singh and say that he is celebrated all over the Punjab. He would strengthen the resolution of Sewapooree in setting affairs. Tell Jewan Singh that he had engaged on behalf of Sewapooree, and that he will suffer if Sewapooree does nothing and that he should arrange for the Punjab as well as he can. If Sewapooree does not attend, encourage him to fulfil his promise. If Sewapooree still does not mind then let Jewan Singh come to me. Give Rs. 100 to Jewan Singh, let Churt Singh take 40 and let 75 be given to Hurdass Singh. Take the money from Lala Doone Chand and divide it.

Translation of Cypher. From Dayaram[10] to Churt Singh bearing Nepal postmark of January 22, 1859

Foreign Political Supplement Proceeding No. 1052, Dated December 30, 1859

Letter No. 6

Bum Bahadur says that the British forces have stopped the war taking place at the points agreed upon. Who can it be that tells the English our plans? Take care, you tell nobody except Sewapooree. If you do, you will suffer. Trust in Gooroo. We shall soon get the upper hand. The news is this, that in the jungle of Uthora and Bichya Khoree and westward in the Kalka jungle in front of Toolseepoor and in other jungles, the Begum, and Nana Rao and Banee Madho and the Helas (i.e., Hindoostanee Sepoys) all are collected and in front of Gorakhpore there is a place named Bustee, near there a great fight has taken place. Nearly 7,000 Sikhs and English have been slain there. Nepal is sending its forces down into the jungle and the Kalas are collected to a number of nearby 2 lakhs. Jeeta[11] has arranged all with Nana Rao and seen their forces. Tell Sewapooree that we, viz., Jung Bahadur and Nana Rao and the Begum say that he must now arrange on his side otherwise such an opportunity will not re-occur.

APPENDIX G

Sarojini Naidu charged the Martial Law Administration with grave outrages on women. The following correspondence between Mr. Montagu, Secretary of State for India and Sarojini Naidu indicates their viewpoint on the subject:

First Letter to Sarojini Naidu.

India Office, White Hall, S.W.I.

9th July, 1920

Madam,

I am directed by the Secretary of State for India to invite your attention to the report of a public meeting at Kingsway Hall on 3rd June, published by organisers of the meeting. You are reported therein to have said: "My sisters were stripped naked, they were flogged, they were outraged." As you have made no correction, the Secretary of State is bound to assume that you were correctly reported.

Mr. Montagu finds it difficult to believe that anybody could for one moment have thought that such occurrences were possible and he finds that these particular allegations do not occur in the Report of the Committee appointed by the Indian National Congress (to which you appeared to refer as the authority for them) or in the Evidence collected by that committee; and nothing in that Report or Evidence justifies the allegation that Indian women were stripped naked, flogged or outraged.

Mr. Montagu has satisfied himself that the statements that women were stripped naked or flogged or outraged during the operation of Martial Law in the Punjab, are of course, absolutely untrue. He therefore requests you to withdraw immediately the charges which are reported, you alone to be responsible, and to give your withdrawal the same publicity as was given to the original statements; or if you are prepared to maintain the accuracy of these specific charges to produce justification for them. The Secretary of State reserves the right of publishing this letter, but before doing so, proposes to await your reply up to Wednesday morning, the 12 of July.

I am, Madam

Your obedient servant

Sd/-S.K.Brown.

Second Letter to Sarojini Naidu

India Office, White Hall, S.W.I.

10 July, 1920

Madam,

Since the despatch of my letter to you yesterday, the attention of the Secretary of State has been called to Statement No. 147 printed on p. 194 of the Report of the National Congress Sub-Committee.

Having regard to the general object of the meeting, to the case which you desired to make to your audience, and to the context of your remarks, the Secretary of State does not think that the charge can be the allegation which you had in mind. It is an allegation wholly unconnected with Martial Law procedure, made against Indian Police Constables and not against what you described as "Martial Authorities". It is not specifically referred to in the Congress Report.

If, however, this allegation which does appear in the Report of the Evidence published by the Congress Sub-Committee, is the foundation of your statement, he asks you to make it clear that you had no reason to make such a charge against any "Martial Authority" and that you had in your mind only an allegation made against the subordinate police in the course of search of stolen property.

I am to add that paragraph 40 of the Government of India's despatch of 3rd May last in which enquiry is promised into such cases of alleged ill-treatment obviously applies to this case. The Secretary of State has also, however, directed special enquiry into this matter and hopes in due course to be in a position to state to the public the results of the enquiry.

I am,

Your most obedient servant,

S.K. Brown.

Sarojini Naidu's Reply

Dear Sir,

I am in receipt of the letters of the 9th and 10th instant sent me by your Secretary at your direction.

I notice that the statements contained in the first letter are considerably modified in the second. While the first categorically denies the existence of any evidence published by the Congress Sub-Committee to justify the remarks made in my Kingsway Hall Speech to which you refer, the second on the contrary admits that there is such evidence, but that the outrages were the work of the police and not of Martial Law authorities.

I am surprised that you should attempt to make such a fine distinction, the materiality of which is not obvious, when the police were an integral part of the Martial Law machinery and admittedly were serving the purposes of Martial Law Authorities inasmuch as these outrages were perpetrated by them to procure evidence for the Martial Law Tribunals.

In any case, if you refer to my speech itself, the report of which is not entirely accurate, you will note that there are only two instances of outrage upon women which I have specifically attributed to Martial Law Authorities. These remarks were based upon several statements made by the women themselves, which read:

Statement 581, Page 868

(Report on the Enquiry Committee, Indian National Congress)

Statement made by twenty-three women

"We were called from our houses wherever we were and collected near the School. We were asked to remove our veils. We were abused and harrassed to give out the name of Bhai Mool Singh as having lectured against the Government. This incident occurred at the end of Baisakhi last in the morning in Mr. Besworth Smith's presence. He spat at us and spoke many bad things. He beat some of us with sticks. We were made to stand in rows and to hold our ears. He abused us also saying: 'Flies, what can you do, if I shoot you?' "

Passage from statement 362, page 387

"While the men were at the Bungalow (where they were detained) he rode to our village, taking back with him all the women who met him on the way carrying food for their men to the bungalow. Reaching the village, he went round the lanes, and ordered all women to come out of their houses, himself forcing them out with sticks. He made us all stand near the village Sarai. The women folded their hands before him. He beat some with his stick and spat at them and used the foulest and most unmentionable language. He hit me twice and spat in my face. He forcibly uncovered the faces of all the women, brushing aside the veils with his own stick.

"He repeatedly called us she-asses, bitches, flies, and swine and said 'You were in the same bed with your husbands, why did you not prevent them from going out to do mischief? Now Your skirts will be looked into by the village constables.' He gave me a kick also and ordered us to undergo the torture of holding our ears by passing our hand round the legs while being bent double."

This treatment was meted out to us in the absence of our men who were away at the Bungalow.

This statement was corroborated by eight other women who made similar statements.

Passage from statement 585 made by Maciaban, p. 869

"On the 5th of Baisakh bullets were fired into our village. The village people ran away hither and thither. One European who was on horseback called some old women together and told them that whatever he had done (firing) was done well. The old women did not give any reply. He then abused them and beat them with a stick. He then asked other women to stand in a row. Those who had veiled their faces were forced to remove their veils, they too were beaten with sticks."

From statement 125, page 177

"...I am a paradanashin. I never appear in public, not even before the servants. I was however called down from my house. I went with a pardah (veil). I was pre-emptively ordered to take off my pardah. I was then asked who assaulted Miss Sahib. They threatened me that unless I named the assailant, I would be given over to the soldiers."

Need I remind you that the pardah is as sacred to the Indian women as is her veil to the Catholic Nun and forcibly to unveil an Indian women constitutes in itself a gross outrage.

The other instances of outrages to which I drew attention in my speech were not specifically attributed to any social individual. My charges however, were based on statement 147, page 194, which as you are aware, is of too indecent a nature to be quoted here or from the public platform.

I would further refer you to statements 130 and 131 which deal with the conduct of soldiers and not of public.

I am deeply grieved to discover that until now you were not cognisant of the statements embodied in the Congress evidence concerning such outrages upon Indian women; and I trust you are causing an exhaustive and impartial enquiry to be made into such cases.

Yours faithfully,

Sd/-Sarojini Naidu

(Mitra, H.N.—Punjab Unrest Before and After, Calcutta, 1921)

APPENDIX H

Mrs. Sonawala's statement before the Court on conditions in the lockup

"I want to say something about the lockup in which we are kept for the last six days. I am in the lockup. I am given a very small room with a small "Chokdi" in it. There is no sort of privacy in it. The doors cannot be closed and the room is open on the road side. Policemen walk up and down in front of the room. It is impossible to take bath, answer calls of nature or even change clothes without being seen from outside. There is no facility for taking bath. The room is not even fit for dogs and cattle. It is a great shame that you have to keep women in such places. There is no light also in the room. I am ready to go to Jail for six years.... Have you no sisters and mothers? How would you like them to be treated like this? I am bringing this matter to your notice not for my own sake but for the sake of many of my sisters who are bound to come after me. If you want to have experience of the lockup, you go and stay there for a day. If you cannot do it at least you can see it.

(Amrita Bazar Patrika, November 1, 1930, p. 9)

Miss Maniben Patel's statement regarding jail treatment to political prisoners

The following are extracts from the statement made by Miss Maniben Patel who was imprisoned in the Satyagraha of 1930:

"The female political prisoners are kept with the ordinary criminals in the same barrack and there is hardly one foot distance between each bedding.

"The criminal may have come for any sort of crime—prostitution, theiving and so forth. They may have venereal diseases, their hair may contain lice, they may smell very badly because of not bathing or keeping their persons clean.

"77 prisoners with four babies including 15 to 16 ordinary criminals are locked up in this one barrack measuring 138 ft. $7^1/_2$ inches by 18 ft. 6 inches, from 5.45 in the evening to 5.45 in the morning. But still the authorities have not yet thought it necessary to make any arrangements for extra latrine. There is one latrine in the barrack which has a door which does not close properly and has no latch. There are three latrines outside in the yard for use in the daytime. These are built in one line with no doors and just a wall standing out in front. Several times the authorities have been requested to have the doors put on these latrines but nothing is done as yet. With the increase of our numbers four more temporary latrines have been erected in the yard but they also have no doors.

" 'C' Class prisoners are not provided with even one bathroom. They may be sick or having any trouble, but they have to bathe in the open under the sky without any privacy. The bathing place has a tap at one end of a long shallow tank with stones on both sides and 6 to 12 or even more are supposed to bathe at one time, in this open space. The authorities have often been spoken to regarding this and the attention of the visitors has been drawn to the necessity of at least one bathroom but 'no bathroom for 'C' Class' has always been the reply.

"Practically the only difference that can be remarked between the criminals and the political prisoners if one may give such a simile is that the treatment of the political prisoners is like that of a stepmother.

"If a political prisoner and a criminal are both ill and lying in the Hospital the matron instead of giving each her medical ration will take away some sugar and milk from the political prisoner and give it to the criminal over and above her own.

"If for some reason or another or by mistake, the ordinary ration of a criminal does not come, the matron goes to the gate, gets it brought from the Kitchen and gives it herself to the criminal. But if some ration of a political prisoner does not come no such promptness is shown.

"The political prisoners have to sweep the barrack and verandah twice a day, clean the vessels which come from the kitchen containing food, wash and clean the latrines (after some two months a special criminal was brought from another jail for this work), washing, bathing places and tank, and fetch the water for the day and night use in the barrack.

"The political prisoners besides the sweeping and cleaning mentioned above, have to sew buttons or do whatever labour is given to them and if the task is not finished in the given time, the matron becomes abusive.

"Females are transferred from one prison to another even at night, with only policemen in charge. There is neither a matron nor any police officer travelling with them."

(Modern Review, Vol. 51, p. 721-722)

Notes and References

1. Jean Baptist, Tavernier, *Travels in India.* Translated by V. Bail, New York, 1889, Vol. II. p. 209.
2. Bernier, *Travels in Moghul Empire,* 2nd edition, 1914, pp. 312-313.
3. She could not influence her daughter who followed the funeral pyre of her husband.
4. *Government of India Act. No. XLV of 1860.*
5. Commissioner of Jabalpur Offg. Agent G.G. for C.I. Governor-General of India, Lt. Governor of Agra, Deputy Commissioner of Jalone, Political Agent of Gwalior, Major Ellis.
6. Bears the Nepal and Benaras postmarks. This letter is really from Maharanee Jindan to Maharaja of Jammu.
7. Supposed to be Maharaja.
8. This means war is brewing.
9. Maharaja of Jammu.
10. Dayaram is an important person. The letter is really from the Maharanee.
11. Maharanee's servant.

BIBLIOGRAPHY

The following are the unpublished records pertaining to the Foreign and Home Political Departments of the Government of India, which have been referred to in the thesis. These records are available in the National Archives, Government of India, New Delhi.

Foreign Political Department

1. Foreign Political A Confidential Consulation No. 153-183, 31 July, 1854.
2. Foreign Political Consulation No. 75 and K.W., 2 March, 1855.
3. Foreign Political Consulation No. 26-31 and K.W., 31 July, 1857.
4. Foreign Political Secret Consulation No. 353, 31 July, 1857.
5. Foreign Political Secret Consulation No. 354, 31 July, 1857.
6. Foreign Political Secret Consulation No. 355, 31 July, 1857.
7. Foreign Political Secret Consulation No. 138, 18 December, 1857.
8. Foreign Political Secret Consulation No. 144-5, 30 April, 1858.
9. Foreign Political Secret Consulation No. 355-362, 30 April, 1858.
10. Foreign Political Secret Consulation No. 73, 28 May, 1858.
11. Foreign Political Secret Consulation No. 127, 28 May, 1858.
12. Foreign Politica A Consulation No. 133, 28 May, 1858.
13. Foreign Political Secret Consulation No. 46-7, 16 July, 1858.
14. Foreign Political Confidential Consulation No. 139/47, August, 1858.
15. Foreign Political Consulation No. 8/12, and K.W., 3 Septemeber, 1858.
16. Foreign Political Secret A Consulation No. 34/38, 26 November, 1858.

17. Foreign Political Secret Consultation No. 3672-3675, 30 December, 1858.
18. Foreign Political Secret Consultation No. 3022, 31 December, 1858.
19. Foreign Political Secret Proceeding No. 1052, 12 February, 1859.
20. Foreign Political A Consulation No. 413/C, 15 July, 1859.
21. Foreign Political A Consulation No. 413/L, 15 July, 1859.
22. Foreign Political A Consulation No. 324, 29 July, 1859.
23. Foreign Political A Consulation No. 183/4, 19 August 1859.
24. Foreign Political Supplement Consulation No. 265, 30 December, 1859.
25. Foreign Political Supplement Consulation No. 266, 30 December, 1859.
26. Foreign Political Supplement Consulation No. 280, 30 December, 1859.
27. Foreign Political Supplement Consulation No. 283, 30 December, 1859.
28. Foreign Political Supplement Consulation No. 284, 30 December, 1859.
29. Foreign Political Supplement Consulation No. 286, 30 December, 1859.
30. Foreign Political Supplement Consulation No. 287, 30 December, 1859.
31. Foreign Political Supplement Consulation No. 288, 30 December, 1859.
32. Foreign Political Consulation No. 617-54 and K.W., 30 December, 1859.
33. Foreign Political Supplement Consultation No. 1764 30 December, 1859.
34. Foreign Political Supplement Consultation No. 1765 30 December, 1859.
35. Foreign Political Supplement No. 1765 30 December, 1859.
36. Foreign Political Proceeding No. 43, February, 1860.
37. Foreign Political A Proceeding No. 395, April, 1860.
38. Foreign Political Secret Proceeding Vol. II, 1862, p. 101.
39. Foreign Political A Proceeding No. 111/112, March, 1867.
40. Foreign Political A Proceeding No. 202/203, February, 1868.
41. Foreign Political A Consultation No. 360, October 1877.
42. Foreign Political A Consultation No. 264, October, 1879.

Home Political Depratment

43. Home Political B Secret Proceeding No. 111, February, 1908.
44. Home Political A Secreat Proceeding No. 48, March, 1908.
45. Home Political B Confidential Proceeding No. 42-49 A, April, 1908.
46. Home Political B Confidential Proceeding No. 161-168, 25 May, 1908.
47. Home Political Confidential Proceeding No. 2, August, 1908.
48. Home Political B Confidential Proceeding No. 18, October 1908.
49. Home Political B Confidential Proceeding No. 63-70, November, 1908.
50. Home Political B Confidential Proceeding No. 135, May, 1909.
51. Home Political (Political Deposits) Confidential Proceeding No. 13, july, 1909.
52. Home Political (Political Deposits) Confidential Proceeding No. 2, April, 1909.
53. Home Political (Political Deposits) Confidential Proceeding No. 1, October, 1909.
54. Home Political B Confidential Proceeding No. 46-52, January, 1910.
55. Home Political B Confidential Proceeding No. 9-16, June, 1910.
56. Home Political B Secret Proceeding No. 18-25, August, 1910.
57. Home Political B Secret Proceeding No. 7-10, December, 1910.
58. Home Political B Secret Proceeding No. 18, January, 1911.
59. Home Political B Confidential Proceeding No. 1-4, July, 1911.
60. Home Political B Confidential Proceeding No. 1, July, 1913.
61. Home Political B Confidential Proceeding No. 37-39, August, 1913.
62. Home Political B Confidential Proceeding No. 169, December, 1914.
63. Home Political B Confidential Proceeding No. 216-217, December, 1914.
64. Home Political B Confidential Proceeding No. 227-28, December, 1914.
65. Home Political Confidential Proceeding No. 166-625, December 1914.
66. Home Political A Confidential Proceeding No. 623-168, December, 1915.

67. Home Political A Confidential Proceeding No. 454-457 and K.W., February, 1916.
68. Home Political B Confidential Proceeding No. 652-653, September, 1916.
69. Home Political A Secret Proceeding No. 53, September, 1916.
70. Home Political Confidential Proceeding No. 129-135, January, 1918.
71. Home Political Confidential Proceeding No. 247 and K.W. March 1918.
72. Home Political Proceeding 1922, File No. 933.

Records in Possession of Bibi Amar Kaur

1. Letter No. 5950 JL-42/544, dated 8 October, 1942, addressed by the Government of Punjab to Amar Kaur.
2. Letter No. 8245 JL-42/73492, dated 31 December, 1942, addressed by the Government of Punjab to Amar Kaur.

Records in Possession of Miss Usha Mehta

1. Paper pertaining to the Congress Radio Calling, Accused No. 3 in the Congress Radio Conspiracy Case, 1939, I and II.
2. Papers in possession of Miss Manmohini Sehgal.

Printed Records of the Government of India and Official Reports available in the National Archives of India, New Delhi, and National Library, Calcutta, which have been referred to in the book

1. Abstract of the Proceedings of the Council of the Governor-General of India, 1870, Vol. IX.
2. Annual Report of the Politics Administration of the Town of Calcutta and its Suburbs, 1932, 1933.
3. Annual Report of the Administration of Bengal, 1932, 1940.
4. A Collection of Extracts from Royal Proclamation, Official Reports and Speeches, New Delhi.
5. British Parliamentary Papers-Education in India, Vol. 4, 1854.
6. Forrest, G.W., Edited-Selections from the Letters, Despatches and Other State Papers, preserved in the Military Department of the Government of India, Calcutta, 1857-58, 1912.
7. Further Papers Relative to the Mutinies in the East Indies, Presented to Both the Houses of Parliament by Command of Her Majesty, 1857-1858.
8. Government of Madhya Pradesh-The History of Freedom Movement, 1956.

9. Health Officer of Calcutta Report, 1913.
10. Hoshiarpur District Gazetteer, Lahore, 1833-34, and 1904.
11. India in 1920.
12. India Gazette, April 15, 1858.
13. Long, J.-Adam's Report on Vernacular Education in Bengal and Bihar, submitted in 1835, 1836, 1839 with a brief review of present conditions, Calcutta, 1868.
14. Multan District Gazetteer, Lahore, 1901-02.
15. Narrative of Events Mutiny in India, 1857-58, Calcutta, 1881.
16. Narrative of Events-Moradabad, J.C. Wilson's Report, 24 December, 1858.
17. Proceedings of the Legislative Council of India, Vol. II, 1857.
18. Parliamentary Debates, House of Commons, 1907, 1917.
19. Report on Native Papers (Confidential), Bengal, 1866, 1869, 1870 and 1876.
20. Report on Native Papers (Confidential), Bombay, 1869, 1870, 1872.
21. Report of the Indian Education Commission, 1882.
22. Report on the Census of Punjab, 1881, 1891, 1901, 1911.
23. Report on the Census of British India, 1881, 1891, 1901, 1911, 1921, 1931, 1941.
24. Report of the Disorders Enquiry Commission (The Hunter Report), London, 1920.
25. Report of the Indian Statutory Commission (Simon Commission), 1930.
26. Rudman, F.R.R.-Central Provinces-District Gazetteer, Mandala District, Vol. A.
27. Selections from the Records of the Government of India connected with Education-Home Department No. LXVII and LXVIII.
28. The Revolt in Central India, 1857-59, compiled in the Intelligence Branch, Division of Chief of Staff, Aramy Headquarters, Simla, India, 1908.
29. Walker, Alexander Colonel.-A Report on Infanticide, 1908.

Records of the Indian National Congress which have been referred to in the book. These records are available in the All India Congress Committee Library, Jantar Mantar Road, New Delhi.

1. Proceedings of the Indian National Congress (annual session) 1918, 1923, 1924, 1927.

2. President Address from 1911 to 1934, Madras.
3. Congress Bulletins, 1930, 1931, 1932, 1937, 1942.
4. Special Bulletins issued by the All India Congress Committee, March 1933.
5. August Struggle Report Parts I and II prepared under the aegis of All India Satyagraha Council, U.P. Branch (unpublished).
6. India Ravaged-Being an Account of Atrocities committed under British aegis over the whole subcontinent of India in the later part of 1942 (unpublished).
7. Report of the Pradesh Congress Committee, Karnataka, 1942.
8. The Report of the Enquiry Committee, Banaras, August 1942 Disturbances (unpublished).
9. Punjab Congress Committee Report on the Disturbances in Lahore, 1942.

JOURNALS

1. *Asiatic Review*, London, 1932.
2. *Calcutta Review*, Calcutta, 1936.
3. *Indian Social Reformer*, Madras and Bombay, 1899, 1900.
4. *Indian Journal of Political Science*, Vol. XIX, 1958.
5. *Indian Ladies Magazine*, Madras, 1908, 1909.
6. *The Indian Review*, Madras, 1923, 1927, 1929, 1937.
7. *Inquiab*-Monthly Journal of the India National Congress, Eastern Zone, 1944.
8. *Illustrated Weekly of India*, Bombay, 1957.
9. *Mahila Pragati Ke Path Par*, Delhi, 1957 (Hindi)
10. *Modern Review*, Calcutta, 1907, 1910, 1911, 1912, 1913, 1916, 1919, 1920, 1926, 1928, 1929, 1932, 1953, 1957.
11. *Stri Dharma*, Madras, 1932, 1933.
12. *Social Welfare*, Delhi, 1959.
13. *Roshni*-Journal published by the All India Women's Council, Delhi, 1947, 1953.
14. *The Indian World*, Calcutta, 1908.
15. *Women on the March*, Delhi, 1957, 1958.

NEWSPAPERS

1. *Amrita Bazar Patrika*, Calcutta, 1919, 1920, 1922, 1923, 1928, 1931, 1932, 10 April, 1930.
2. *Advance*, Calcutta, 1930, 1931, 1932, 1942.
3. *Bengalee*, Calcutta, 1921, 1928.

4. *Civil and Military Gazette*, Lahore, 1922.
5. *Friend of India*, Calcutta, 1858, 1865, 1866.
6. *The Hindustan Times*, Delhi, 1954.
7. *Hindoo Patriot*, Madras, 1871, 1878, 1905, 1909.
8. *Hindustan Standard*, Calcutta, 1942.
9. *Independent*, December 1921 (Unregistered Paper edited by Mahadev Desai, All India Congress Committee Library, New Delhi).
10. *The Times of India*, Bombay, 1929, 1930.
11. *The Tribune*, Ambala, 1932, 1946.
12. *Saddiq-Ali Akhbar*, Delhi, 8 July 1857 (Urdu).
13. *New India*, Madras.

BOOKS

Aiyer, A., Rangaswami, *Dr. Annie Besant--Her Work for Swaraj*, Madras, 1955.

Altekar, A.S., *Position of Women in Hindu Civilisation from Prehistoric Times to the Present Day*, Banaras, 1938.

Andrews, C.F. and Mukerjee, G., *Rise and Growth of the Indian National Congress*, 1938.

Arnold, Edwin, *The Marquis of Dalhousie, Administration of the British India*, London, 1865.

——, *A Brief Account of the National Activities of Bibi Amar Kaur Ahluwalia* (Handbill).

Bagal, J.C., *History of the Indian Association, 1876-1951*, Calcutta.

Bahadur Mal, *A Story of Indian Culture*, Hoshiarpur.

Ball, Charles, *History of the Indian Mutiny*, 2 Volumes, London and New York.

Benarjee, S.N., *A Nation in Making*, London, 1925.

Benarjee, B., *Indian War of Independence*.

Basu, Dr. K.K., *An Article-Story of a Century Old Sati Case in Bihar* contributed to the History Department, Panjab University, Chandigarh.

Bell, Major Evans, *The Empire in India, Letters*, London.

Bernier, F., *Travels in Mughal Empire*, 2nd Edition, 1914.

Besant, Annie, *Wake Up India*, Madras, 1913

——, *India, A Nation*, Madras, 1925.

——, *India Bonded or Free*, Great Britain, 1926.

——, *The Future of Indian Politics*, 1922.

Bright, J.S., *The Great Nehrus*.

Brockway, A.F., *Indian Crisis*, London, 1930.

Brown, John Cave, *Indian Infanticide, Its Origin, Progress and Suppression*, London, 1857.

Buch, M.L., *Rise and Growth of Liberalism*, Baroda, 1938.

Chattopadhya, K., *The Awakening of Indian Womanhood*, Madras, 1939.

Chriol, Valentine, *Indian Unrest*, London, 1910.

——, *India*, London, 1926.

Cormackam, Rev. J., *Accounts of Abolition of Female Infanticide in Gujarat*, London, 1815.

Cousins, M.E., *The Awakening of Asian Womanhood*, Madras, 1922.

——, *Indian Womanhood Today*, Allahabad, 1941.

Cousins, J.H., *The Annie Besant Centenary Book*.

Desai, A.R., *Social Background of Indian Nationalism*, Bombay, 1948.

Desai, Mahadev, *Story of Bardoli* (Being a History of the Bardoli Satyagraha of 1928 and its Sequel), Ahmedabad, 1929.

Desai, Neera, Woman in Modern India, Bombay, 1957.

Diwakar, R.R., *Satyagraha in Action—A Brief Outline of Gandhiji's Satyagraha Campaign*, Calcutta, 1949.

Dutta, Kalpana, Chittagong Armoury Raiders: *Reminiscences*, Calcutta, 1949.

Edger, Lilan, *Elements of Theosophy*, 1903.

Farquahar, J.N., The Crown of Hinduism, 2nd Edition, Oxford, 1915.

——, *Modern Religious Movements*, New York, 1924.

Fazal, Abul, *Aine-e-Akbari*, Vol. I, English Translation by Blockmann, 1873.

Forbas, Mitchell W., *Reminiscences of the Great Mutiny, 1857-59*, London, 1910.

Fuller M.B., *The Wrongs of Indian Womanhood*, New York, 1900.

G.A. Nateson and Co., Madras, *Speeches and Writings of Sarojini Naidu*.

Gandhi, M.K., *Women and Social Injustice*, Ahmedahad, 1945.

——, *Satyagraha in South Africa*, Madreas, 1928.

Giani, K.S., *Indian Independence Movement in East Asia*, Lahore, 1947.

Gedge, E.C. and Choksi, M., *Women in Modern India*, Bombay, 1929.

Gleig, G.R., *The Life of Sir Thomas Munro*, London,

Gordon Alexandra, U. Col., W., *Recollections of a Highland Subaltern During the Campaign*, London, 1948.

Sen, Gupta, Padmini, *Pioneer Women of India*, 1944.

Gough, General Sir H., *Old Memries,* Edinburgh, 1897.

Hardass Bal Shastri, *Armed Struggle for Freedom,* Rendered into English by S.S. Apte, Poona, 1958.

H.H. Nawab Sultan Jahan Begum, *Al-Hijab or Why Purdah is Necessary,* Calcutta, 1922.

Holmes, T.R., *History of the Indian Mutiny,* London, 1898.

Horner, I.B., *Women Under Primitive Buddhism.* London.

Innes, Lt. General, J.J. Mcleod, *Lucknow and Allahabad in Mutiny,* London, 1896.

Jack, A. Homer, *The Gandhi Reader,* Bloomington, 1956.

Kane, P.V., *History of Dharamshastras, Ancient and Medieval Religions and Civil Law,* Poona.

Keye, John William, *History of the Sepoy War,* Vol. III, London, 1876.

Khan, Abdul Majid, *The Great Daughter of India,* Lahore, 1946.

Lajpat Rai, *The Arya Samaj* (An Account of its Aims, Doctrines and Activities with a Biographical Sketch of the Leader), Lahore, 1932.

Lajpat Rai, *Young India,* Lahore, 1916.

Lang, J., *Wanderings in India and Other Sketches of Life in Hindustan,* London, 1859.

Leitner, G.W., *History of Indigenous Education in the Panjab Since Annexation and in 1882,* Calcutta, 1882.

Lowe, Thomas, *Central India, During the Rebellion of 1857-1858,* London, 1960.

Macdonald, Ramsay, *The Awakening of India,* London, 1918.

Malleson, G.B., *History of the India Mutiny, 1857-58,* Second Edition, 1879, Vol. II.

————, *History of the Indian Mutiny, 1857-58,* London, 1870, Vol. I.

Mazumdar, R.C., *The Sepoy Mutiny and the Revolt of 1857,* Calcutta, 1957.

Mitra, Bejan and Chakraborty, P., *Rebel India,* Calcutta, 1946.

Mitra, R.N., *Panjab Unrest Before and After,* Calcutta, 1921.

Mitra, N.N., *Annual Register,* Calcutta, 1932, 1933, 1942, 1945.

Montague, Edwin, *An Indian Diary,* London, 1930.

Mookerjee, H. and Mookerjee, *Uma, India's Fight for Freedom, 1905-1906,* Calcutta.

Mookerjee, R.K., *Hindu Civilisation,* 1936.

Morton, E., *The Women in Gandhi's Life,* New York, 1953.

Mullick, B., *The Hindu Family in Bengal,* Calcutta, 1882.

Murdoch, John, *Twelve Years of Indian Progress.*

Muir, Ramsay, *A Short History of British Commonwealth,* New York, 1923.

Nehru, Jawaharlal, *An Autobiography*, 1935.

——, *The Unity of India—Collected Writings, 1937-1940,* London, 1941.

——, Towards Freedom, New York, 1941.

Nehru, Shyama Kumari (Edited), *Our Cause*, Allahabad.

Nivedita, Sister, *Selected Essays of Sister Nivedita,* 3rd Edition, Madras.

——, *Studies from an Eastern Home*, 1913.

O'Malley, L.S.S. (Edited), *Modern India and the West*, Oxford, 1941.

Pandit, Vijayalakshmi, *So I Became a Minister*, Allahabad, 1939.

Pal, B.C., *Brahmo Samaj and the Battle of Swaraj in India,* Calcutta, 1926.

Parvate, T.V., *Bal Gangadhar Tilak*, Ahmedabad, 1558.

Peggs, *India's Cries to British Humanity*, 2nd Edition, 1913.

Prakasa, Sri, Annie Besant, Bombay, 1945.

Publications Division, Government of India, Delhi, *Women in India,* Delhi, 1958.

Pyare Lal, *Mahatma Gandhi, The Last Phase.*

Ray, P.C., *Life and Times of C.R. Das*, 1927.

Reddy, Dr. Muthulakshmi, *My Experiences as a Legislator,* Madras, 1930.

Russel, Sir W.H., *My Diary in India in the Year 1858-1859,* London, 1860, 2 Vols.

Sahai, Gobind, *42 Rebellion*, Delhi, 1947.

Sen, Surendra Nath, *Eighteen Fifty-Seven*, Delhi, 1957.

Stephen, Leslie, *Dictionary of National Biography*, London, 1887, Vol. IX.

Sitaramayya, Dr. P., *History of the Indian National Congress,* 1946, Vol. 1 and II.

——, *Nationalist Movement in India*, Bombay, 1950.

Shaw, G.B., *John Bill's Other Island,* London, 1907.

Smith, A., Vincent, *Oxford History of India.*

Sorabji, Cornella, *The Position of Hindu Women Fifty Years Ago.*

Swami Pavitrananda, *Ramakrishna Mission,* Almora.

Tahmankar, D.V., Lokmanya Tilak, London, 1956.

Tavernier, Jean Baptiste, *Travels in India,* New York, 1889.

Thesophical Publishing House, Madras, *The Besant Spirit*, Vol. III and IV, 1939.

Theosophical Publishing House, Madras Annie Besant-*Builder of New India.*

Thompson, E. & Garrett G., *Rise and Fulfilment of British Rule in India*, 1936.

Tod, J., *Annals and Antiquities of Rajasthan.*

University of Calcutta, *Convocation of Addresses, 1889-1906,* Calcutta, 1914.

Vincent, Sheen, *Lead Kindly Light,* New York, 1949.

Walter, Wallbank, Short History of India and Pakistan, New York, 1958.

West, Geofry, *The Life of Annie Besant.*

Weinbrecht, Mrs. M., *Women in India and Christian Work in the Zenana,* London.

Wheeler, P., *India Against the Strom,* New York, 1944.

Wilson, J., *History of the Suppression of Infanticide in Western India,* Bombay.

Women's India Association, Madras, *Mrs. M. Cousins and Her Work in India.*

W. & R. Chambers, *The History of Indian Revolt, 1857-58,* London, 1859.

Zacharia, H.C.E., *Renascent India from Rammohun Roy to Mohan Das Gandhi,* London, 1933.

Books in Indian Vernacular

Mufti Intazamula Sahibi (Ed.), *Begum Oudh Ke Khatute* (Urdu), Delhi.

Uttar Pradesh Freedom Movement Board, *Sangharsh Kalin Netaon Ki Jiwanian* (Hindi), 1957.

Taliwar, D.R., *Bharatvarsh Ki Vibhutian* (Hindi)

Mehta, Mrs. Gurcharan, *Azad Hind Fauj* (Gurmukhi), Amitsar.

GLOSSARY

Ashram	...	Originally a hermitage. It usually means a home where wokers devoted to social, religions, political service live together and observe a common discipline.
Ayah	...	A nursemaid.
Baee(Bai)	...	A lady.
Bhang	...	Narcotic leaves of hemp.
Baithak	...	Sit-stand exercise.
Bhieste	...	Water carrier.
Chauri	...	A sort of fan.
Charkha	...	A Spinning wheel.
Daroga	...	A jail offical.
Durbar	...	Gathering of nobles-assembled by a king or a chief.
Elaqua	...	Jurisdiction.
Guru	...	A religious guide, a spiritual percepter.
Hartal	...	Cessation of work.
Hind	...	India.
Hooka	...	Hubble-bubble, the Indian pipe for smoking through water.
Jee (Ji)	...	A common suffix of respect corresponding to Sir or Mister.
Khaddar	...	Homespun cloth.
Khureeta	...	The silk bag in which a noble encloses his letter, hence a letter.
Kutchery	...	A court house.
Lathi	...	A long stick.
Mahajans	...	Moneylenders.
Mahatama	...	Great soul.
Nazarana	...	A ceremonial offering.

Nazim	...	A court official.
Nari	...	Woman
Nari Samiti	...	Women's Association.
Pan	...	Betelnut.
Puja	...	Worship.
Purdah	...	Curtain.
Pultan	...	A Battalion or Platoon.
Perwanah	...	Message, letter.
Prabhatpheri	...	Morning procession with the chanting of hymns.
Prasad	...	A sweet offering distributed to devotes in religious places.
Prachar	...	Propagate, preach.
Pradesh	...	Province.
Raj	...	Kindom, rule.
Rajya Sabha	...	Council of States (Upper House of Parliament).
Risaldar	...	Commander of a body horses.
Raksha Bandhan	...	A ceremony of tying a thread around the wrist of male members usually a brother.
Sultan-e-Alam	...	King Emperor.
Smt.	...	Srimati, normally used for Mrs.
Subedar	...	The chief Indian officer of a Company of Infantry.
Satyagraha	...	Truth force or Soul force.
Swadeshi	...	Belonging to one's own country.
Swaraj	...	Self-rule.
Sarkar	...	Government.
Tehsildar	...	A revnue collector.
Takli	...	Spinning needle.
Zenana	...	Women's apartment.
Sjt.	...	Shrijut-A common title equivalent to Esquire.

INDEX